MEASUREMENT
AND
REPRESENTATION
OF
SENSATIONS

SCIENTIFIC PSYCHOLOGY SERIES
Stephen W. Link and James T. Townsend, Series Editors

MONOGRAPHS

Louis Narens • *Theories of Meaningfulness*

R. Duncan Luce • *Utility of Gains and Losses: Measurement-Theoretical and Experimental Approaches*

William R. Uttal • *The War Between Mentalism and Behaviorism: On the Accessibility of Mental Processes*

William R. Uttal • *Toward a New Behaviorism: The Case Against Perceptual Reductionism*

Gordon M. Redding and Benjamin Wallace • *Adaptive Spatial Alignment*

John C. Baird • *Sensation and Judgment: Complementarity Theory of Psychophysics*

John A. Swets • *Signal Detection Theory and ROC Analysis in Psychology and Diagnostics: Collected Papers*

William R. Uttal • *The Swimmer: An Integrated Computational Model of a Perceptual–Motor System*

Stephen W. Link • *The Wave Theory of Difference and Similarity*

EDITED VOLUMES

Christian Kaernbach, Erich Schröger, and Hermann Müller • *Psychophysics Beyond Sensation: Laws and Invariants of Human Cognition*

Michael Wenger and James Townsend • *Computational, Geometric, and Process Perspectives on Facial Cognition: Contests and Challenges*

Jonathan Grainger and Arthur M. Jacobs • *Localist Connectionist Approaches to Human Cognition*

Cornilia E. Dowling, Fred S. Roberts, and Peter Theuns • *Recent Progress in mathematical Psychology*

F. Gregory Ashby • *Multidimensional Models of Perception and Cognition*

Hans-Georg Geissler, Stephen W. Link, and James T. Townsend • *Cognition, Information Processing, and Psychophysics: Basic Issues*

TEXTBOOKS

Norman H. Anderson • *Empirical Direction in Design and Analysis*

MEASUREMENT AND REPRESENTATION OF SENSATIONS

Edited by

Hans Colonius
Universität Oldenburg

Ehtibar N. Dzhafarov
Purdue University

Psychology Press
Taylor & Francis Group

New York   London

Copyright © 2006 by Lawrence Erlbaum Associates, Inc.

First published by
Lawrence Erlbaum Associates, Inc., Publishers
10 Industrial Avenue
Mahwah, New Jersey 07430

This edition published 2013 by Psychology Press

Psychology Press   Psychology Press
Taylor & Francis Group   Taylor & Francis Group
711 Third Avenue   27 Church Road, Hove
New York, NY 10017   East Sussex BN3 2FA

First issued in paperback 2014

Psychology Press is an imprint of the Taylor & Francis Group, an informa business

Cover design by Tomai Maridou

Library of Congress Cataloging-in-Publication Data

Measurement and representation of sensations / Hans Colonius and Ehtibar N. Dzhafarov, editors.
      p. cm.
Includes bibliographical references and index.
ISBN 0-8058-5353-7 (alk. paper)
1. Sensory stimulation—Measurement. 2. Sensory descrimination.
   3. Senses and sensations. I. Colonius, Hans, Dr. rer. nat. II. Dzhafarov, Ehtibar N.
QP435.M285   2006
152.1—dc22   2005052082
                                              CIP

ISBN 13: 978-0-8058-5353-7 (hbk)
ISBN 13: 978-0-415-65000-7 (pbk)

Contents

Foreword

A. A. J. Marley

University of Victoria

An important open issue in many areas of mathematical behavioral science concerns the extent to which probabilistic (nondeterministic) models are necessary to explain the data. This issue is distinct from, though related to, statistical issues that arise in testing deterministic models. To a significant extent, when researchers do propose probabilistic interpretations of the data, they leave the source of the underlying variability unspecified – this is less so in the study of psychophysics than in, say, the study of choice or voting behavior. As this book shows, both the deterministic and the probabilistic perspective are contributing significantly to modern psychophysics.

The book, which should interest both behavioral scientists and applied mathematicians, includes a sample of the most sophisticated current mathematical approaches to psychophysical problems. Most of the problems studied are classical, dating back to Fechner, von Helmholtz, Schrödinger, Stevens, and other founders of modern psychophysics. However, the techniques – both deterministic and probabilistic – presented in the book's six chapters are all original and recent. The chapters present rigorous mathematical definitions of theoretical concepts and discuss relatively simple procedures for the empirical evaluation of these concepts.

The volume, although not comprehensive in its coverage, encompasses a broad spectrum of psychophysical problems and approaches. Dzhafarov and Colonius, and, separately, Zhang, discuss probabilistic models of (subjective) similarity. In their first chapter, Dzhafarov and Colonius show that if probabilistic same-different judgments satisfy two quite general properties, which appear to hold for available data, then a large class of probabilistic models for such judgments are ruled out; in the second chapter, they apply one of these principles in a novel manner to derive subjective metrics from probabilistic same-different judgments. Zhang's chapter presents a somewhat similar approach and applies a variant of one of Dzhafarov and Colonius's general principles to situations where the two stimuli being compared have qualitatively distinct psychological representations. Luce and Steingrimsson present behavioral conditions that are sufficient for a deterministic representation of the psychophysical and weighting function involved in magnitude production. These behavioral conditions are formulated in terms of the joint effect of pairs of stimuli and of judgments of intervals separating two pairs of stimuli. Townsend, Aisbett, Busemeyer, and Assadi define and classify the possible forms of perceptual separability.

They do so by combining the language of differential geometry with general recognition theory, the latter being a multidimensional generalization of signal detection theory proposed earlier by Ashby and Townsend. And Balakhrishnan defines carefully the concept of observable probabilities and illustrates their use in the evaluation of the (sub)optimality of a decision rule. In doing so, he proposes a new probabilistic language that is applicable to all psychophysical tasks in which a participant's responses can be classified as either correct or incorrect, and uses this language to show how the classical concepts of psychophysical decision making (such as in the theory of signal detection) can be defined directly in terms of observable properties of behavior.

After thinking about this book and the possible strengths and weaknesses of the presented modeling approaches, I concluded that several factors encourage researchers to focus their attention on either deterministic or probabilistic models, usually to the relative exclusion of the other model class. The factor that I want to consider here is the complexity of the empirical situation. Focussing on psychophysics, there are at least two places where the empirical situation can be less or more complex: first, in the physical complexity of the stimuli; second, in the complexity of the task posed to the participant. I consider each in turn.

First, consider the complexity of the stimuli. For instance, consider a task where the participant is asked to make a "same-different" judgment, such as is studied in this book by Dzhafarov and Colonius, and by Zhang. This might be considered a fairly "simple" judgment to make. Now consider possible stimulus spaces for such a "same-different" task. If lines of varying length are the stimuli, then we have a relatively "simple" stimulus space, whereas if the stimuli are small spatiotemporal patches differing in color[1], then we have a "complex" stimulus space. There are then two relatively standard ways to carry out the experiment. In one, various pairs of stimuli are presented and the participant has to decide whether they are the "same" or "different"; in the second, one stimulus is presented and the participant has to adjust a second one until it "matches" the first. Independent of the experimental task, if the behavior is deterministic, then I think that, in the line length case, we will be surprised if there is more than one stimulus that "exactly" matches another[2]. However, in the color case,

---

[1] Note that line length can be measured physically, whereas "color" depends on the visual system being studied. However, in both cases, the stimuli being used can be specified in terms of physical variables. Also, when participants are asked to make color judgments, they are instructed to ignore other qualities of the stimulus such as hue or saturation.

[2] The matching lines may not be of the same length due to biases such as time-order effects. However, I think such effects can be considered minor in terms of the points I wish to make.

there will be a subspace of the stimulus space that matches any given color. Thus, assuming deterministic data, there is relatively little information in the "same-different" line length judgments, whereas there is considerable information in the "same-different" color judgments. This perspective is confirmed by the extensive deterministic representational theory concerning (metameric) color matching and its empirical evaluations, with no parallel (deterministic) theory and data concerning the matching of line-lengths. Of course, the data are probabilistic – or at least "noisy" – in both the line length and the color task when the stimuli are (psychologically) very similar. Thus, one would expect the development of probabilistic models for such "local" judgments, and attempts to use these "local" models and data to develop "global" representations. This is the approach taken in this book by Dzhafarov and Colonius, and by Zhang.

Second, consider the complexity of the participant's task. For instance, as in the chapter by Luce and Steingrimsson, assume that the basic stimulus is a pair (x, u) where x is a pure tone of some fixed frequency and intensity presented to the left ear of a participant and u is a pure tone of the same frequency and phase but a (possibly) different intensity presented to the right ear. The basic task is to judge which of two such pairs, (x, u) and (y, v), is the louder. However, in line with the intent of this paragraph to consider more complex tasks, now consider the additional task of *ratio production*, which involves the presentation to a participant of a positive number p and the stimuli (x, x) and (y, y), with y less intense than x, and asking the participant to produce the stimulus (z, z) for which the loudness "interval " from (y, y) to (z, z) is perceived to stand in the ratio p to the loudness "interval " from (y, y) to (x, x). As mentioned above, Luce and Steingrimsson show that, under a specific set of deterministic behavioral conditions, there is a numerical representation of these judgments that involves a psychophysical and a weighting function. And, though their data are somewhat "noisy" (probabilistic?), the behavioral properties are quite well-supported by the data.

Summarizing the above ideas, it appears that one can develop, and test, interesting deterministic psychological representations both for complex stimuli in simple tasks and for simple stimuli in (relatively) complex tasks. Of course, one can then combine these approaches to study complex stimuli in complex tasks. This is not to deny that there is likely some nondeterminism in each set of data, and that locally – when the stimuli are quite (psychologically) "similar" – there may be considerable nondeterminsm. Thus, a major challenge is to develop and test theories that have "local" nondeterminism in conjunction with "global" determinism. The chapters in this book present significant contributions to various parts of this challenge, some emphasizing "local" nondeterminism, some emphasizing "global" determinism, and some dealing with both aspects of the problem. I look forward to future work that builds on these sophisticated results by further integrating the study of "local" (nondeterminsitic) and "global" (deterministic) representations, continues the authors' initial contributions to the study of dynamic effects, such as sequential dependencies, and extends the approaches to include response times.

1

Regular Minimality: A Fundamental Law of Discrimination

Ehtibar N. Dzhafarov[1] and Hans Colonius[2]

[1] Purdue University
[2] Universität Oldenburg

1. INTRODUCTION

The term *discrimination* in this chapter is understood in the meaning of *telling stimuli apart*. More specifically, it refers to a process or ability by which a perceiver judges two stimuli to be different or identifies them as being the same (overall or in a specified respect). We postpone until later the discussion of the variety of meanings in which one can understand the terms *stimuli, perceiver,* and *same–different judgments*. For now, we can think of discrimination as pertaining to the classical psychophysical paradigm in which stimuli are being chosen from a certain set (say, of colors, auditory tones, or geometric shapes) two at a time, and presented to an observer or a group of observers who respond by saying that the two stimuli are the same, or that they are different. The response to any given pair of stimuli $(\mathbf{x}, \mathbf{y})$ in such a paradigm can be viewed as a binary random variable whose values (same–different) vary, in the case of a single observer, across the potential infinity of replications of this pair, or, in the case of a group, across the population of observers the group represents. As a result, each stimulus pair $(\mathbf{x}, \mathbf{y})$ can be assigned a certain probability, $\psi(\mathbf{x}, \mathbf{y})$, with which a randomly chosen response to $\mathbf{x}$ and $\mathbf{y}$ (paired in this order) is "the two stimuli are different,"

$$\psi(\mathbf{x}, \mathbf{y}) = \Pr[\mathbf{x} \text{ and } \mathbf{y} \text{ are judged to be different}]. \qquad (1)$$

The empirical basis for considering $(\mathbf{x}, \mathbf{y})$ as an ordered pair, distinct from $(\mathbf{y}, \mathbf{x})$, is the same as for considering $(\mathbf{x}, \mathbf{x})$ as a pair of two identical stimuli rather than a single stimulus. Stimuli $\mathbf{x}$ and $\mathbf{y}$ presented to a perceiver for comparison are necessarily different in some respect, even when

1

one refers to them as being physically identical and writes $\mathbf{x} = \mathbf{y}$: thus, $\mathbf{x}$ (say, a tone) may be presented first and followed by $\mathbf{y}$ (another tone, perhaps otherwise identical to $\mathbf{x}$); or $\mathbf{x}$ and $\mathbf{y}$ (say, aperture colors) may be presented side-by-side, one on the left, the other on the right. Dzhafarov (2002b) introduced the term *observation area* to reflect and generalize this distinction: two stimuli being compared belong to two distinct observations areas (in the examples just given, spatial locations, or ordinal positions in time). This seemingly trivial fact plays a surprisingly prominent role in the theory of perceptual discrimination. In particular, it underlies the formulation of the law of Regular Minimality, on which we focus in this chapter.

There is more to the notion of an observation area than the difference between spatiotemporal locations of stimuli, but this need not be discussed now. Formally, we refer to $\mathbf{x}$ in $(\mathbf{x}, \mathbf{y})$ as belonging to the *first observation area*, and to $\mathbf{y}$ as belonging to the *second observation area*, the adjectives "first" and "second" designating the ordinal positions of the symbols in the pair rather than the chronological order of their presentation. The difference between the two observation areas, whatever their physical meaning, is always perceptually conspicuous, and the observer is supposed to ignore it: thus, when asked to determine whether the stimulus on the left (or presented first) is identical to the stimulus on the right (presented second), the observer would normally perceive two stimuli rather than a single one, and understand that the judgment must not take into account the difference between the two spatial (or temporal) positions. In the history of psychophysics, this aspect of discrimination has not received due attention, although G. T. Fechner did emphasize its importance in his insightful discussion of the "non-removable spatiotemporal non-coincidence" of two stimuli under comparison (1887, p. 217; see also the translation in Scheerer, 1987).

It should be noted that the meaning of the term *discrimination*, as used by Fechner and by most psychophysicists after him, was different from ours. In this traditional usage, the notion of discrimination is confined to semantically unidimensional attributes (such as loudness, brightness, or attractiveness) along which two stimuli, $\mathbf{x}$ and $\mathbf{y}$, are compared in terms of which of them contains more of this attribute (greater–less judgments, as opposed to same–different ones). Denoting this semantically unidimensional attribute by $\mathcal{P}$, each ordered pair $(\mathbf{x}, \mathbf{y})$ in this paradigm is assigned probability $\gamma(\mathbf{x}, \mathbf{y})$, defined as

$$\gamma(\mathbf{x}, \mathbf{y}) = \Pr[\mathbf{y} \text{ is judged to be greater than } \mathbf{x} \text{ with respect to } \mathcal{P}]. \quad (2)$$

As a rule, although not necessarily, subjective attribute $\mathcal{P}$ is being related to its "physical correlate," a physical property representable by an axis of nonnegative reals (e.g., sound pressure, in relation to loudness). In this case, stimuli $\mathbf{x}, \mathbf{y}$ can be identified by values x, y of this physical property, and probability $\gamma(\mathbf{x}, \mathbf{y})$ can be written as $\gamma(x, y)$.[3] The physical correlate is always chosen so that $y \to \gamma(x, y)$; (i.e., function γ considered as a function of y only, for a fixed value of x) is a strictly increasing function for any value of x, as illustrated in Fig. 1, left. Clearly then, $x \to \gamma(x, y)$ is a strictly decreasing function for any value of y. Note, in Fig. 1 (left), the important notion of a *Point of Subjective Equality* (PSE). The difference between x, in the first observation area, and its PSE in the second observation area, is sometimes called the *constant error* associated with x (the term "systematic error" being preferable, because the difference between x and its PSE need not be constant in value across different values of x). The systematic error associated with y, in the second observation area, is defined analogously.

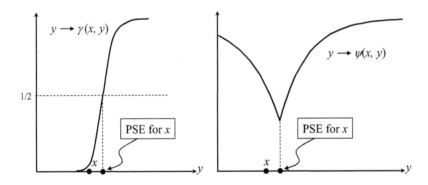

Fig. 1:   Possible   appearance   of   discrimination   probability   functions
$\gamma(x, y)$ =   Pr $[y$ is greater than x in attribute $\mathcal{P}]$ (left)   and $\psi(x, y)$ =
Pr $[x$ is different from $y]$ (right), both shown for a fixed value of x, with x and y represented by real numbers (unidimensional stimuli). For $\gamma(x, y)$, the median value of y is taken as the Point of Subjective Equality (PSE) for x (with respect to $\mathcal{P}$). For $\psi(x, y)$, PSE for x is the value of y at which $\psi(x, y)$ achieves its minimum.

Same–different discrimination also may involve a semantically unidimensional attribute (e.g., "do these two tones differ in loudness?"), but it does not have to: the question can always be formulated "generically": are the two stimuli different (in anything at all, ignoring however the difference

---

[3]Here and throughout, we use boldface lowercase letters to denote stimuli, and lightface lowercase letters when dealing with their real-number attributes; by convenient abuse of language, however, we may refer to "stimulus x" in place of "stimulus $\mathbf{x}$ with value x."

between the observation areas). It is equally immaterial whether stimuli $\mathbf{x}, \mathbf{y}$ can be represented by real numbers, vectors of real numbers, or any other mathematical construct: physical measurements only serve as labels identifying stimuli. For convenience of graphical illustrations, however, we will assume in the beginning of our discussion that $\mathbf{x}, \mathbf{y}$ are matched in all respects except for a unidimensional physical attribute (so they can be written x, y). In such a case, discrimination probability function might look as shown in Fig. 1, right. The important notion of PSE here acquires a new meaning: for x, in the first observation area, its PSE is the stimulus in the second observation which is least discriminable from x (and analogously for PSE for y in the second observation area). That such a point exists is part of the formulation of the Regular Minimality principle.[4]

Our last introductory remark relates to a possible confusion in understanding of functions $\mathbf{y} \rightarrow \psi(\mathbf{x}, \mathbf{y})$ and $\mathbf{x} \rightarrow \psi(\mathbf{x}, \mathbf{y})$; (this remark equally applies to functions $\mathbf{y} \rightarrow \gamma(\mathbf{x}, \mathbf{y})$ and $\mathbf{x} \rightarrow \gamma(\mathbf{x}, \mathbf{y})$ for greater–less discriminations). The mathematical meaning of $\mathbf{y} \rightarrow \psi(\mathbf{x}, \mathbf{y})$, for example, is that $\mathbf{x}$ is being held constant whereas $\mathbf{y}$ varies, with ψ varying as a function of $\mathbf{y}$. It is important to keep in mind that whenever we use such a construction, the distinction between $\mathbf{x}$ and $\mathbf{y}$ is purely conceptual, and not procedural: it is *not* assumed that $\mathbf{x}$ is being held constant physically within a certain block of trials whereas $\mathbf{y}$ changes from one trial to another. To emphasize this fact, we often refer to $\mathbf{y} \rightarrow \psi(\mathbf{x}, \mathbf{y})$ and $\mathbf{x} \rightarrow \psi(\mathbf{x}, \mathbf{y})$ as *cross-sections* of function $\psi(\mathbf{x}, \mathbf{y})$, made at a fixed value of $\mathbf{x}$ or $\mathbf{y}$, respectively. The ideal procedure our analysis pertains to involves all possible pairs $(\mathbf{x}, \mathbf{y})$ being presented with equal likelihoods and with no sequential dependences. All necessary and optional deviations from this ideal procedure are only acceptable under the assumption (more easily stated than tested) that they yield discrimination probabilities $\psi(\mathbf{x}, \mathbf{y})$ which approximate those obtainable by means of the ideal procedure. Among necessary deviations from the ideal procedure, the most obvious one is that we have to use samples of $(\mathbf{x}, \mathbf{y})$ pairs with a finite number of replications per pair, rather than all possible pairs of stimuli of a certain type replicated infinite number of times each. Among optional deviations, we have various partial randomization schemes (including, as a marginal case, blocking trials with constant $\mathbf{x}$ or $\mathbf{y}$). One should contrast this understanding with Zhang's analysis (2004; see also Zhang's chapter in this volume) of the situations where $\psi(\mathbf{x}, \mathbf{y})$ critically depends on the blocking of constant-$\mathbf{x}$ or constant-$\mathbf{y}$ trials, or on which of

---

[4] The reason $y \rightarrow \psi(x, y)$ in Fig. 1 (right) is drawn with a "pencil-sharp" rather than rounded minimum is that the latter can be shown (Dzhafarov, 2002b, 2003a, 2003b; Dzhafarov & Colonius, 2005a) to be incompatible with the conjunction of Regular Minimality and Nonconstant Self-Dissimilarity, discussed later.

the two stimuli in a trial is semantically labeled as the "reference" to which the other stimulus is to be compared.

2. REGULAR MEDIALITY

It is useful for our discussion to stay a while longer with the greater–less discrimination probabilities, to formulate a principle which is analogous to Regular Minimality but has a simpler mathematical structure. Refer to Figs. 2 and 3. Think, for concreteness, of x, y being independently varying lengths of two otherwise identical horizontal line segments presented side-by-side, x on the left, y on the right; γ being the probability of judging y longer than x.

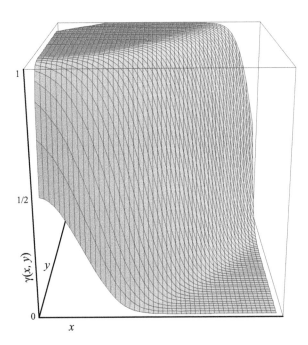

Fig. 2: Possible appearance of psychometric function $\gamma(x, y)$ for unidimensional stimuli. (This particular function was generated by a classical Thurstonian model in which x and y are mapped into independent normally distributed random variables whose means and variances change as functions of these stimuli.)

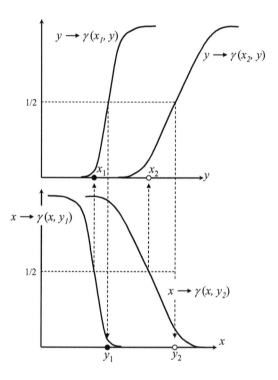

Fig. 3: Cross-sections of psychometric function $\gamma(x, y)$ shown in Fig. 2 made at two fixed values of x (upper panel) and two fixed values of y (lower panel). The figure illustrates the Regular Mediality principle for greater–less discriminations: y is the Point of Subjective Equality (PSE) for x if and only if x is the PSE for y. Thus, $\gamma(x_1, y)$ achieves level $\frac{1}{2}$ at $y = y_1$, and this is equivalent to $\gamma(x, y_1)$ achieving level $\frac{1}{2}$ at $x = x_1$ (and analogously for x_2, y_2).

We assume that, for any given x, as y changes from 0 to ∞ (or whatever the full range of presented lengths might be), function $y \to \gamma(x, y)$ increases from some value below $\frac{1}{2}$ to some value above $\frac{1}{2}$ (in Fig. 3, from 0 to 1). Because of this, the function attains $\frac{1}{2}$ at some unique value of y, by definition taken to be the PSE of x. We have therefore the following statement:

(S1) every x in $\mathcal{O}_1$ has a unique PSE y in $\mathcal{O}_2$,

where $\mathcal{O}_1, \mathcal{O}_2$ abbreviate the two observation areas. The value of y may but does not have to be equal to x. That is, we allow for a systematic error, interpretable, say, as indicating that one's perception of a given length depends on whether the segment is on the left or on the right (perceptual bias), or that the observer is predisposed to say "y is longer than x" less often or more often than to say "y is shorter than x" (response bias).

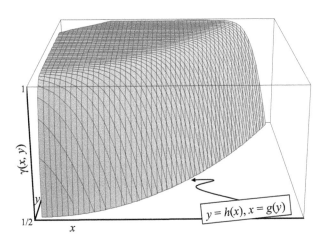

Fig. 4: The upper half of psychometric function $\gamma(x, y)$ shown in Fig. 2. The horizontal cross-section of the function at level $\frac{1}{2}$ is the PSE line, representing bijective maps h and g between the sets of all possible values for x and for y, $g \equiv h^{-1}$. By construction, $\gamma(x, h(x)) = \frac{1}{2}$ for all x; equivalently, $\gamma(g(y), y) = \frac{1}{2}$ for all y.

We further assume that, for any given y, as x changes from 0 to ∞, function $x \rightarrow \gamma(x, y)$ decreases from some value above $\frac{1}{2}$ to some value below $\frac{1}{2}$, because of which it reaches $\frac{1}{2}$ at some unique value of x, the PSE for y. We have the next statement:

(S2) every y in $\mathcal{O}_2$ has a unique PSE x in $\mathcal{O}_1$.

On a moment's reflection, we also have the third statement:

$$y \text{ in } \mathcal{O}_2 \text{ is the PSE for } x \text{ in } \mathcal{O}_1$$
(S3)   if and only if
$$x \text{ in } \mathcal{O}_1 \text{ is the PSE for } y \text{ in } \mathcal{O}_2.$$

Indeed, $\gamma(x, y) = \frac{1}{2}$ means, by definition, that both y is a PSE for x and x is a PSE for y; and due to S1 and S2, these PSEs are unique. The seeming redundancy in the formulation of S3 serves to emphasize that the statement does not involve any switching of the physical locations of the two lines as we state their PSE relations: x remains on the left, y on the right.

The three statements just formulated, S1 to S3, constitute what can be called the *Regular Mediality* principle (Dzhafarov, 2003a). Its significance in this context is in that the formulation of Regular Minimality, as we see in the next section, is essentially identical, with the following caveats: in the Regular Minimality principle, the PSEs are defined differently, the formulations of S1 to S3 are not confined to unidimensional stimuli, and S3 is an independent statement rather than a consequence of S1 and S2.

Before we turn to Regular Minimality, however, it is useful to observe the following, in reference to Fig. 4. Statement S1 is equivalent to saying that there is a function $y = h(x)$ such that $\gamma(x, h(x)) = \frac{1}{2}$, for all x. Analogously for S2, there is a function $x = g(y)$ such that $\gamma(g(y), y) = \frac{1}{2}$, for all y. The meaning of S3 then is that g and h are inverses of each other (hence they are both bijective maps, one-to-one and onto). Geometrically, there is a single PSE line in the xy-plane, equivalently representable by $y = h(x)$ and $x = g(y)$.

3.   REGULAR MINIMALITY

We give the formulation of Regular Minimality in full generality, for stimuli of arbitrary nature.

Discrimination probability function $\psi(\mathbf{x}, \mathbf{y})$ satisfies Regular Minimality if the following three statements are satisfied:

(RM1) There is a function $\mathbf{y} = \mathbf{h}(\mathbf{x})$ such that, for every $\mathbf{x}$ in $\mathcal{O}_1$, function $\mathbf{y} \rightarrow \psi(\mathbf{x}, \mathbf{y})$ achieves its minimum at $\mathbf{y} = \mathbf{h}(\mathbf{x})$ in $\mathcal{O}_2$;

(RM2) There is a function $\mathbf{x} = \mathbf{g}\left(\mathbf{y}\right)$ such that, for every $\mathbf{y}$ in $\mathcal{O}_2$, function $\mathbf{x} \to \psi\left(\mathbf{x}, \mathbf{y}\right)$ achieves its minimum at $\mathbf{x} = \mathbf{g}\left(\mathbf{y}\right)$ in $\mathcal{O}_1$;

(RM3) $\mathbf{g} \equiv \mathbf{h}^{-1}$.

Remark 1. Strictly speaking, the formulation of Regular Minimality requires a caveat: physical labels for stimuli in the two observation areas have been assigned so that, in $\mathcal{O}_1$, $\mathbf{x}_1 = \mathbf{x}_2$ if and only if they are "psychologically indistinguishable," in the sense that $\psi\left(\mathbf{x}_1, \mathbf{y}\right) = \psi\left(\mathbf{x}_2, \mathbf{y}\right)$ for all $\mathbf{y}$; and analogously for $\mathbf{y}_1, \mathbf{y}_2$ in $\mathcal{O}_2$. The notion of psychological equality (indistinguishability) is discussed later, in Section 10).

Remark 2. It follows from RM1 to RM3 that both $\mathbf{h}$ and $\mathbf{g}$ are bijective maps (one-to-one and onto), from all possible values of $\mathbf{x}$ onto all possible values of $\mathbf{y}$, and vice versa.

Remark 3. Statement RM3 can also be formulated in the form of S3 for Regular Mediality:

$$\mathbf{y} \text{ in } \mathcal{O}_2 \text{ is the PSE for } \mathbf{x} \text{ in } \mathcal{O}_1$$
$$\text{if and only if}$$
$$\mathbf{x} \text{ in } \mathcal{O}_1 \text{ is the PSE for } \mathbf{y} \text{ in } \mathcal{O}_2.$$

Figures 5 and 6 provide an illustration using unidimensional stimuli. Focusing on x_1 (in $\mathcal{O}_1$) and y_1 (in $\mathcal{O}_2$), they are PSEs of each other because $y \to \psi\left(x_1, y\right)$ achieves its minimum at $y = y_1$ and $x \to \psi\left(x, y_1\right)$ achieves its minimum at $x = x_1$. Note that x_1 and y_1 need not coincide (we see later that this depends on our choice of physical labeling). Note also that the two cross-sections, $y \to \psi\left(x_1, y\right)$ and $x \to \psi\left(x, y_1\right)$, may very well have different shapes and generally cannot be reconstructed from each other. Their minima, however, are necessarily on the same level (see Fig. 7), because, due to Regular Minimality, this level is, for the first of these cross-sections, $\psi\left(x_1, y = y_1\right)$, and for the second, $\psi\left(x = x_1, y_1\right)$.

Unlike Regular Mediality, where the uniqueness of the PSE relation (statements S1 and S2) is generally lost outside the context of unidimensional stimuli, Regular Minimality applies to stimuli of arbitrary nature, including multidimensional stimuli, such as colors identified by Commission Internationale de l'Eclairage (CIE) or Munsell coordinates, discrete stimuli (such as letters of alphabet), and more complex stimuli (such as human faces or variable-trajectory variable-speed motions of a visual target), representable by one or several functions of several arguments. Figure 8 illustrates Regular Minimality for two-dimensional stimuli (the analogue of Fig. 5, being a four-dimensional hypersurface, cannot, of course, be shown graphically).

A toy example demonstrates Regular Minimality in the case of a discrete stimulus set. Symbols $\mathbf{x}_a$, $\mathbf{x}_b$, $\mathbf{x}_c$, $\mathbf{x}_d$ represent stimuli in the first

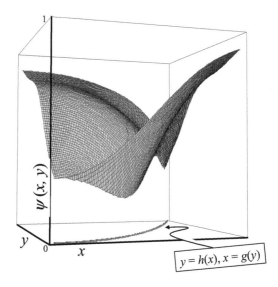

Fig. 5: Possible appearance of discrimination probability function $\psi(x, y)$ for uni-dimensional stimuli. (This particular function was generated by the "quadrilateral dissimilarity" model described in Section 7.2.) The function satisfies Regular Minimality. The curve in the xy-plane is the PSE line, representing bijective maps h and g between the sets of all possible values for x and for y, $g \equiv h^{-1}$. By definition of PSE, for any fixed x, $\psi(x, y)$ achieves its minimum at $y = h(x)$; and for any fixed y, $\psi(x, y)$ achieves its minimum at $x = g(y)$.

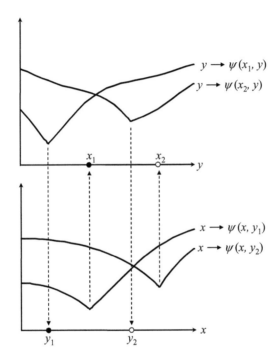

Fig. 6: Cross-sections of discrimination probability function $\psi(x, y)$ shown in Fig. 5 made at two fixed values of x (upper panel) and two fixed values of y (lower panel). The figure illustrates the Regular Minimality principle for same-different discriminations: y is the PSE for x if and only if x is the PSE for y. Thus, $\psi(x_1, y)$ achieves its minimum at $y = y_1$, while $\psi(x, y_1)$ achieves its minimum at $x = x_1$ (and analogously for x_2, y_2).

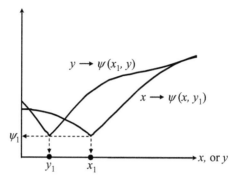

Fig. 7: The superposition of functions $\psi(x_1, y)$ and $\psi(x, y_1)$ from Fig. 6. Minimum level ψ_1 is the same in these two (generally different) functions because in both cases it equals $\psi(x_1, y_1)$.

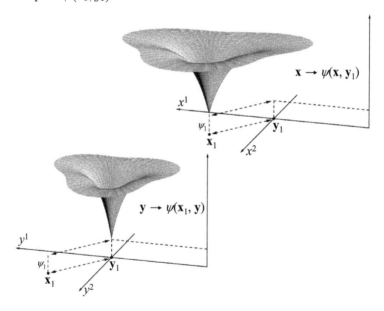

Fig. 8: Two cross-sections of a discrimination probability function, $\psi(\mathbf{x}, \mathbf{y})$, $\mathbf{x} = (x^1, x^2)$, $\mathbf{y} = (y^1, y^2)$, made at a fixed value of $\mathbf{x}$ ($\mathbf{x} = \mathbf{x}_1$, lower panel) and a fixed value of $\mathbf{y}$ ($\mathbf{y} = \mathbf{y}_1$, upper panel). The figure illustrates the Regular Minimality principle for same–different discriminations of two–dimensional stimuli: $\psi(\mathbf{x}_1, \mathbf{y})$ achieves its minimum at at $\mathbf{y} = \mathbf{y}_1$ (i.e., $\mathbf{y}_1$ is the PSE for $\mathbf{x}_1$) if and only if $\psi(\mathbf{x}, \mathbf{y}_1)$ achieves its minimum at $\mathbf{x} = \mathbf{x}_1$ (i.e., $\mathbf{x}_1$ is the PSE for $\mathbf{y}_1$). Minimum level ψ_1 is the same in the two panels because in both cases it equals $\psi(\mathbf{x}_1, \mathbf{y}_1)$. This is essentially a two-dimensional analogue of Figs. 6 and 7.

observation area, $\mathbf{y}_a$, $\mathbf{y}_b$, $\mathbf{y}_c$, $\mathbf{y}_d$ represent the same four stimuli in the second observation area. (We discuss later that, in general, stimulus sets in the two observation areas need not be the same.) The entries of the matrix represent discrimination probabilities $\psi(\mathbf{x}, \mathbf{y})$.

TOY$_1$	$\mathbf{y}_a$	$\mathbf{y}_b$	$\mathbf{y}_c$	$\mathbf{y}_d$
$\mathbf{x}_a$	0.6	0.6	0.1	0.8
$\mathbf{x}_b$	0.9	0.9	0.8	0.1
$\mathbf{x}_c$	1	0.5	1	0.6
$\mathbf{x}_d$	0.5	0.7	1	1

Here, Regular Minimality manifests itself in the fact that

1. every row contains a single minimal cell;
2. every column contains a single minimal cell;
3. a cell is minimal in its row if and only if it is minimal in its column.

The four PSE pairs in this example are $(\mathbf{x}_a, \mathbf{y}_c)$, $(\mathbf{x}_b, \mathbf{y}_d)$, $(\mathbf{x}_c, \mathbf{y}_b)$, and $(\mathbf{x}_d, \mathbf{y}_a)$.

4. NONCONSTANT SELF-DISSIMILARITY

Another important feature exhibited by our matrix TOY$_1$ is that the minima achieved by function $\psi(\mathbf{x}, \mathbf{y})$ at PSE pairs are not all on the same level:

$\mathcal{O}_1$	$\mathbf{x}_a$	$\mathbf{x}_b$	$\mathbf{x}_c$	$\mathbf{x}_d$
$\mathcal{O}_2$	$\mathbf{y}_c$	$\mathbf{y}_d$	$\mathbf{y}_b$	$\mathbf{y}_a$
ψ	0.1	0.1	0.5	0.5

The same is true for the discrimination probability function shown in Fig. 5. This is best illustrated by the "wall" erected vertically from the PSE line until it touches the surface representing $\psi(x, y)$, as shown in Fig. 9. The upper contour of the "wall" is function $\omega_1(x) = \psi(x, h(x))$ or equivalently, $\omega_2(y) = \psi(g(y), y)$, the values attained by $\psi(x, y)$ when x and y are mutual PSEs.

In general, we call the values of $\psi(\mathbf{x}, \mathbf{y})$ attained when the two arguments are each other's PSEs (i.e., $\mathbf{y} = \mathbf{h}(\mathbf{x})$, $\mathbf{x} = \mathbf{g}(\mathbf{y})$), the *self-dissimilarity values*, and we call either of functions $\omega_1(\mathbf{x}) = \psi(\mathbf{x}, \mathbf{h}(\mathbf{x}))$ and $\omega_2(\mathbf{y}) = \psi(\mathbf{y}, \mathbf{h}(\mathbf{y}))$, the *minimum level function*. Although $\omega_1(\mathbf{x})$ and $\omega_2(\mathbf{y})$ may be different functions, geometrically they describe one and the same set of

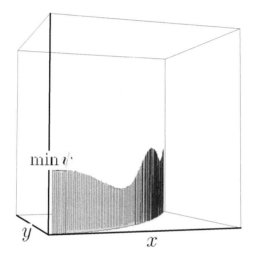

Fig. 9: The "wall" whose bottom contour is PSE line $y = h(x)$ (equivalently, $x = g(y)$) for function $\psi(x,y)$ shown in Fig. 5, and the top contour is minimum level function $\psi(x, h(x))$ (equivalently, $\psi(g(y),y)$) for the same function. The figure illustrates, in addition to Regular Minimality, the notion of Nonconstant Self-Dissimilarity: the minimum level function is not constant..

points in the $\mathbf{xy}\psi$-coordinates (in the same way $\mathbf{h}(\mathbf{x})$ and $\mathbf{g}(\mathbf{y})$ describe one and the same set of points in $\mathbf{xy}$-coordinates).

According to the principle of Nonconstant Self-Dissimilarity, $\omega_1(\mathbf{x})$ (or, equivalently, $\omega_2(\mathbf{y})$) is not *necessarily* a constant function. The modal quantifier "is not necessarily" should be understood in the following sense. For a given stimulus set presented to a given perceiver it may happen that $\omega_1(\mathbf{x})$ has a constant value across all values of $\mathbf{x}$. It may only happen, however, as a numerical coincidence rather than by virtue of a law that compels $\omega_1(\mathbf{x})$ to be constant: $\omega_1(\mathbf{x})$ considered across all possible sets of stimuli pairwise presented in all possible experiments with all possible perceivers will at least sometimes be a nonconstant function. If $\omega_1(\mathbf{x})$ is nonconstant for a particular discrimination probability function $\psi(\mathbf{x}, \mathbf{y})$, we say that Nonconstant Self-Dissimilarity is *manifest* in this function. This is the most conservative formulation of the principle. With less caution, one might hypothesize that minimum level function $\omega_1(\mathbf{x})$, at least in psychophysical applications involving same–different judgments, is never constant, provided the probabilities are measured precisely enough.

For completeness, Fig. 10 illustrates Nonconstant Self-Dissimilarity for two-dimensional stimuli, like the ones in Fig. 8. The surface that contains the minima of the cross-sections $\mathbf{y} \to \psi(\mathbf{x}, \mathbf{y})$ is the minimum level function $\omega_2(\mathbf{y})$.

5. FUNCTIONS VIOLATING REGULAR MINIMALITY

Unlike Regular Mediality, which can be mathematically deduced from the monotonicity of cross-sections $x \to \gamma(x, y)$ and $y \to \gamma(x, y)$, Regular Minimality is not reducible to more elementary properties of $\psi(\mathbf{x}, \mathbf{y})$.

It is easy to see how Regular Minimality can be violated in discrete stimulus sets.

TOY_2	$\mathbf{y}_a$	$\mathbf{y}_b$	$\mathbf{y}_c$	$\mathbf{y}_d$	TOY_3	$\mathbf{y}_a$	$\mathbf{y}_b$	$\mathbf{y}_c$	$\mathbf{y}_d$
$\mathbf{x}_a$	0.1	0.6	0.1	0.8	$\mathbf{x}_a$	0.7	0.4	0.2	0.8
$\mathbf{x}_b$	0.9	0.9	0.8	0.1	$\mathbf{x}_b$	0.9	0.9	0.8	0.4
$\mathbf{x}_c$	1	0.5	1	0.6	$\mathbf{x}_c$	1	0.6	0.7	0.8
$\mathbf{x}_d$	0.5	0.7	1	1	$\mathbf{x}_d$	0.4	0.7	1	1

Using the same format as in matrix TOY_1, the first of the two matrices above has two equal minima in the first row, in violation of RM1. One can say here that $\mathbf{x}_a$ in $\mathcal{O}_1$ has two PSEs in $\mathcal{O}_2$ ($\mathbf{y}_a$ and $\mathbf{y}_c$), or (if the

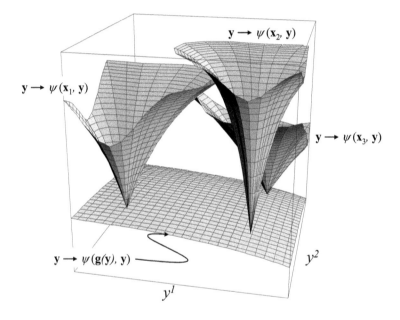

Fig. 10: An illustration of Nonconstant Self-Dissimilarity for two-dimensional stimuli. Shown are three cross-sections $\mathbf{y} \to \psi(\mathbf{x}, \mathbf{y})$, $\mathbf{x} = \mathbf{x}_1, \mathbf{x}_2, \mathbf{x}_3$, of discrimination probability function $\psi(\mathbf{x}, \mathbf{y})$, whose minima, $\mathbf{h}(\mathbf{x}_1)$, $\mathbf{h}(\mathbf{x}_2)$, and $\mathbf{h}(\mathbf{x}_3)$, lie on minimum level surface $\psi(\mathbf{g}(\mathbf{y}), \mathbf{y})$, where $\mathbf{g} \equiv \mathbf{h}^{-1}$. This surface is not parallel to the $y^1 y^2$-plane, manifesting Nonconstant Self-Dissimilarity.

uniqueness of a PSE is considered part of its definition) that the PSE for $\mathbf{x}_a$ is not defined. Matrix TOY_3 above is of a different kind: it satisfies properties RM1 and RM2 but violates RM3. Stimulus $\mathbf{x}_c$ in $\mathcal{O}_1$ has $\mathbf{y}_b$ in $\mathcal{O}_2$ as its unique PSE; the unique PSE in $\mathcal{O}_1$ for $\mathbf{y}_b$, however, is not $\mathbf{x}_c$ but $\mathbf{x}_a$ (one could continue: and the PSE for $\mathbf{x}_a$ is not $\mathbf{y}_b$ but $\mathbf{y}_c$). In a situation like this one can say that the relation "is the PSE of" is not symmetrical, and the notion of a *"PSE pair"* is not well defined.

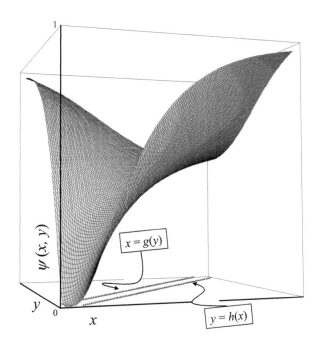

Fig. 11: An example of function $\psi(x, y)$ that violates Regular Minimality. (This particular function was generated by Luce-Galanter's Thurstonian-type model described in Section 7.1.) For a fixed value of x, $\psi(x, y)$ achieves its minimum at $y = h(x)$; for a fixed value of y, $\psi(x, y)$ achieves its minimum at $x = g(y)$. But g is not the inverse of h: the lines $y = h(x)$ and $x = g(y)$ (nearly straight lines in this example) do not coincide. Compare to Fig. 5.

Figures 11, 12, and 13 present an analogue for TOY_3 in a continuous (unidimensional) domain. The function depicted in these figures satisfies properties RM1 and RM2, but violates RM3: if y is the PSE for x, the latter generally will not (in this example, never) be the PSE for y, and vice versa. The notion of a PSE pair is not well defined here. Specifically,

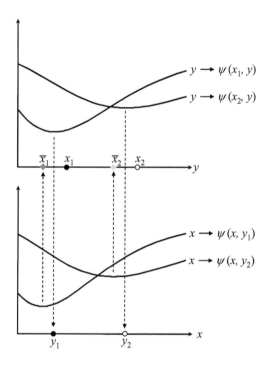

Fig. 12: Cross-sections of function $\psi(x,y)$ shown in Fig. 11 made at two fixed values of x (upper panel) and two fixed values of y (lower panel). The figure details violations of the Regular Minimality principle in this function: $\psi(x_1,y)$ achieves its minimum at $y = y_1$, but $\psi(x,y_1)$ achieves its minimum at a point different from $x = x_1$ (and analogously for x_2, y_2). One cannot speak of PSE pairs unambiguously in this case: for example., (x_1, y_1) and $(\bar{x}_1, y_1)$ are both "PSE pairs," with one and the same y_1 in the second observation area.

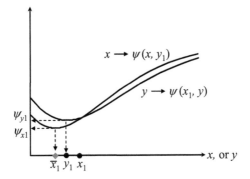

Fig. 13: The superposition of functions $\psi(x_1, y)$ and $\psi(x, y_1)$ from Fig. 12. Minimum level ψ_{x1} for the former is not the same as minimum level ψ_{y1} for the latter. Compare with Fig. 7.

one and the same stimulus (say, $x = a$ in $\mathcal{O}_1$) can be paired either with y at which $\psi(a, y)$ achieves its minimum, or with $\bar{y}$ such that $x \to \psi(x, \bar{y})$ achieves its minimum at $x = a$.

It may be useful to look at this issue more schematically. Regular Minimality can be represented by the diagram

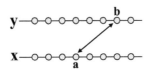

in which the two "beaded strings" stand for stimuli in the two observation areas, and arrows stand for relation "is the PSE for." Starting at any point and traveling along the arrows, one is bound to return to this point after having visited just one other point, its PSE in the other observation area. If Regular Minimality is violated, the traveling along the arrows between the observation areas becomes more adventurous, with the potential of "wandering away" indefinitely far:

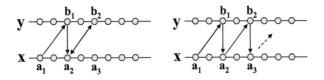

6.   EMPIRICAL EVIDENCE

Discrimination probabilities of the same–different type have not been studied as intensively as those of the greater–less type. The available empirical evidence, however, seems to be in good agreement with the hypothesis that discrimination probabilities (a) satisfy Regular Minimality and (b) manifest Nonconstant Self-Dissimilarity.

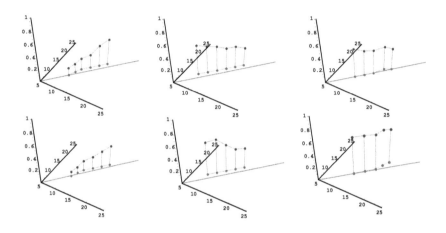

Fig. 14: An empirical version of Fig. 9, based on one of the experiments described in Dzhafarov and Colonius (2005a). x and y are lengths of two horizontal line segments, in pixels (1 pixel $\approx$ 0.86 min arc), presented side-by-side; each panel represents an experiment with a single observer. The bottom line shows estimated positions of PSEs, $y = h(x)$, the upper line shows the corresponding probabilities, $\psi(x, h(x))$ (the minimum level function). Straight lines in the xy-planes are bisectors. Each probability estimate is based on 500 to 600 replications.

In an experiment reported in Dzhafarov and Colonius (2005a), observers were asked to compare two side-by-side presented horizontal line segments (identical except for their lengths, x on the left, y on the right). The results of such an experiment are represented by a matrix of pairwise probabilities $\psi(x, y)$, with x and y values providing a dense sample of length values within a relatively small interval. Except for an occasional necessity to interpolate a minimum between two successive values, the compliance with Regular Minimality in such a matrix is verified by showing that the matrix is structured essentially like TOY$_1$ in Section 3 rather than TOY$_2$ or TOY$_3$ in Section 5. If (and only if) Regular Minimality is established, one can draw a single line through PSE pairs, $(x, h(x))$ or, equivalently, $(g(y), y)$, in the

xy-plane. Plotting the discrimination probability against each of these PSE pairs, we get an empirical version of the minimum level function. The results presented in Fig. 14 clearly show that Regular Minimality is satisfied, and that $\psi\left(x, h\left(x\right)\right)$ is generally different for different x (i.e., Nonconstant Self-Dissimilarity is manifest). Note, in relation to the issue of canonical transformations, considered in Section 9, that x and y in a PSE pair (x, y) in these data are generally physically different, y (the length on the right) tends to be larger, indicating that the right lengths tend to be underestimated with respect to the left ones ("systematic error"). Analogous results are reported in Dzhafarov (2002b) and Dzhafarov and Colonius (2005a) for same–different discriminations of apparent motions (two-dot displays with temporal asynchrony between the dots) presented side-by-side or in a succession.

Figure 15 shows the results of an experiment by Zimmer and Colonius (2000), in which listeners made same–different judgments in response to successively presented sinusoidal tones varying in intensity (x followed by y). Regular Minimality here holds in the simplest form: x and y are mutual PSEs if (and only if) $x = y$. The minimum level function here is therefore $\psi\left(x, x\right)$ (equivalently, $\psi\left(y, y\right)$), and it clearly manifests Nonconstant Self–Dissimilarity.

Indow, Robertson, von Grunau, and Fielder (1992) and Indow (1998) reported discrimination probabilities for side-by-side presented colors varying in CIE chromaticity-luminance coordinates (a three-dimensional continuous stimulus space). With the right-hand color $\mathbf{y}$ serving as a fixed reference stimulus, function $\mathbf{x} \to \psi\left(\mathbf{x}, \mathbf{y}\right)$ in this study reached its minimum at $\mathbf{x} = \mathbf{y}$,

$$\mathbf{x} \neq \mathbf{y} \Longrightarrow \psi\left(\mathbf{y}, \mathbf{y}\right) < \psi\left(\mathbf{x}, \mathbf{y}\right).$$

The experiment was not conducted with fully randomized color pairs, and it was not replicated with the left-hand color $\mathbf{x}$ used as a reference. One cannot therefore check for the compliance with Regular Minimality directly. It is reasonable to assume, however, that $\psi\left(\mathbf{x}, \mathbf{y}\right)$ for side-by-side presented colors is order-balanced,

$$\psi\left(\mathbf{x}, \mathbf{y}\right) = \psi\left(\mathbf{y}, \mathbf{x}\right),$$

and under this assumption, it is easily seen, the inequality above implies Regular Minimality in the simplest form: $\mathbf{x}$ and $\mathbf{y}$ are mutual PSEs if (and only if) $\mathbf{x} = \mathbf{y}$. Nonconstant Self-Dissimilarity is a prominent feature of Indow's data: for instance, with reference color $\mathbf{y}$ changing from grey to red to yellow to green to blue, the probability $\psi\left(\mathbf{y}, \mathbf{y}\right)$ for one observer increased from 0.07 to 0.33.

The conjunction of the simplest form of Regular Minimality with prominent Nonconstant Self-Dissimilarity was also obtained in two large data sets

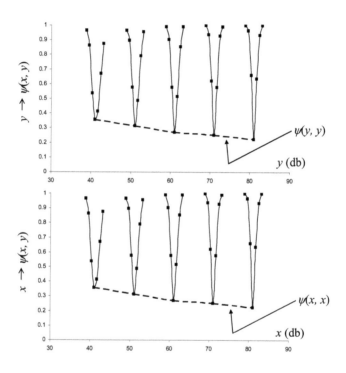

Fig. 15: An empirical version of Fig. 6, based on an experiment reported in Zimmer and Colonius (2000). x and y represent intensity of pure tones of a fixed frequency. The data are shown for a single listener. The PSEs in this case are physically identical, $h(x) = x$; that is, for any x, $\psi(x, y)$ achieves its minimum at $y = x$, and for any y, $\psi(x, y)$ achieves its minimum at $x = y$. The value of $\psi(x, x)$ decreases with increasing x.

involving discrete stimuli (36 Morse codes for letters and digits in Rothkopf, 1957, and 32 Morse code-like stimuli in Wish, 1967; sequential presentation in both cases). Below is a small fragment of Rothkopf's matrix: $\psi\,(\mathbf{x}, \mathbf{y})$ in each cell, for $\mathbf{x}, \mathbf{y} = D, H, K, S, W$. Each value on the main diagonal is the smallest probability in both its row and its column (Regular Minimality), and this value varies along the diagonal from 0.04 to 0.14 (Nonconstant Self-Dissimilarity). (A single deviation from this pattern found in Wish's data can be attributed to a statistical estimation error; for details, see Chapter 2 in this volume.)

RO	D	H	K	S	W
D	.12	.64	.19	.71	.82
H	.75	.13	.91	.63	.91
K	.27	.89	.09	.98	.67
S	.70	.41	.87	.04	.88
W	.78	.85	.71	.88	.14

7.   THE CONJUNCTION OF REGULAR MINIMALITY AND NONCONSTANT SELF-DISSIMILARITY

When dealing with stimulus sets containing finite number of elements, it is easy to construct examples of discrimination probability matrices that both satisfy Regular Minimality and manifest Nonconstant Self-Dissimilarity (as our matrix TOY$_1$ shown earlier). Here is a simple algorithm: given an n-element stimulus set, create any sequence (i_1, j_1), ..., (i_n, j_n), with $(i_1, ..., i_n)$ and $(j_1, ..., j_n)$ being two complete permutations of $(1, ..., n)$; fill in cells (i_1, j_1), ..., (i_n, j_n) with probability values $\psi_1 \geq ... \geq \psi_n$; fill in the rest of the i_1th row and j_1th column by values greater than ψ_1; fill in the rest of the i_2th row and j_2th column by values greater than ψ_2; etc. In thus a created matrix, the i_kth row stimulus (interpreted as a stimulus in $\mathcal{O}_1$) and the j_kth column stimulus (in $\mathcal{O}_2$) will be mutual PSEs ($k = 1, ..., n$), and Nonconstant Self-Dissimilarity will be manifest if at least one of the inequalities in $\psi_1 \geq ... \geq \psi_n$ is strict. It is equally easy to construct examples that do not satisfy Regular Minimality (as TOY$_2$ and TOY$_3$ matrices above) or do not manifest Nonconstant Self-Dissimilarity (set $\psi_1 = ... = \psi_n$ in the algorithm just given).

The construction of examples is less obvious in the case of continuous stimulus sets, as in our Fig. 5 and Fig. 11. It is instructive therefore to consider theoretical models which generate functions $\psi(\mathbf{x}, \mathbf{y})$ that always satisfy the conjunction of Regular Minimality and Nonconstant Self-Dissimilarity, as well as theoretical models whose generated functions $\psi(\mathbf{x}, \mathbf{y})$ always violate this conjunction of properties. We consider the latter class of models first.

7.1. Thurstonian-type models

To avoid technicalities, we confine our discussion here to the unidimensional case, with x, y taking on their values on intervals of reals, finite or infinite. The results to be mentioned, however, generalize to arbitrary continuous spaces of stimuli.

Consider the following scheme, well familiar to psychophysicists. Let any pair (x, y) presented to an observer for a same–different comparison be mapped into a pair of perceptual images, (P_x, Q_y), and let P_x and Q_y be mutually independent random entities taking on their values in some perceptual space, of arbitrary nature.[5] In any given trial, the observer experiences two realizations of these random entities, (p, q), and there is a decision rule that maps some of the possible (p, q)-pairs into response "same" and the remaining ones into response "different." The decision rule can be arbitrary, and so can be the distributions of P_x and Q_y in the perceptual space, except for the following critical constraint: we assume that P_x and Q_y are "well-behaved" in response to small changes in x and y. This means the following. The distribution of P_x is determined by the probabilities with which p falls within various measurable subsets of the perceptual space, and these probabilities generally change as x changes within an arbitrarily small interval of values. Intuitively, P_x is well-behaved if the rate of these changes cannot get arbitrarily high. The well-behavedness of Q_y is defined analogously.[6] As shown in Dzhafarov (2003a), no $\psi(x, y)$ generated by such a model can both satisfy Regular Minimality and manifest

---

[5] Notation conventions: P_x, Q_y, and $S_{x,y}$ designate random entities whose distributions depend on their index. Random entities are called random variables if their realizations p, q, s, are real numbers (with the Lebesgue sigma-algebra).

[6] In terminology of Dzhafarov (2003a), this is the "well-behavedness in the narrow (or absolute) sense": for any $x = a$, the right-hand and left-hand derivatives of $\Pr[P_x \in \mathfrak{p}]$ with respect to x exist and are bounded across all measurable sets $\mathfrak{p}$ and all values of x within an arbitrarily small interval $[a - \varepsilon, a + \varepsilon]$ (and analogously for y and Q_y). This requirement can be considerably weakened, with respect to both the class of (x, y)-values and the class of measurable sets for which it is supposed to hold (details in Dzhafarov, 2003a, b). The simplest and perhaps most important example of a non-well-behaved P_x is a deterministic entity, having a single possible value for every x.

Nonconstant Self-Dissimilarity. This means, in particular, that with such a model,

1. if $\psi(x, y)$ satisfies Regular Minimality, then $\psi(x, y) \equiv$ *constant* across all PSE pairs (x, y) (i.e., Regular Minimality can only coexist with *Constant* Self-Dissimilarity);
2. if $y \to \psi(x, y)$ achieves a minimum at $y = h(x)$, if $x \to \psi(x, y)$ achieves a minimum at $x = g(y)$, and if either $\psi(x, h(x))$ or $\psi(g(y), y)$ is nonconstant across, respectively, x and y values, then g cannot coincide with h^{-1} (i.e., even if RM1 and RM2 are satisfied, Nonconstant Self-Dissimilarity forces RM3 of Regular Minimality to be violated).

The class of such models has its historical origins in Thurstone's analysis of greater–less discriminations (Thurstone, 1927a, 1927b), because of which in Dzhafarov (2003a, 2003b) such models are referred to as "Thurstonian-type" (see Fig. 16). The simplest Thurstonian-type model for same–different discriminations is presented in Luce and Galanter (1963): the perceptual space is the set of reals, P_x and Q_y are normally distributed, and the decision rule is "respond 'different' if and only if $|p - q| > \varepsilon$," for some $\varepsilon > 0$. If the means and the variances of these normal distributions, $(\mu_P(x), \sigma_P^2(x))$ and $(\mu_Q(y), \sigma_Q^2(y))$, are piecewise smooth functions of x and y (which is sufficient although not necessary for P_x and Q_y to be well-behaved), then the resulting $\psi(x, y)$ must violate the conjunction of Regular Minimality and Nonconstant Self-Dissimilarity. Figures 11, 12, and 13 are generated by means of such a model (with x, y positive, and $\mu_P(x)$, $\sigma_P^2(x)$, $\mu_Q(y)$, $\sigma_Q^2(y)$ linear transformations of their arguments).

Most Thurstonian-type models proposed in the literature for same–different discriminations involve univariate or multivariate normal distributions for perceptual images of stimuli (Dai, Versfeld, & Green, 1996; Ennis, 1992; Ennis, Palen, & Mullen, 1988; Luce & Galanter, 1963; Sorkin, 1962; Suppes & Zinnes, 1963; Thomas, 1996; Zinnes & MacKay, 1983). With these and other distributions possessing finite density in $\mathbb{R}^n$ ($n \geq 1$), a piecewise smooth dependence of their parameters on x or y implies their well-behavedness, hence the impossibility of generating a discrimination probability function with both Regular Minimality and Nonconstant Self-Dissimilarity. Luce (1977) called Thurstonian models the "essence of simplicity": "this conception of internal representation of signals is so simple and so intuitively compelling that no one ever really manages to escape from it. No matter how one thinks about psychophysical phenomena, one seems to come back to it" (p. 462). Luce refers here to the simplest Thurstonian models, involving unidimensional random representations and simple decision rules based on values of $p - q$. These models do work well for greater–less discriminations, generating functions like the one shown in

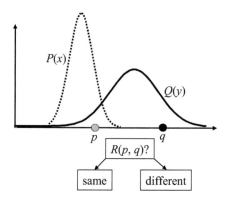

Fig. 16: Schematic representation of a Thurstonian-type model. Stimuli x and y are mapped into their "perceptual images," random variables $P(x)$ and $Q(y)$ (here, independently normally distributed on a set of reals). Response "same" or "different" is given depending on whether the realizations p, q of $P(x)$ and $Q(y)$ in a given trial stand or do not stand in a particular relation, R, to each other (e.g., $|p - q|$ exceeds or does not exceed some ε, or p, q fall or do not fall within one and the same interval in some partitioning of the set of reals). In general, p and q may be elements of an arbitrary set, the decision rule may be probabilistic (i.e., every pair p, q may lead to response "different" with some probability $\pi(p,q)$), and "perceptual images" $P(x)$ and $Q(y)$ may be stochastically interdependent, provided they are selectively attributable to x and y, respectively (in the sense of Dzhafarov, 2003c).

Figs. 2-4, subject to Regular Mediality. In the context of same–different discriminations, however, if the properties of Regular Minimality and Non-constant Self-Dissimilarity do hold empirically, as data seem to suggest, Thurstonian-type models fail even if one allows for arbitrary decision rules and arbitrarily complex (but well-behaved) distributions for P_x and Q_y.[7] Moreover, the failure in question extends to the models in which decision rules are probabilistic rather than deterministic, that is, where each pair (p, q) can lead to both responses, "same" and "different," with certain probabilities (Dzhafarov, 2003b).

Finally, the failure in question extends to models with stochastically interdependent P_x and Q_y, provided P_x can still be considered an image of x (and not also of y) whereas Q_y is considered an image of y (and not also of x). The *selective attribution* of P_x and Q_y to x and y, respectively, is understood in the meaning explicated in Dzhafarov (2003c): one can find mutually independent random entities C, C_1, C_2, whose distributions do not depend on either x or y, such that

$$P_x = \pi\left(x, C, C_1\right), \quad Q_y = \theta\left(y, C, C_2\right), \tag{3}$$

where π, θ are some measurable functions. In other words, P_x and Q_y depend on x and y selectively, and their stochastic interdependence is due to a *common source of variability*, C. The latter may represent, for example, random fluctuations in the arousal or attention level, or in receptive fields' sensitivity profiles. P_x and Q_y then are *conditionally independent* at any fixed value c of C, because random entities $\pi\left(x, c, C_1\right)$ and $\theta\left(y, c, C_2\right)$ have independent sources of variability, C_1, C_2. As shown in Dzhafarov (2003b), if, for any c, $\pi\left(x, c, C_1\right)$ and $\theta\left(y, c, C_2\right)$ are well-behaved in the sense explained earlier (in which case we call P_x and Q_y themselves well-behaved), the resulting discrimination probability functions cannot both satisfy Regular Minimality and manifest Nonconstant Self-Dissimilarity.

The selectiveness in the attribution of P_x to x and Q_y to y is an important caveat. In Dzhafarov's (2003a, 2003b) terminology which we follow here, it is a necessary condition for calling a stochastic model Thurstonian-type. *Any* function $\psi\left(x, y\right)$ can be accounted for by a model in which x and y jointly map into a perceptual property, $S_{x,y}$, which then either maps into responses "same" and "different" probabilistically, or is a random entity itself, mapped into the responses by means of a certain decision rule (these two conceptual schemes are mathematically equivalent). For example, $S_{x,y}$ may be a nonnegative random variable interpretable as a measure

---

[7] The well-behavedness constraint, in some form, is critical here: as shown in Dzhafarov (2003a), *any* function $\psi\left(x, y\right)$ can be generated by a Thurstonian-type model if $P\left(x\right)$ and $Q\left(y\right)$ are allowed to have arbitrary distributions arbitrarily depending on, respectively, x and y. The well-behavedness constraint, however, is unlikely to be violated in a model designed to fit or simulate empirical data.

of "subjective dissimilarity" between x and y, and the decision rule be as in the classical signal detection theory: respond "different" if and only if the realization of s of $S_{x,y}$ exceeds some $\varepsilon > 0$. A model of the latter variety can be found, for example, in Takane and Sergent (1983). With this approach, $S_{x,y}$ can always be set up in such a way that $\psi(x,y)$ possesses both Regular Minimality and Nonconstant Self-Dissimilarity. Once this is done, Dzhafarov's (2003a, 2003b) results would indicate that $S_{x,y}$ cannot be computed from any two well-behaved random entities P_x and Q_y selectively attributable to x and y (e.g., subjective dissimilarity $S_{x,y}$ cannot be presented as $|P_x - Q_y|$ in Luce and Galanter's model mentioned earlier). In other words, $S_{x,y}$ must be an "emergent property," not reducible to the separate (and well-behaved) perceptual images of x and of y. We discuss such models next, but we prefer to do this within the conceptually more economic (but equivalent) theoretical language in which $S_{x,y}$ is treated as a deterministic quantity, $S(x,y)$, mapped into responses "same" and "different" probabilistically.

7.2.   "Quadrilateral dissimilarity," "uncertainty blobs," etc.

At this point, we can switch back to stimuli $\mathbf{x}, \mathbf{y}$ of arbitrary nature, as the case of unidimensional stimuli is technically no simpler than the general case. We consider a measure of subjective dissimilarity, $S(\mathbf{x},\mathbf{y})$, a deterministic quantity (i.e., having a fixed value for any $\mathbf{x},\mathbf{y}$) related to discrimination probabilities by

$$\psi(\mathbf{x},\mathbf{y}) = \beta(S(\mathbf{x},\mathbf{y})), \tag{4}$$

where β is some strictly increasing function. Such a model is distinctly non-Thurstonian as it does not involve individual random images for individual stimuli. Rather the models of this class are in the spirit of what Luce and Edwards (1958) called "the old, famous psychological rule of thumb: equally often noticed differences are equal" (p. 232), provided one keeps in mind that the "difference," understood to mean dissimilarity $S(\mathbf{x},\mathbf{y})$, cannot be a true distance (as this would force constant minima at $\mathbf{x} = \mathbf{y}$).[8] As it turns out, for a broad class of possible definitions of $S(\mathbf{x},\mathbf{y})$, such

---

[8] The Probability-Distance hypothesis, as it is termed in Dzhafarov (2002a), according to which $\psi(\mathbf{x},\mathbf{y})$ is an increasing transformation of some distance $D(\mathbf{x},\mathbf{y})$, is as traditional in psychophysics as is the Thurstonian-type modeling. In the context of unidimensional stimuli and greater–less discrimination probabilities $\gamma(x,y)$ this hypothesis is known as the "Fechner problem" (Falmagne, 1971; Luce & Edwards, 1958). See Dzhafarov (2002a) for history and a detailed discussion.

models only generate discrimination probability functions that are subject
to both Regular Minimality and Nonconstant Self-Dissimilarity. Intuitively,
the underlying idea is that the dissimilarity between stimulus $\mathbf{x}$ in $\mathcal{O}_1$ and
stimulus $\mathbf{y}$ in $\mathcal{O}_2$ involves (a) the distance between $\mathbf{x}$ and the PSE $\mathbf{g}\left(\mathbf{y}\right)$ of
$\mathbf{y}$ (both in $\mathcal{O}_1$), (b) the distance between $\mathbf{y}$ and the PSE $\mathbf{h}\left(\mathbf{x}\right)$ of $\mathbf{x}$ (both
in $\mathcal{O}_2$), and (c) some slowly changing "residual" dissimilarities within the
PSE pairs themselves, $(\mathbf{x}, \mathbf{h}\left(\mathbf{x}\right))$ and $(\mathbf{g}\left(\mathbf{y}\right), \mathbf{y})$.[9]

As before, the "beaded strings" in the diagram below schematically
represent stimulus sets in the two observation areas, but the arrows now
designate the components of a possible dissimilarity measure between $\mathbf{x_a}$
and $\mathbf{y_b}$. The PSE relation is indicated by identical index at $\mathbf{x}$ and $\mathbf{y}$: thus,
$(\mathbf{x_a}, \mathbf{y_a})$ and $(\mathbf{x_b}, \mathbf{y_b})$ are PSE pairs.

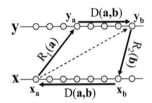

We assume some distance measure D among stimuli *within* either of the
observation areas: the notation $D\left(\mathbf{a}, \mathbf{b}\right)$ indicates that the distance between
$\mathbf{x_a}$ and $\mathbf{x_b}$ in $\mathcal{O}_1$ is the same as that between their respective PSEs, $\mathbf{y_a}$ and
$\mathbf{y_b}$, in $\mathcal{O}_2$. By definition of distance, $D\left(\mathbf{a}, \mathbf{b}\right) \geq 0$, $D\left(\mathbf{a}, \mathbf{b}\right) = 0$ if and only
if $\mathbf{a} = \mathbf{b}$, $D\left(\mathbf{a}, \mathbf{b}\right) = D\left(\mathbf{b}, \mathbf{a}\right)$, and $D\left(\mathbf{a}, \mathbf{b}\right) + D\left(\mathbf{b}, \mathbf{c}\right) \geq D\left(\mathbf{a}, \mathbf{c}\right)$.[10] We
also assume the existence of the "residual" dissimilarity within the PSE
pairs, *across* the two observation areas: for any PSE pair $(\mathbf{x_c}, \mathbf{y_c})$, this
dissimilarity is a nonnegative number denoted $R_1\left(\mathbf{c}\right)$ if computed from $\mathcal{O}_1$
to $\mathcal{O}_2$, and $R_2\left(\mathbf{c}\right)$ if computed from $\mathcal{O}_2$ to $\mathcal{O}_1$. Generally, $R_1\left(\mathbf{c}\right) \neq R_2\left(\mathbf{c}\right)$.
The overall dissimilarity is computed as

$$S\left(\mathbf{x_a}, \mathbf{y_b}\right) = R_1\left(\mathbf{a}\right) + 2D\left(\mathbf{a}, \mathbf{b}\right) + R_2\left(\mathbf{b}\right). \tag{5}$$

Note that

$$S\left(\mathbf{x_b}, \mathbf{y_a}\right) = R_2\left(\mathbf{a}\right) + 2D\left(\mathbf{a}, \mathbf{b}\right) + R_1\left(\mathbf{b}\right)$$

---

[9] The choice of β is irrelevant for our discussion, because the properties of
Regular Minimality and Nonconstant Self-Dissimilarity are invariant under all
strictly increasing transformations of $\psi\left(\mathbf{x}, \mathbf{y}\right)$. This is a fact with considerable
theoretical implications, some of which is discussed in Chapter 2 of this volume
(possible transformation of discrimination probabilities).

[10] Note that the first and the second $\mathbf{a}$ in $(\mathbf{a}, \mathbf{a})$, as well as in $(\mathbf{a}, \mathbf{b})$ and $(\mathbf{b}, \mathbf{a})$,
generally stand for different stimuli, $\mathbf{x_a}$, and $\mathbf{y_a}$. We are essentially using here a
canonical transformation of stimuli, formally introduced in Section 9.

is generally different from $S(\mathbf{x_a}, \mathbf{y_b})$, and for $\mathbf{a} = \mathbf{b}$,

$$S(\mathbf{x_a}, \mathbf{y_a}) = R_1(\mathbf{a}) + R_2(\mathbf{a}).$$

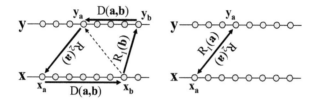

The conjunction of Regular Minimality and Nonconstant Self-Dissimilarity is ensured by positing that $R_1(\mathbf{c})$, $R_2(\mathbf{c})$ need not be the same for all $\mathbf{c}$, and that

$$|R_1(\mathbf{a}) - R_1(\mathbf{b})| < 2D(\mathbf{a}, \mathbf{b}), \quad |R_2(\mathbf{a}) - R_2(\mathbf{b})| < 2D(\mathbf{a}, \mathbf{b}).$$

These inequalities are a form of the Lipschitz condition imposed on the growth rate of R_1 and R_2. Figures 5 to 7 were generated in accordance with this "quadrilateral dissimilarity" model: we chose $\beta(s)$ in (4) as $1 - \exp(-\theta s - \eta)$, and put $D(a, b) = \gamma|a - b|$, $R_1(a) = \sin(\theta_1 a - \eta_1)$, $R_2(b) = \sin(\theta_2 b - \eta_2)$, with all Greek letters representing appropriately chosen positive constants; labels a, b in this example are related to stimuli x_a, y_b by $x_a = \sqrt{a}$ and $y_b = b$ (so that x and y are mutual PSEs if and only if $x = \sqrt{y}$).

Except for technicalities associated with R_1 and R_2 and for the fact that identically labeled $\mathbf{x}$ and $\mathbf{y}$ in (5) are generally different stimuli, the mathematical form of (5) is essentially the same as in Krumhansl's (1978) model. Somewhat more directly, the "quadrilateral dissimilarity" in (5) is related to the dissimilarity between two "uncertainty blobs," as introduced in Dzhafarov (2003b). Figure 17 provides an illustration. The "common space" in which the blobs are defined has the same meaning as the set of indices $\mathbf{a}, \mathbf{b}$ assigned to stimuli $\mathbf{x}, \mathbf{y}$ in the description of the quadrilateral dissimilarity above: that is, $\mathbf{x_a}$ and $\mathbf{y_b}$ are mapped into blobs centered at $\mathbf{a}$ and $\mathbf{b}$, respectively. The intrinsicality of metric D^* means that for a certain class of curves in the space, one can compute their lengths, and the distance between two points is defined as the length of the shortest line connecting them (a geodesic). By the assumptions made, a D^*-geodesic line connecting $\mathbf{a}$ to $\mathbf{b}$ can be produced beyond these points until it crosses the borders of the two blobs, at points $\mathbf{aa}$ and $\mathbf{bb}$. It is easy to see that no point in the first blob and no point in the second one are separated by D^*-distance exceeding $D^*(\mathbf{aa}, \mathbf{bb})$. Taking this largest possible distance for $S(\mathbf{x_a}, \mathbf{y_b})$,

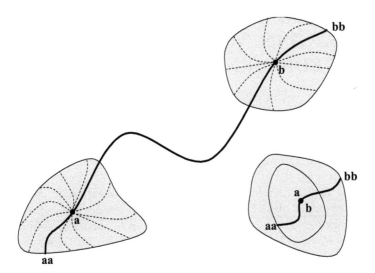

Fig. 17: Schematic representation of the "uncertainty blobs" model (Dzhafarov, 2003b). The figure plane represents a "common space" $\mathfrak{S}$ with some intrinsic metric D^* such that any two points in the space can be connected by a geodesic curve, and each geodesic curve can be produced beyond its endpoints. Each stimulus $\mathbf{x}$ in $\mathcal{O}_1$ (or $\mathbf{y}$ in $\mathcal{O}_2$) is mapped into a "blob," a D^*-circle in $\mathfrak{S}$ centered at $\mathbf{a} = \mathbf{f}_1(\mathbf{x})$ with radius $R_1(\mathbf{a})$ (respectively, centered at $\mathbf{b} = \mathbf{f}_2(\mathbf{y})$ with radius $R_2(\mathbf{b})$), such that $\mathbf{f}_1(\mathbf{x}) = \mathbf{f}_2(\mathbf{y})$ if and only if $\mathbf{x}, \mathbf{y}$ are mutual PSEs (as shown in the right lower corner). Dissimilarity $S(\mathbf{x}, \mathbf{y})$ is defined as the largest D^*-distance between the two blobs, here shown as the length of the geodesic line connecting points $\mathbf{aa}$ and $\mathbf{bb}$.

we have then

$$S\left(\mathbf{x_a}, \mathbf{y_b}\right) = R_1\left(\mathbf{a}\right) + D^*\left(\mathbf{a}, \mathbf{b}\right) + R_2\left(\mathbf{b}\right),$$

which is identical to (5) on putting $D^*\left(\mathbf{a}, \mathbf{b}\right) = 2D\left(\mathbf{a}, \mathbf{b}\right)$. To make this identity complete, all we have to do is stipulate that the radii of the blobs change relatively slowly, in the same meaning as shown earlier,

$$\left|R_1\left(\mathbf{a}\right) - R_1\left(\mathbf{b}\right)\right| < D^*\left(\mathbf{a}, \mathbf{b}\right), \quad \left|R_2\left(\mathbf{a}\right) - R_2\left(\mathbf{b}\right)\right| < D^*\left(\mathbf{a}, \mathbf{b}\right).$$

8. RANDOM VARIABILITY IN STIMULI AND IN NEUROPHYSIOLOGICAL REPRESENTATIONS OF STIMULI

In the foregoing, we tacitly assumed that once stimulus labels have been assigned, they are always identified correctly. In a continuous stimulus set, however, stimuli are bound to be identified with only limited precision. Confining, for simplicity, the discussion to unidimensional stimuli, one and the same "apparent" physical label (i.e., the value of stimulus as known to the experimenter, say, 10 min arc, 50 cd/m^2, 30 dB) generally corresponds to at least slightly different "true" stimuli in different trials. To put this formally, apparent stimuli x, y chosen from a stimulus set correspond to random variables P_x, Q_y taking on their values in the same set of stimuli (quantities $P_x - x$, $Q_y - y$ being the measurement, or identification errors). In every trial, a pair of apparent stimuli (x, y) is probabilistically mapped into a pair of true stimuli (p, q), which in turn is mapped into the response "different" with probability $\psi\left(p, q\right)$ (about which we assume that it satisfies Regular Minimality). We have therefore

$$\psi_{app}\left(x, y\right) = \int_{q \in \mathfrak{I}} \int_{p \in \mathfrak{I}} \psi\left(p, q\right) \mathrm{d}F_x\left(p\right) \mathrm{d}F_y\left(q\right), \qquad (6)$$

where $\psi_{app}\left(x, y\right)$ is discrimination probability as a function of apparent stimuli; $F_x\left(p\right)$, $F_y\left(q\right)$ are the distribution functions for true stimuli P_x, Q_y with apparent values x and y; and $\mathfrak{I}$ is the interval of all possible stimulus values.

If we assume that P_x, Q_y are stochastically independent and well-behaved (e.g., if they possess finite densities whose parameters change smoothly with the corresponding apparent stimuli, as in the classical Gaussian measurement error model), then the situation becomes formally equivalent to a Thurstonian-type model, only "perceptual space" here is replaced with the set of true stimuli. Applying the results described in Section 7.1, we come to the following conclusion: although the true discrimination probability function, $\psi\,(p,q)$, satisfies Regular Minimality, the apparent discrimination probability function, $\psi_{app}\,(x,y)$, generally does not. Indeed, it is easy to show that the minimum values of functions $y \to \psi_{app}\,(x,y)$ and $x \to \psi_{app}\,(x,y)$ computed from (6) will not generally be on a constant level (across, respectively, all possible x and all possible y); and we know that $\psi_{app}\,(x,y)$, being computed from a Thurstonian-type model with well-behaved random variables, cannot simultaneously exhibit the properties of Nonconstant Self-Dissimilarity and Regular Minimality. If the independent measurement errors for x and y are not negligible, therefore, one can expect apparent violations of Regular Minimality even if the principle does hold true.

This analysis, as we know, can be generalized to stochastically interdependent P_x, Q_y, provided they are selectively attributable to x and y, respectively. Stated explicitly, if P_x and Q_y are representable as in (3) (with C being a source of error common to both observation areas and C_1, C_2 being error sources specific to the first and second observation areas), and if $\pi\,(x,c,C_1)$ and $\theta\,(y,c,C_2)$ are well-behaved for any value c of C, then Regular Minimality can be violated in $\psi_{app}\,(x,y)$. Conversely, if $\psi_{app}\,(x,y)$ does not violate Regular Minimality, then the aforementioned model for measurement error cannot be correct: either measurement errors for x and y cannot be selectively attributed to x and y, or $\pi\,(x,c,C_1)$ and $\theta\,(y,c,C_2)$ are not well behaved. As an example of the latter, $\pi\,(x,c,C_1)$ and $\theta\,(y,c,C_2)$ may be deterministic quantities (see Footnote 6), or equivalently, representation (3) may have the form

$$P_x = \pi\,(x,C)\,, \quad Q_y = \theta\,(y,C)\,. \qquad (7)$$

Clearly, when statistical error in estimating $\psi_{app}\,(x,y)$ is involved, all such statements should be "gradualized": thus, the aforementioned measurement error model may hold, but the variability in $\pi\,(x,c,C_1)$ and $\theta\,(y,c,C_2)$ may be too small to make the expected violations of Regular Minimality observable on a sample level.

Now, the logic of this discussion remains valid if instead of understanding P_x and Q_y as stimulus values we use these random entities to designate certain neurophysiological states, or processes evoked by stimuli x and y (which we now take as identified precisely). The mapping from stimuli to responses involves brain activity, and at least at sufficiently peripheral levels thereof we can speak of "separate" neurophysiological representations of x and y. Clearly, the response given in a given trial (same or different) depends on the values of these representations, $P_x = p$ and $Q_y = q$, irrespective of which stimuli x, y they represent. We need not decide here where the neurophysiological representation of stimuli ends and the response formation begins. Whatever the nature and complexity of P_x, Q_y, our conclusion will be the same: if $\psi\left(x,y\right)$ satisfies Regular Minimality (and manifests Nonconstant Self-Dissimilarity), then either P_x, Q_y cannot be selectively attributed to x and y, respectively (in which case they probably should not be called neurophysiological representations of x and y in the first place), or else, they are not well-behaved: for example, they covary in accordance with (7), or still simpler, are deterministic entities,

$$P_x = \pi\left(x\right), \quad Q_y = \theta\left(y\right)$$

(perhaps a kind of neurophysiological analogues of the "uncertainty blobs" depicted in Fig. 17).

A word of caution is due here: the mathematical justification for this analysis is derived from Dzhafarov (2003a, 2003b) and, strictly speaking, is confined to continuous stimulus spaces only (although not just unidimensional spaces considered here for simplicity): the definition of well-behavedness is based on the behavior of random entities P_x, Q_y in response to arbitrarily small changes in x and y. Restrictions imposed by the Regular Minimality and Nonconstant Self-Dissimilarity on possible representations of discrete stimulus sets remain to be investigated.

9. CANONICAL REPRESENTATION OF STIMULI AND DISCRIMINATION PROBABILITIES

We have seen that the conjunction of Regular Minimality and Nonconstant Self-Dissimilarity has a powerful restrictive effect on the possible theories of perceptual discrimination. In particular, it rules out two most traditional ways of modeling discrimination probabilities: by monotonically relating them to some distance measure imposed on stimulus space, and by deriving them from well-behaved random representations selectively attributable to stimuli being compared. The following characterization therefore is well worth emphasizing. Regular Minimality and Nonconstant Self-Dissimilarity are *purely psychological* properties, in the sense this term is used in Dzhafarov and Colonius (2005a, 2005b): they are completely independent of the physical measures or descriptions used to identify the individual stimuli in a stimulus space. If $\psi\left(\mathbf{x}, \mathbf{y}\right)$ satisfies Regular Minimality and manifests Nonconstant Self-Dissimilarity, then the same remains true after all stimuli $\mathbf{x}$ (in $\mathcal{O}_1$) and/or all stimuli $\mathbf{y}$ (in $\mathcal{O}_2$) have been relabeled by means of arbitrary bijective transformations. In other words, insofar as the identity of a stimulus is preserved, its physical description is irrelevant. In the next section, we see that the preservation of a stimulus's identity itself has a prominent "psychological" (nonphysical) aspect.

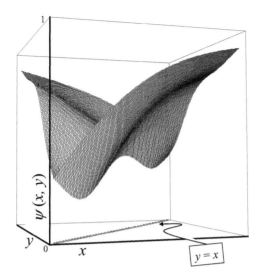

Fig. 18: A canonical form for discrimination probability function $\psi\left(\mathbf{x}, \mathbf{y}\right)$ shown in Fig. 5. The PSE line $y = h\left(x\right)$ transforms into $y = x$.

In this section, we consider the identity-preserving transformations of stimuli that make the formulation of Regular Minimality especially convenient for theoretical developments. We have already used this device (*canonical transformation* of stimuli, or bringing $\psi\left(\mathbf{x}, \mathbf{y}\right)$ into a *canonical form*) in the previous section. It only remains to describe it systematically.

The simplest form of Regular Minimality is observed when $\mathbf{x}$ and $\mathbf{y}$ are mutual PSEs if and only if $\mathbf{x} = \mathbf{y}$. That is,

$$\mathbf{x} \neq \mathbf{y} \implies \psi\left(\mathbf{x}, \mathbf{y}\right) > \max\left\{\psi\left(\mathbf{x}, \mathbf{x}\right), \psi\left(\mathbf{y}, \mathbf{y}\right)\right\}, \tag{8}$$

or equivalently,

$$\mathbf{x} \neq \mathbf{y} \implies \psi\left(\mathbf{x}, \mathbf{x}\right) < \min\left\{\psi\left(\mathbf{x}, \mathbf{y}\right), \psi\left(\mathbf{y}, \mathbf{x}\right)\right\}. \tag{9}$$

It is possible that in the case of discrete stimuli (such as letters of alphabet or Morse codes), Regular Minimality always holds in this form. In general, however, PSE function $\mathbf{y} = \mathbf{h}\left(\mathbf{x}\right)$ may deviate from the identity function. Thinking of the situations when the stimulus sets in the two observation areas are different (see Section 11), $\mathbf{x} = \mathbf{y}$ may not even be a meaningful equality.

It is always possible, however, to relabel the stimuli in the two observation areas in such a way that (a) the stimulus sets in $\mathcal{O}_1$ and $\mathcal{O}_2$ are identical

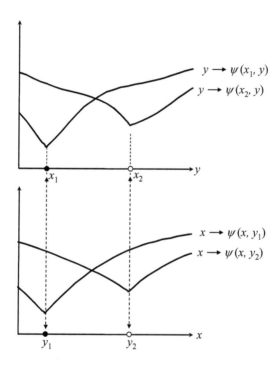

Fig. 19: Analogous to Fig. 6, but the cross-sections are those of discrimination probability function $\psi(\mathbf{x}, \mathbf{y})$ in a canonical form, as shown in Fig. 18. y is the PSE for x (equivalently, x is the PSE for y) if and only if $x = y$.

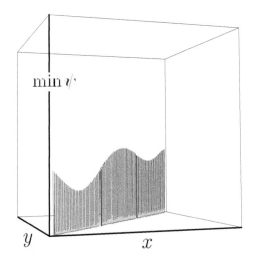

Fig. 20: Analogous to Fig. 9, but for discrimination probability function $\psi(\mathbf{x}, \mathbf{y})$ in a canonical form, as shown in Fig. 18. The transformation of the PSE line into $y = x$ does not, of course, change the contour of the minimum level function, exhibiting Nonconstant Self-Dissimilarity.

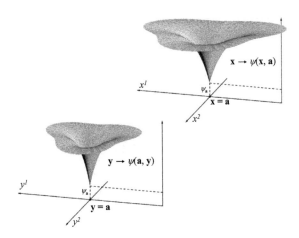

Fig. 21: Analogous to Fig. 8, but the two cross-sections are those of discrimination probability function $\psi(\mathbf{x}, \mathbf{y})$ in a canonical form. The cross-sections are made at $\mathbf{x} = \mathbf{a}$ (lower panel, with $\psi(\mathbf{a}, \mathbf{y})$ reaching its minimum at $\mathbf{y} = \mathbf{a}$) and $\mathbf{y} = \mathbf{a}$ (upper panel, with $\psi(\mathbf{x}, \mathbf{a})$ reaching its minimum at $\mathbf{x} = \mathbf{a}$).

and (b) Regular Minimality is satisfied in the simplest form, (8) to (9). We know that Regular Minimality implies a bijective correspondence between the stimulus sets in $\mathcal{O}_1$ and $\mathcal{O}_2$. It is always possible, therefore, to form a set $\mathbf{S}$ of "common stimulus labels" (or simply, "common stimuli") and to map it by means of two bijective functions, $\mathbf{f}_1^{-1}$ and $\mathbf{f}_2^{-1}$, onto the stimulus sets in $\mathcal{O}_1$ and $\mathcal{O}_2$ in such a way that, for any $\mathbf{a} \in \mathbf{S}$, $\left(\mathbf{f}_1^{-1}(\mathbf{a}), \mathbf{f}_1^{-1}(\mathbf{a})\right)$ is a pair of mutual PSEs. Equivalently, $\mathbf{f}_1(\mathbf{x}) = \mathbf{f}_2(\mathbf{y})$ if and only if $(\mathbf{x}, \mathbf{y})$ is a pair of mutual PSEs (see the legend to Fig. 17). Once this is done, one can redefine ψ by

$$\psi_{old}(\mathbf{x}, \mathbf{y}) = \psi_{new}(\mathbf{f}_1(\mathbf{x}), \mathbf{f}_2(\mathbf{y})).$$

As an example, matrix TOY_1 in Section 3 allows for the relabeling shown below,

$\mathcal{O}_1$	$\mathbf{x}_a$	$\mathbf{x}_b$	$\mathbf{x}_c$	$\mathbf{x}_d$
$\mathcal{O}_2$	$\mathbf{y}_c$	$\mathbf{y}_d$	$\mathbf{y}_b$	$\mathbf{y}_a$
common label	A	B	C	D

The following, therefore, is a canonical transformation of TOY_1:

TOY_1	$\mathbf{y}_a$	$\mathbf{y}_b$	$\mathbf{y}_c$	$\mathbf{y}_d$
$\mathbf{x}_a$	0.6	0.6	0.1	0.8
$\mathbf{x}_b$	0.9	0.9	0.8	0.1
$\mathbf{x}_c$	1	0.5	1	0.6
$\mathbf{x}_d$	0.5	0.7	1	1

$\Longrightarrow$

TOY_0	A	B	C	D
A	0.1	0.8	0.6	0.6
B	0.8	0.1	0.9	0.9
C	1	0.6	0.5	1
D	1	1	0.7	0.5

For continuous stimuli, given a PSE function, $\mathbf{y} = \mathbf{h}(\mathbf{x})$, any pair of functions $\mathbf{f}_1 \equiv \mathbf{f}$, $\mathbf{f}_2 \equiv \mathbf{h} \circ \mathbf{f}$, for any (bijective) $\mathbf{f}$, provides a canonical transformation. Figures 18, 19, 20, and 21 illustrate canonical forms for our earlier examples.

10.   PSYCHOLOGICAL IDENTITY OF STIMULI

Up to this point, we implicitly assumed that all stimuli in either of the observation areas are psychologically distinct, in the following sense: if $\mathbf{x}_1 \neq \mathbf{x}_2$ in $\mathcal{O}_1$, then at least for one stimulus $\mathbf{y}$ in $\mathcal{O}_2$,

$$\psi(\mathbf{x}_1, \mathbf{y}) \neq \psi(\mathbf{x}_2, \mathbf{y});$$

and analogously for any $\mathbf{y}_1 \neq \mathbf{y}_2$ in $\mathcal{O}_2$. Put differently, if $\psi(\mathbf{x}_1, \mathbf{y}) = \psi(\mathbf{x}_2, \mathbf{y})$ for all $\mathbf{y}$ in $\mathcal{O}_2$, then $\mathbf{x}_1 = \mathbf{x}_2$; and if $\psi(\mathbf{x}, \mathbf{y}_1) = \psi(\mathbf{x}, \mathbf{y}_2)$ for all $\mathbf{x}$ in $\mathcal{O}_1$, then $\mathbf{y}_1 = \mathbf{y}_2$. On a moment's reflection, this is not a real constraint. If $x_1 \neq x_2$, but $\psi(x_1, y) = \psi(x_2, y)$ for all y in $\mathcal{O}_2$ (in which case, one can say that that x_1 and x_2 are *"psychologically equal"*), one can always relabel the stimuli so that x_1 and x_2 receive identical labels. For example, if aperture colors are initially labeled by their radiometric spectra (radiometric intensity as a function of wavelength), we know that there are an infinity of distinct spectra that are, for a given level of adaptation, equally distinguishable from any given spectrum (metameric). As a result, all mutually metameric colors can be merged and assigned a single label, say, a triple of CIE color coordinates. Figure 22 provides a schematic illustration.

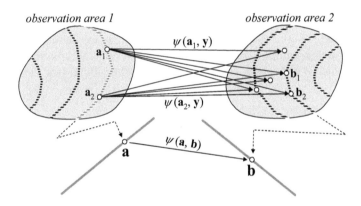

Fig. 22: Equivalence class of psychologically equal stimuli (shown by striped lines). a_1 and a_2 in $\mathcal{O}_1$ are psychologically equal because $\psi(a_1, y) = \psi(a_2, y)$ for every y in $\mathcal{O}_2$; these two stimuli therefore are assigned a common label, a. Equivalence classes a and b are treated as single stimuli in $\mathcal{O}_1$ and $\mathcal{O}_2$, respectively, with $\psi(a, b)$ put equal to $\psi(x, y)$ for any $x \in a$, $y \in b$. The Regular Minimality condition is assumed to hold for these "reduced" stimulus sets (sets of equivalence classes, shown by the two straight lines).

The example below shows a matrix of discrimination probabilities that, following the procedure of "lumping together" psychologically equal stimuli, yields our matrix TOY_1.

TOY$_{11}$	y_a		y_b		y_c	y_d	
	y_1	y_2	y_3	y_4	y_5	y_6	y_7
x_a x_1	0.6	0.6	0.6	0.6	0.1	0.8	0.8
x_2	0.6	0.6	0.6	0.6	0.1	0.8	0.8
x_b x_3	0.9	0.9	0.9	0.9	0.8	0.1	0.1
x_4	0.9	0.9	0.9	0.9	0.8	0.1	0.1
x_c x_5	1	1	0.5	0.5	1	0.6	0.6
x_d x_6	0.5	0.5	0.7	0.7	1	1	1
x_7	0.5	0.5	0.7	0.7	1	1	1

$\Longrightarrow$

TOY$_1$	y_a	y_b	y_c	y_d
x_a	0.6	0.6	0.1	0.8
x_b	0.9	0.9	0.8	0.1
x_c	1	0.5	1	0.6
x_d	0.5	0.7	1	1

Thus, $\{x_1, x_2\} \to x_a$, $\{y_1, y_2\} \to y_a$, and so forth. In this example, each equivalence class of psychologically equal stimuli in $\mathcal{O}_1$ bijectively maps onto an equivalence class of psychologically equal stimuli in $\mathcal{O}_2$: $\{x_1, x_2\} \longleftrightarrow \{y_1, y_2\}$, $\{x_5\} \longleftrightarrow \{y_5\}$, and so forth. Although we cannot think of a realistic counterexample, on this level of abstraction there is no reason to postulate such a correspondence. The matrix below illustrates the point.

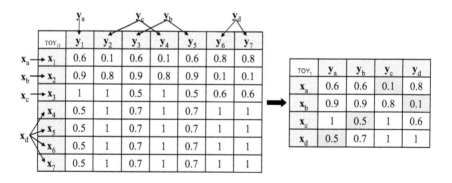

TOY$_{12}$	y_a	y_c	y_b		y_d		
	y_1	y_2	y_3	y_4	y_5	y_6	y_7
$x_a \to x_1$	0.6	0.1	0.6	0.1	0.6	0.8	0.8
$x_b \to x_2$	0.9	0.8	0.9	0.8	0.9	0.1	0.1
$x_c \to x_3$	1	1	0.5	1	0.5	0.6	0.6
x_4	0.5	1	0.7	1	0.7	1	1
x_d x_5	0.5	1	0.7	1	0.7	1	1
x_6	0.5	1	0.7	1	0.7	1	1
x_7	0.5	1	0.7	1	0.7	1	1

$\Longrightarrow$

TOY$_1$	y_a	y_b	y_c	y_d
x_a	0.6	0.6	0.1	0.8
x_b	0.9	0.9	0.8	0.1
x_c	1	0.5	1	0.6
x_d	0.5	0.7	1	1

This matrix, too, following the relabeling shown, yields matrix TOY$_1$, but the equivalence classes in $\mathcal{O}_1$ cannot be paired with equinumerous equivalence classes in $\mathcal{O}_2$ (e.g., $\{x_4, x_5, x_6, x_7\}$ does not have a four-element counterpart in $\mathcal{O}_2$). It is critical for the requirement of Regular Minimality, however, that the resulting sets of the equivalence classes themselves contain equal numbers of elements in the two observation areas: $\{x_a, x_b, x_c, x_d\}$ and $\{y_a, y_b, y_c, y_d\}$. Regular Minimality, in effect, says that one can establish a bijection between the equivalence classes in $\mathcal{O}_1$ and the equivalence classes in $\mathcal{O}_2$ in such a way that the corresponding elements (equivalence classes treated as redefined stimuli) are mutual PSEs.

11. VARIETY OF PARADIGMS

Here, we describe a variety of meanings in which one can understand same-different judgments, observation areas, and the very terms *stimuli* and *perceiver*.

It was mentioned in the introductory paragraph of this chapter that the sameness or difference of two stimuli can be judged "overall" or "in a specified respect." Expanding on that, the definition of a discrimination probability function, (1), can be generalized in two ways:

$$\psi\left(\mathbf{x},\mathbf{y}\right) = \Pr\left[\mathbf{x} \text{ and } \mathbf{y} \text{ are different with respect to } \mathcal{A}\right], \qquad (10)$$

meaning that all differences other than those in a designated property $\mathcal{A}$ (shape, size, color, etc.) should be ignored; and

$$\psi\left(\mathbf{x},\mathbf{y}\right) = \Pr\left[\mathbf{x} \text{ and } \mathbf{y} \text{ are different in any respect other than } \mathcal{B}\right], \qquad (11)$$

meaning that any differences in a designated property $\mathcal{B}$ (which again can be shape, size, color, etc.) should be ignored. As follows from our discussion of the two distinct observation areas, the "generic" definition (1) is in fact a special case of (11), with $\mathcal{B}$ designating the perceptual difference between the two observation areas.

In psychophysical experiments, the observation areas usually mean different locations in space or time, but the scope of possible meanings is much broader. Thus, $\mathcal{O}_1$ and $\mathcal{O}_2$ may be defined by the modality of stimulus, as in the grapheme-morpheme comparisons (e.g., a written syllable $\mathbf{x}$ compared with a pronounced syllable $\mathbf{y}$): in this case, the ordering of two stimuli in $\left(\mathbf{x},\mathbf{y}\right)$ is determined by which of them is written and which pronounced, irrespective of their temporal order. As another example, when a green color patch and a red color patch of variable intensities are compared in brightness, the two fixed colors serve to define the two observation areas, irrespective of the spatial positions or temporal order of the patches.

A combination of several such observation-area-defining attributes (say, colors × locations) or simply more than just two values of a given attribute (say, several locations) may lead to multiple observation areas, in which case stimulus pairs should be encoded as $\left(\left(\mathbf{x},o\right),\left(\mathbf{y},o'\right)\right)$, where $\mathbf{x},\mathbf{y}$ are labels identifying the stimuli in all respects except for their observation areas, the latter being designated by o, o' (with $o \neq o'$). Although the relation among $\psi\left(\left(\mathbf{x},o\right),\left(\mathbf{y},o'\right)\right)$ for different pairs of distinct o, o' is beyond the scope of this chapter, our hypothesis is that Regular Minimality should be satisfied for all such pairs.

In some applications, the difference between the observation areas is known or assumed to be immaterial. Thus, when asked to compare the attractiveness of two photographs, their spatial arrangement may very well be immaterial (or even undefined, if the perceiver is allowed to move them freely). Our analysis still applies to such cases: although formally distinguishing $(\mathbf{a}, \mathbf{b})$ and $(\mathbf{b}, \mathbf{a})$, we simply impose the order-balance, or symmetry condition, $\psi(\mathbf{x}, \mathbf{y}) = \psi(\mathbf{y}, \mathbf{x})$. Counterintuitive as it may sound, the order-balancedness does not imply that Regular Minimality can only be satisfied in a canonical form. If $\psi(\mathbf{x}, \mathbf{y}) = \psi(\mathbf{y}, \mathbf{x})$, the PSE relation $\mathbf{y} = \mathbf{h}(\mathbf{x})$ is equivalent to the PSE relation $\mathbf{x} = \mathbf{h}(\mathbf{y})$. Comparing this to properties (RM1 to RM3), in Section 3, we see that $\mathbf{h} \equiv \mathbf{h}^{-1}$. The functional equation $\mathbf{h} \equiv \mathbf{h}^{-1}$ is known as Babbage's equation (see Kuczma, Choczewski, & Ger, 1990), and it has more solutions than just an identity function, although the latter often is the only realistic solution (e.g., it is the only nondecreasing solution in the case of unidimensional stimuli).

One can significantly broaden the class of paradigms which can be treated as same-different comparisons by applying the term *stimuli*, in a purely formal way, to any two sets of entities, $\mathbf{M}_1$ and $\mathbf{M}_2$ (stimuli in the first and second observation areas, respectively), that can be endowed with a probability function $\psi : \mathbf{M}_1 \times \mathbf{M}_2 \to [0, 1]$. The term *perceiver* then, may designate any device or computational procedure which, in response to any ordered pair $\mathbf{x} \in \mathbf{M}_1$, $\mathbf{y} \in \mathbf{M}_2$, produces a certain output with probability $\psi(\mathbf{x}, \mathbf{y})$. We propose that this output can be interpreted as meaning "$\mathbf{x}$ is different from $\mathbf{y}$" if and only if function $\psi(\mathbf{x}, \mathbf{y})$ satisfies Regular Minimality. In other words, Regular Minimality may serve as a criterion (necessary and sufficient condition) for the inclusion of otherwise vastly different paradigms in the category of same-different comparisons.

To give a very "nonpsychophysical" example, consider a class $\mathbf{M}$ of statistical models, and a class $\mathfrak{D}$ of possible results of some experiment. Each model from $\mathbf{M}$ can be fitted to each possible result, and rejected or retained in accordance with some statistical criterion $\mathcal{C}$. Given two models, $\mathbf{x}, \mathbf{y} \in \mathbf{M}$, and a certain experimental outcome $d_0 \in \mathfrak{D}$, consider a procedure that consists of (a) fitting $\mathbf{x}$ to d_0 and specifying thereby all free parameters of $\mathbf{x}$ (b) repeatedly generating outcomes $d \in \mathfrak{D}$ by means of thus specified $\mathbf{x}$; and (c) fitting $\mathbf{y}$ to every generated outcome d and rejecting or retaining it in accordance with criterion $\mathcal{C}$. Then the probability $\psi(\mathbf{x}, \mathbf{y})$ with which model $\mathbf{y}$ is rejected by an outcome generated by model $\mathbf{x}$ can be taken as the probability of discriminating $\mathbf{y}$ from $\mathbf{x}$, provided $\psi(\mathbf{x}, \mathbf{y})$ satisfies Regular Minimality. In this example, the "observation area" of a model is defined by the role in which this model is employed: $\mathbf{M}_1$ represents the models specified by fitting them to d_0 and used to generate outcomes d, whereas $\mathbf{M}_2$ represents the models tested by applying them to thus generated d. The "perceiver" in this case, from whose "point of view" the models are being compared, is the entire computational procedure, specified by d_0 and $\mathcal{C}$. One would normally expect that Regular Minimality for a well-defined class of models should be satisfied canonically, (8) to (9). This is, however, a secondary consideration, because the models in $\mathbf{M}_2$, as we know, can always be relabeled so that the PSE of model $\mathbf{x} \in \mathbf{M}_1$ is assigned label $\mathbf{x}$.

As another example, let $\mathbf{M}_1$ be a set of categories or sources, each of which can be exemplified by a variety of entities (e.g., lung dysfunctions exemplified by X-ray films), and let $\mathbf{M}_2$ be the same set of categories or sources when they are judged to be or not to be exemplified by a given entity ("does this X-ray film indicate this lung dysfunction?"). The probability with which an entity exemplifying category $\mathbf{x}$ is judged not to belong to category $\mathbf{y}$ then can be taken as $\psi(\mathbf{x}, \mathbf{y})$, provided ψ satisfies Regular Minimality. Again, in a well-calibrating expert system, one would expect Regular Minimality to hold canonically, but any form of Regular Minimality can be recalibrated into a canonical form.

12. CONCLUSION

The principle according to which any well-defined discrimination probability function $\psi(\mathbf{x}, \mathbf{y})$, defined by (1), (10), or (11), should satisfy Regular Minimality, seems to have all the hallmarks of a fundamental law:

(A) It cannot be derived from more elementary properties of discrimination probabilities. In this respect, it is very different from the Regular Mediality principle for greater-less judgments (Section 2).

(B) It is conceptually simple, almost obvious, yet has unexpectedly restrictive consequences for theoretical modeling of discrimination probabilities (Sections 7.1, 7.2, and 8), especially when combined with the property of Nonconstant Self-Dissimilarity (Section 4).

(C) Its conceptual plausibility allows one to use it as a criterion for classifying a paradigm into the category of same-different judgments (Section 11).

(D) It is born out by available experimental evidence (although much more work remains to be done before one can call this evidence abundant; see Section 6).

(E) It can serve as a benchmark against which to consider empirical evidence: if the latter exhibits deviations from Regular Minimality, one is warranted to look for other possible causes before discarding the principle itself (Section 8).

We conclude this chapter by a brief comment on the last characterization. Stimulus uncertainty, which we discussed in Section 8 is only one of many factors which, if Regular Minimality does in fact hold true, predictably leads to its apparent violations in data. Skipping over the relatively obvious issue of sampling errors (both in estimating probabilities and in choosing a representative subset of a stimulus space), perhaps the most important factor working against the principle of Regular Minimality in real-life experiments is the possibility of mixing together discrimination probability functions with different PSE functions. It is easy to see that if Regular Minimality is satisfied in both $\psi_1(\mathbf{x}, \mathbf{y})$ and $\psi_2(\mathbf{x}, \mathbf{y})$, defined on the same set of stimuli, and if their respective PSE functions are $\mathbf{y} = \mathbf{h}_1(\mathbf{x})$ and $\mathbf{y} = \mathbf{h}_2(\mathbf{x})$, then linear combinations $\alpha\psi_1(\mathbf{x}, \mathbf{y}) + (1-\alpha)\psi_2(\mathbf{x}, \mathbf{y})$ ($0 \le \alpha \le 1$) will generally violate Regular Minimality, unless $\mathbf{h}_1 \equiv \mathbf{h}_2$. In a psychophysical experiment with continuous stimuli (like the one related to Fig. 14), it seems desirable to use very large numbers of replications per stimulus pair to increase the reliability of the statistical estimates of discrimination probabilities. In a very long experiment, however, it seems likely that the discrimination probability function would gradually change, because of which the resulting probability estimates will be those of a linear combination of functions $\psi_t(\mathbf{x}, \mathbf{y})$, with t being the time at which $(\mathbf{x}, \mathbf{y})$ was presented. If PSE functions $\mathbf{y} = \mathbf{h}_t(\mathbf{x})$ also vary in time, this mixture may very well exhibit violations of Regular Minimality. Analogous considerations apply to group experiments: there we may have to deal with heterogeneous mixtures of functions $\psi_k(\mathbf{x}, \mathbf{y})$, with k representing different members of a group.

Acknowledgment. This research was supported by National Science Foundation grant SES 0318010 to Purdue University.

References

Dai, H., Versfeld, N. J., & Green, D. M. (1996). The optimum decision rules in the same-different paradigm. *Perception and Psychophysics*, 58, 1–9.

Dzhafarov, E. N. (2002a). Multidimensional Fechnerian scaling: Probability-distance hypothesis. *Journal of Mathematical Psychology*, 46, 352–374.

Dzhafarov, E. N. (2002b). Multidimensional Fechnerian scaling: Pairwise comparisons, regular minimality, and nonconstant self-similarity. *Journal of Mathematical Psychology*, 46, 583–608.

Dzhafarov, E. N. (2003a). Thurstonian-type representations for "same-different" discriminations: Deterministic decisions and independent images. *Journal of Mathematical Psychology*, 47, 208–228.

Dzhafarov, E. N. (2003b). Thurstonian-type representations for "same-different" discriminations: Probabilistic decisions and interdependent images. *Journal of Mathematical Psychology*, 47, 229–243.

Dzhafarov, E. N. (2003c). Selective influence through conditional independence. *Psychometrika*, 68, 7–26.

Dzhafarov, E. N., & Colonius, H. (2005a). Psychophysics without physics: A purely psychological theory of Fechnerian Scaling in continuous stimulus spaces. *Journal of Mathematical Psychology*, 49, 1–50.

Dzhafarov, E.N., & Colonius, H. (2005b). Psychophysics without physics: Extension of Fechnerian Scaling from continuous to discrete and discrete-continuous stimulus spaces. *Journal of Mathematical Psychology*, 49, 125–141.

Ennis, D. M. (1992). Modeling similarity and identification when there are momentary fluctuations in psychological magnitudes. In F. G. Ashby (Ed.), *Multidimensional models of perception and cognition* (pp. 279–298). Hillsdale, NJ: Lawrence Erlbaum Associates, Inc.

Ennis, D. M., Palen, J. J., & Mullen, K. (1988). A multidimensional stochastic theory of similarity. *Journal of Mathematical Psychology*, 32, 449–465.

Falmagne, J.-C. (1971). The generalized Fechner problem and discrimination. *Journal of Mathematical Psychology*, 8, 22–43.

Fechner, G. T. (1887). Über die psychischen Massprinzipien und das Webersche Gesetz [On the principles of mental measurement and Weber's Law]. Philosophische Studien, 4, 161–230.

Indow, T. (1998). Parallel shift of judgment-characteristic curves according to the context in cutaneous and color discrimination. In C. E. Dowling, F. S. Roberts, P. Theuns (Eds.), *Recent progress in mathematical psychology* (pp. 47–63). Mahwah, NJ: Erlbaum Associates, Inc.

Indow, T., Robertson, A. R., von Grunau, M., & Fielder, G. H. (1992). Discrimination ellipsoids of aperture and simulated surface colors by matching and paired comparison. *Color Research and Applications*, 17, 6–23.

Krumhansl, C. L. (1978). Concerning the applicability of geometric models to similarity data: The interrelationship between similarity and spatial density. *Psychological Review*, 85, 445–463.

Kuczma, M., Choczewski, B., & Ger, R. (1990). *Iterative functional equations.* Cambridge, England: Cambridge University Press.

Luce, R. D. (1977). Thurstone's discriminal processes fifty year later. *Psychometrika*, 42, 461–489.

Luce, R. D., & Edwards, W. (1958). The derivation of subjective scales from just noticeable differences. *Psychological Review*, 65, 222–237.

Luce, R. D., & Galanter, E. (1963). Discrimination. In R. D. Luce, R. R. Bush, & E. Galanter (Eds.), *Handbook of mathematical psychology*, v. 1 (pp. 103–189). New York: Wiley.

Rothkopf, E. Z. (1957). A measure of stimulus similarity and errors in some paired-associate learning tasks. *Journal of Experimental Psychology*, 53, 94–102.

Scheerer, E. (1987). The unknown Fechner. *Psychological Research*, 49, 197–202.

Sorkin, R. D. (1962). Extension of the theory of signal detectability to matching paradigms in psychoacoustics. *Journal of the Acoustical Society of America*, 34, 1745–1751.

Suppes, P., & Zinnes, J. L. (1963). Basic measurement theory. In R. D. Luce, R. R. Bush, & E. Galanter (Eds.), *Handbook of mathematical psychology*, v. 1 (pp. 3–76). New York: Wiley.

Takane, Y., & Sergent, J. (1983). Multidimensional scaling models for reaction times and same-different judgments, *Psychometrika*, 48, 393–423.

Thomas, R. D. (1996). Separability and independence of dimensions within the same-different judgment task. *Journal of Mathematical Psychology*, 40, 318–341.

Thurstone, L. L. (1927a). Psychophysical analysis. *American Journal of Psychology*, 38, 368–389.

Thurstone, L. L. (1927b). A law of comparative judgments. *Psychological Review*, 34, 273–286.

Wish, M. (1967). A model for the perception of Morse code-like signals. *Human Factors*, 9, 529–540.

Zhang, J. (2004). Dual scaling of comparison and reference stimuli in multidimensional psychological space. *Journal of Mathematical Psychology*, 48, 409–424.

Zimmer, K., & Colonius, H. (2000). Testing a new theory of Fechnerian scaling: The case of auditory intensity discrimination. *Journal of the Acoustical Society of America*, 108, 2596.

Zinnes, J. L., & MacKay, D. B. (1983). Probabilistic multidimensional scaling: Complete and incomplete data. *Psychometrika*, 48, 27–48.

2

Reconstructing Distances Among Objects from Their Discriminability

Ehtibar N. Dzhafarov[1] and Hans Colonius[2]

[1] Purdue University
[2] Universität Oldenburg

1. INTRODUCTION

The problem of reconstructing distances among stimuli from some empirical measures of pairwise dissimilarity is old. The measures of dissimilarity are numerous, including numerical ratings of (dis)similarity, classifications of stimuli, correlations among response variables, errors of substitution, and many others (Everitt & Rabe-Hesketh, 1997; Suppes, Krantz, Luce, & Tversky, 1989; Sankoff & Kruskal, 1999; Semple & Steele, 2003). Formal representations of proximity data, like Multidimensional Scaling (MDS; Borg & Groenen, 1997; Kruskal & Wish, 1978) or Cluster Analysis (Corter, 1996; Hartigan, 1975), serve to describe and display data structures by embedding them in low-dimensional spatial or graph-theoretical configurations, respectively. In MDS, one embeds data points in a low-dimensional Minkowskian (usually, Euclidean) space so that distances are monotonically (in the metric version, proportionally) related to pairwise dissimilarities. In Cluster Analysis, one typically represents proximity relations by a series of partitions of the set of stimuli resulting in a graph-theoretic tree structure with ultrametric or additive-tree metric distances.

Discrimination probabilities,

$$\psi\left(\mathbf{x}, \mathbf{y}\right) = \Pr\left[\mathbf{x} \text{ and } \mathbf{y} \text{ are judged to be different}\right], \tag{1}$$

which we discussed in Chapter 1, occupy a special place among available measures of pairwise dissimilarity. The ability of telling two objects apart or identifying them as being the same (in some respect or overall) is arguably the most basic cognitive ability in biological perceivers and the most basic requirement of intelligent technical systems. At least this seems to be a plausible view, granting it is not self-evident. It is therefore a plausible position that a metric appropriately computed from the values of $\psi\left(\mathbf{x},\mathbf{y}\right)$ may be viewed as the "subjective metric," a network of distances "from the point of view" of a perceiver.

As discussed in Chapter 1, the notion of a perceiver has a variety of possible meanings, including even cases of "paper-and-pencil" perceivers, abstract computational procedures assigning to every pair $\mathbf{x},\mathbf{y}$ the probability $\psi\left(\mathbf{x},\mathbf{y}\right)$ (subject to Regular Minimality). The example given in Chapter 1 was that of $\psi\left(\mathbf{x},\mathbf{y}\right)$ being the probability with which a data set (in a particular format) generated by a statistical model, $\mathbf{x}$, rejects (in accordance with some criterion) a generally different statistical model, $\mathbf{y}$. The pairwise determinations of sameness/difference in this example (meaning, model $\mathbf{y}$ is retained/rejected when applied to a data set generated by model $\mathbf{x}$) are usually readily available and simple. It is an attractive possibility, therefore, to have a general algorithm in which one can use these pairwise determinations to compute distances among conceptual objects (here, statistical models). The alternative, an a priori choice of a distance measure between two statistical models, may be less obvious and more difficult to justify.

This chapter provides an informal introduction to Fechnerian Scaling, a metric-from-discriminability theory which has been gradually developed by the present authors in the recent years (Dzhafarov, 2002a, 2002b, 2002c, 2002d; 2003a, 2003b; Dzhafarov & Colonius, 1999, 2001, 2005a, 2005b). Its historical roots, however, can be traced back to the work of G. T. Fechner (1801–1887). To keep the presentation on a nontechnical level, we provide details for only the mathematically simplest case of Fechnerian Scaling, the case of discrete stimulus sets (such as letters of alphabets or Morse codes); only a simplified and abridged account of the application of Fechnerian Scaling to continuous stimulus spaces is given. Notation conventions are the same as in Chapter 1.

1.1. Example

Consider the toy matrix used in Chapter 1, presented in a canonical form,

TOY$_0$	A	B	C	D
A	0.1	0.8	0.6	0.6
B	0.8	0.1	0.9	0.9
C	1	0.6	0.5	1
D	1	1	0.7	0.5

This matrix is used throughout to illustrate various points. We describe a computational procedure, *Fechnerian Scaling,* which, when applied to such matrices, produces a matrix of distances we call *Fechnerian.* Intuitively, they reflect the degree of subjective dissimilarity among the stimuli, "from the point of view" of the perceiver (organism, group, technical device, or a computational procedure) to whom stimuli $x, y \in \{A, B, C, D\}$ were presented pairwise and whose responses (interpretable as "same" and "different") were used to compute the probabilities $\psi(x, y)$ shown as the matrix entries. In addition, when the set of stimuli is finite, Fechnerian Scaling produces a set of what we call *geodesic loops,* the shortest (in some well-defined sense) chains of stimuli leading from one given object to another given object and back. Thus, when applied to our matrix TOY_0, Fechnerian Scaling yields the following two matrices:

L_0	A	B	C	D
A	A	ACBA	ACA	ADA
B	BACB	B	BCB	BDCB
C	CAC	CBC	C	CDC
D	DAD	DCBD	DCD	D

G_0	A	B	C	D
A	0	1.3	1	1
B	1.3	0	0.9	1.1
C	1	0.9	0	0.7
D	1	1.1	0.7	0

We can see in matrix L_0, for instance, that the shortest (geodesic) loop connecting A and B within the four-element space $\{A, B, C, D\}$ is

$$A \to C \to B \to A,$$

whereas the geodesic loop connecting A and C in the same space is

$$A \to C \to A.$$

The lengths of these geodesic loops (whose computation will be explained later) are taken to be the Fechnerian distances between A and B and between A and C, respectively. As we see in matrix G_0, the Fechnerian distance between A and B is 1.3 times the Fechnerian distance between A and C.

We should recall some basic facts from Chapter 1:

(1) The row stimuli and the column stimuli in TOY_0 belong to two *distinct observation areas* (say, row stimuli are those presented on the left, or chronologically first, the column stimuli are presented on the right, or second).

(2) $\{A, B, C, D\}$ are psychologically distinct, that is, no two rows or two columns in the matrix are identical (if they were, they would be merged into a single one).

(3) TOY_0 may be the result of a canonical relabeling of a matrix in which the minima lie outside the main diagonal, such as

TOY,	$\mathbf{y}_a$	$\mathbf{y}_b$	$\mathbf{y}_c$	$\mathbf{y}_d$
$\mathbf{x}_a$	0.6	0.6	0.1	0.8
$\mathbf{x}_b$	0.9	0.9	0.8	0.1
$\mathbf{x}_c$	1	0.5	1	0.6
$\mathbf{x}_d$	0.5	0.7	1	1

The physical identity of the $\{\mathbf{A}, \mathbf{B}, \mathbf{C}, \mathbf{D}\}$ in TOY_0 may therefore be different for the row stimuli and the column stimuli.

1.2. Features of Fechnerian Scaling

(A) Regular Minimality is the cornerstone of Fechnerian Scaling, and in the case of discrete stimulus sets, it is essentially the only prerequisite for Fechnerian Scaling. Due to Regular Minimality, we can assume throughout most of this chapter that our stimulus sets are canonically (re)labeled (as in TOY_0), so that

$$\mathbf{x} \neq \mathbf{y} \implies \psi(\mathbf{x}, \mathbf{y}) > \max\{\psi(\mathbf{x}, \mathbf{x}), \psi(\mathbf{y}, \mathbf{y})\}, \tag{2}$$

or equivalently,

$$\mathbf{x} \neq \mathbf{y} \implies \psi(\mathbf{x}, \mathbf{x}) < \min\{\psi(\mathbf{x}, \mathbf{y}), \psi(\mathbf{y}, \mathbf{x})\}. \tag{3}$$

In accordance with the discussion of the fundamental properties of discrimination probabilities (Chapter 1), Fechnerian Scaling does not presuppose that $\psi(\mathbf{x}, \mathbf{x})$ is the same for all $\mathbf{x}$ (Nonconstant Self-Dissimilarity), or that $\psi(\mathbf{x}, \mathbf{y}) = \psi(\mathbf{y}, \mathbf{x})$ (Asymmetry).

(B) The logic of Fechnerian Scaling is very different from the existing techniques of metrizing stimulus spaces (such as MDS) in the following respect: Fechnerian distances are computed *within* rather than *across* the two observation areas. In other words, the Fechnerian distance between $\mathbf{a}$ and $\mathbf{b}$ does not mean a distance between $\mathbf{a}$ presented first (or on the left) and $\mathbf{b}$ presented second (or on the right). Rather, we should logically distinguish $G^{(1)}(\mathbf{a}, \mathbf{b})$, the distance between $\mathbf{a}$ and $\mathbf{b}$ in the first observation area, from $G^{(2)}(\mathbf{a}, \mathbf{b})$, the distance between $\mathbf{a}$ and $\mathbf{b}$ in the second observation area. This must not come as a surprise if one keeps in mind that $\mathbf{a}$ and $\mathbf{b}$ in the first observation area are generally perceived differently from $\mathbf{a}$ and $\mathbf{b}$ in the second observation area. As it turns out, however, if Regular Minimality is satisfied and the stimulus set is put in a canonical form, then it follows from the general theory that

$$G^{(1)}(\mathbf{a}, \mathbf{b}) = G^{(2)}(\mathbf{a}, \mathbf{b}) = G(\mathbf{a}, \mathbf{b}).$$

This is illustrated in the diagram below, where the line connecting a stimulus in $\mathcal{O}1$ with a stimulus in $\mathcal{O}1$ ($\mathcal{O}$ standing for observation area) represents the probability ψ of their discrimination. Note that, for a given $\mathbf{a}, \mathbf{b}$, distance $G(\mathbf{a}, \mathbf{b})$ is computed, in general, from $\psi(\mathbf{x}, \mathbf{y})$ for all $\mathbf{x}, \mathbf{y}$, and not just from $\psi(\mathbf{a}, \mathbf{b})$. Later all of this is explained in detail.

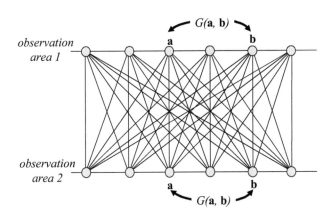

(C) In TOY_0, a geodesic loop containing two given stimuli is defined uniquely. In general, however, this need not be the case: there may be more than one loop of the shortest possible length. Moreover, when the set of stimuli is infinitely large, whether discrete or continuous, geodesic loops may not exist at all, and the Fechnerian distance between two stimuli is then defined as the greatest lower bound (rather than minimum) of lengths of all loops that include these two stimuli.

1.3.   Fechnerian Scaling and Multidimensional Scaling

MDS, when applied to discrimination probabilities, serves as a convenient reference against which to consider the procedure of Fechnerian Scaling. Assuming that discrimination probabilities $\psi(\mathbf{x}, \mathbf{y})$ are known precisely, the classical MDS is based on the assumption that for some metric $d(\mathbf{x}, \mathbf{y})$ (distance function) and some increasing transformation β,

$$\psi(\mathbf{x}, \mathbf{y}) = \beta(d(\mathbf{x}, \mathbf{y})). \tag{4}$$

This is a prominent instance of what is called the *probability-distance hypothesis* in Dzhafarov (2002b). Recall that the defining properties of a metric d are as follows: (A) $d(\mathbf{a}, \mathbf{b}) \geq 0$; (B) $d(\mathbf{a}, \mathbf{b}) = 0$ if and only if $\mathbf{a} = \mathbf{b}$; (C) $d(\mathbf{a}, \mathbf{c}) \leq d(\mathbf{a}, \mathbf{b}) + d(\mathbf{b}, \mathbf{c})$; (D) $d(\mathbf{a}, \mathbf{b}) = d(\mathbf{b}, \mathbf{a})$. In addition, one assumes in MDS that metric d belongs to a predefined class, usually the class of Minkowski metrics with exponents between 1 and 2.

It immediately follows from (A), (B), (D), and the monotonicity of β that for any distinct $\mathbf{x}, \mathbf{y}$,

$$
\begin{aligned}
\psi\left(\mathbf{x}, \mathbf{y}\right) &= \psi\left(\mathbf{y}, \mathbf{x}\right) \quad \text{(Symmetry)} \\
\psi\left(\mathbf{x}, \mathbf{x}\right) &= \psi\left(\mathbf{y}, \mathbf{y}\right) \quad \text{(Constant Self-Dissimilarity)} \\
\psi\left(\mathbf{x}, \mathbf{x}\right) &< \begin{cases} \psi\left(\mathbf{x}, \mathbf{y}\right) \\ \psi\left(\mathbf{y}, \mathbf{x}\right) \end{cases} \text{(Regular Minimality)}
\end{aligned}
\tag{5}
$$

We know from Chapter 1 that although the property of Regular Minimality is indeed satisfied in all available experimental data, the property of Constant Self-Dissimilarity is not. The latter can clearly be seen in the table below, a 10×10 excerpt from Rothkopf's (1957) well-known study of Morse code discriminations. In his experiment, a large number of respondents made same–different judgments in response to 36×36 auditorily presented pairs of Morse codes for letters of the alphabet and digits.[3]

Ro	B	0	1	2	3	4	5	6	7	8	9
B	16	88	83	86	60	68	26	57	83	96	96
0	95	16	37	87	92	90	92	81	68	43	45
1	86	38	11	46	80	95	86	80	79	84	89
2	92	82	36	14	69	77	59	84	83	92	90
3	81	95	74	56	11	58	56	68	90	97	97
4	55	86	90	70	31	10	58	76	90	94	95
5	20	85	86	74	76	83	14	31	86	95	86
6	67	78	71	82	85	88	39	15	30	80	87
7	77	58	71	84	84	91	40	40	11	39	74
8	86	43	61	91	88	96	89	58	44	9	22
9	97	50	74	91	89	95	78	83	48	19	6

Regular Minimality here is satisfied in the canonical form, and one can see, for example, that the Morse code for digit 6 was judged different from itself by 15% of respondents, but only by 6% for digit 9. Symmetry is clearly violated as well: thus, digits 4 and 5 were discriminated from each other in 83% of cases when 5 was presented first in the two-code sequence, but in only 58% when 5 was presented second. Nonconstant Self-similarity and

---

[3] This particular 10-code subset is chosen so that it forms a self-contained subspace of the 36 codes: a geodesic loop (as explained later) for any two of its elements is contained within the subset.

Asymmetry are also manifest in the 10×10 excerpt below from a similar study of Morse-code-like signals by Wish (1967).[4]

Wi	S	U	W	X	0	1	2	3	4	5
S	6	16	38	45	35	73	81	70	89	97
U	28	6	44	24	59	56	49	51	71	69
W	44	42	4	11	78	40	79	55	48	83
X	64	71	26	3	86	51	73	27	31	44
0	34	55	56	46	6	52	39	69	39	95
1	84	75	22	33	70	3	69	17	40	97
2	81	44	62	31	45	50	7	41	35	26
3	94	85	44	17	85	19	84	2	63	47
4	89	73	26	20	65	38	67	45	3	49
5	100	94	74	11	83	95	58	67	25	3

We can conclude, therefore, that MDS, or any other data-analytic technique based on the probability-distance hypothesis, is not supported by discrimination probability data. By contrast, Fechnerian Scaling, in the case of discrete stimulus sets, is only based on Regular Minimality, which is supported by data. Although prior to Dzhafarov (2002d), Regular Minimality has not been formulated as a basic property of discrimination, independent of its other properties (such as Constant Self-Dissimilarity), the violations of Symmetry and Constant Self-Dissimilarity have long since been noted. Tversky's (1977) contrast model and Krumhansl's (1978) distance-and-density scheme are two best known theoretical schemes dealing with these issues.

2. Multidimensional Fechnerian Scaling

MDFS (*Multidimensional Fechnerian Scaling*) is Fechnerian Scaling performed on a stimulus set whose physical description can be represented by an open connected region $\mathbf{E}$ of n-dimensional ($n \geq 1$) real-valued vectors, such that $\psi(\mathbf{x}, \mathbf{y})$ is continuous with respect to its Euclidean topology. This simply means that as $(\mathbf{x}_k, \mathbf{y}_k) \to (\mathbf{x}, \mathbf{y})$, in the conventional sense,

---

[4] 32 stimuli in this study were five-element sequences $T_1 P_1 T_2 P_2 T_3$, where T stands for a tone (short or long) and P stands for a pause (1 or 3 units long). We arbitrarily labeled the stimuli $A, B, ..., Z, 0, 1, ..., 5$, in the order they are presented in Wish's (1967) article. The criterion for choosing this particular subset of 10 stimuli is the same as for matrix Ro.

$\psi\left(\mathbf{x}_k, \mathbf{y}_k\right) \rightarrow \psi\left(\mathbf{x}, \mathbf{y}\right)$. The theory of Fechnerian Scaling has been developed for continuous (arcwise connected) spaces of a much more general structure (Dzhafarov & Colonius, 2005a), but a brief overview of MDFS should suffice for understanding the main ideas underlying Fechnerian Scaling. Throughout the entire discussion, we tacitly assume that Regular Minimality is satisfied in a canonical form.

2.1. Oriented Fechnerian Distances in Continuous Spaces

Any $\mathbf{a}, \mathbf{b} \in \mathbf{E}$ can be connected by a smooth arc $\mathbf{x}\left(t\right)$, a piecewise continuously differentiable mapping of an interval $[\alpha, \beta]$ of reals into $\mathbf{E}$, such that $\mathbf{x}\left(\alpha\right) = \mathbf{a}$, $\mathbf{x}\left(\beta\right) = \mathbf{b}$ Refer to Fig. 1. The main intuitive idea underlying Fechnerian Scaling is that

(a) Any point $\mathbf{x}\left(t\right)$ on this arc, $t \in [\alpha, \beta)$, can be assigned a local measure of its difference from its "immediate neighbors," $\mathbf{x}\left(t + dt\right)$.

(b) By integrating this local difference measure along the arc, from α to β, one can obtain the "psychometric length" of this arc.

(c) By taking the infimum (the greatest lower bound) of psychometric lengths across all possible smooth arcs connecting $\mathbf{a}$ to $\mathbf{b}$, one obtains the distance from $\mathbf{a}$ to $\mathbf{b}$ in space $\mathbf{E}$.

As argued in Dzhafarov and Colonius (1999), this intuitive scheme can be viewed as the essence of Fechner's original theory for unidimensional stimulus continua (Fechner, 1860). The implementation of this idea in MDFS is as follows (see Fig. 2).

As t for a smooth arc $\mathbf{x}\left(t\right)$ moves from α to β, the value of self-discriminability $\psi\left(\mathbf{x}\left(t\right), \mathbf{x}\left(t\right)\right)$ may vary (Nonconstant Self-Dissimilarity property). Therefore, to see how distinct $\mathbf{x}\left(t\right)$ is from $\mathbf{x}\left(t + dt\right)$ it would not suffice to look at $\psi\left(\mathbf{x}\left(t\right), \mathbf{x}\left(t + dt\right)\right)$, or $\psi\left(\mathbf{x}\left(t + dt\right), \mathbf{x}\left(t\right)\right)$; one should compute instead the *increments* in discriminability

$$\begin{aligned} \phi^{(1)}\left(\mathbf{x}\left(t\right), \mathbf{x}\left(t + dt\right)\right) &= \psi\left(\mathbf{x}\left(t\right), \mathbf{x}\left(t + dt\right)\right) - \psi\left(\mathbf{x}\left(t\right), \mathbf{x}\left(t\right)\right), \\ \phi^{(2)}\left(\mathbf{x}\left(t\right), \mathbf{x}\left(t + dt\right)\right) &= \psi\left(\mathbf{x}\left(t + dt\right), \mathbf{x}\left(t\right)\right) - \psi\left(\mathbf{x}\left(t\right), \mathbf{x}\left(t\right)\right). \end{aligned} \quad (6)$$

Both $\phi^{(1)}$ and $\phi^{(2)}$ are positive due to the Regular Minimality property (in a canonical form). They are referred to as *psychometric differentials* of the *first kind* (or in the first observation area) and *second kind* (in the second observation area), respectively.

The assumptions of MDFS guarantee that the cumulation of $\phi^{(1)}\left(\mathbf{x}\left(t\right), \mathbf{x}\left(t + dt\right)\right)$ (i.e., integration of $\phi^{(1)}\left(\mathbf{x}\left(t\right), \mathbf{x}\left(t + dt\right)\right)/dt+$) from $t = \alpha$ to $t = \beta$ always yields a positive quantity.[5] We call this quan-

---

[5] Aside from Regular Minimality and continuity of $\psi\left(\mathbf{x}, \mathbf{y}\right)$, the only other essential assumption of MDFS is that of the existence of a "global psychometric

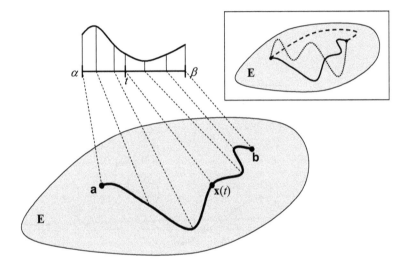

Fig. 1: The underlying idea of MDFS. $[\alpha, \beta]$ is a real interval, $\mathbf{a} \to \mathbf{x}(t) \to \mathbf{b}$ a smooth arc. The psychometric length of this arc is the integral of "local difference" of $\mathbf{x}(t)$ from $\mathbf{x}(t + dt)$, shown by vertical spikes along $[\alpha, \beta]$. The inset shows that one should compute the psychometric lengths for all possible smooth arcs leading from $\mathbf{a}$ to $\mathbf{b}$. Their infimum is the oriented Fechnerian distance from $\mathbf{a}$ to $\mathbf{b}$.

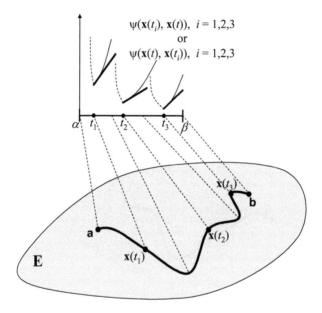

Fig. 2: The "local difference" of $\mathbf{x}(t)$ from $\mathbf{x}(t+dt)$ (as $dt \to 0+$) at a given point, $t = t_i$, is the slope of the tangent line drawn to $\psi(\mathbf{x}(t_i), \mathbf{x}(t))$, or to $\psi(\mathbf{x}(t), \mathbf{x}(t_i))$, at $t = t_i+$. Using $\psi(\mathbf{x}(t_i), \mathbf{x}(t))$ yields derivatives of the first kind, using $\psi(\mathbf{x}(t), \mathbf{x}(t_i))$ yields derivatives of the second kind. Their integration from α to β yields oriented Fechnerian distances (from $\mathbf{a}$ to $\mathbf{b}$) of, respectively, first and second kind.

tity the *psychometric length* of arc $\mathbf{x}(t)$ of the first kind, and denote it $L^{(1)}[\mathbf{a} \to \mathbf{x} \to \mathbf{b}]$, where we use the suggestive notation for arc $\mathbf{x}$ connecting $\mathbf{a}$ to $\mathbf{b}$: this notation is justified by the fact that the choice of the function $\mathbf{x}:[\alpha, \beta] \to \mathbf{E}$ is irrelevant insofar as the graph of the function (the curve connecting $\mathbf{a}$ to $\mathbf{b}$ in $\mathbf{E}$) remains invariant. It can further be shown that the infimum of all such psychometric lengths $L^{(1)}[\mathbf{a} \to \mathbf{x} \to \mathbf{b}]$, across all possible smooth arcs connecting $\mathbf{a}$ to $\mathbf{b}$, satisfies all properties of a distance except for symmetry. Denoting this infimum by $G_1(\mathbf{a}, \mathbf{b})$, we have (A) $G_1(\mathbf{a}, \mathbf{b}) \geq 0$; (B) $G_1(\mathbf{a}, \mathbf{b}) = 0$ if and only if $\mathbf{a} = \mathbf{b}$; (C) $G_1(\mathbf{a}, c) \leq G_1(\mathbf{a}, \mathbf{b}) + G_1(\mathbf{b}, c)$; but it is not necessarily true that $G_1(\mathbf{a}, \mathbf{b}) = G_1(\mathbf{b}, \mathbf{a})$. Such geometric constructs are called *oriented distances*. We call $G_1(\mathbf{a}, \mathbf{b})$ the *oriented Fechnerian distance of the first kind* from $\mathbf{a}$ to $\mathbf{b}$.

By repeating the whole construction with $\phi^{(2)}(\mathbf{x}(t), \mathbf{x}(t + dt))$ in place of $\phi^{(1)}(\mathbf{x}(t), \mathbf{x}(t + dt))$ we get the psychometric lengths $L^{(2)}[\mathbf{a} \to \mathbf{x} \to \mathbf{b}]$ *of the second kind* (for arcs $\mathbf{x}(t)$ connecting $\mathbf{a}$ to $\mathbf{b}$), and, as their infima, the oriented Fechnerian distances $G_2(\mathbf{a}, \mathbf{b})$ of the second kind (from $\mathbf{a}$ to $\mathbf{b}$).

2.2. Multidimensional Fechnerian Scaling and Multidimensional Scaling

The following observation provides additional justification for computing the oriented Fechnerian distances in the way just outlined.

A metric d (symmetrical or oriented) on some set $\mathbf{S}$ is called *intrinsic* if $d(\mathbf{a}, \mathbf{b})$ for any $\mathbf{a}, \mathbf{b} \in \mathbf{S}$ equals the infimum of the lengths of all "allowable" arcs connecting $\mathbf{a}$ and $\mathbf{b}$ (i.e., arcs with some specified properties). The oriented Fechnerian distances $G_1(\mathbf{a}, \mathbf{b})$ and $G_2(\mathbf{a}, \mathbf{b})$ are intrinsic in this sense, provided the allowable arcs are defined as smooth arcs. In reference to the classical MDS, all Minkowski metrics are (symmetrical) intrinsic metrics, in the same sense.

---

transformation" Φ which makes the limit ratios

$$\lim_{s \to 0+} \frac{\Phi\left[\phi^{(\iota)}(\mathbf{x}(t), \mathbf{x}(t + s))\right]}{s} \qquad (\iota = 1, 2)$$

nonvanishing, finite, and continuous in $(\mathbf{x}(t), \dot{\mathbf{x}}(t))$, for all arcs. (Actually, this is the "First Main Theorem of Fechnerian Scaling," a consequence of some simpler assumptions.) As it turns out (Dzhafarov, 2002d), together with Nonconstant Self-Dissimilarity, this implies that $\Phi(h)/h \to k > 0$ as $h \to 0+$. That is, Φ is a scaling transformation in the small and can therefore be omitted from formulations, on putting $k = 1$ with no loss of generality. The uniqueness of extending $\Phi(h) = h$ to arbitrary values of $h \in [0, 1]$ is analyzed in Dzhafarov and Colonius (2005b). In this chapter, $\Phi(h) = h$ is assumed tacitly.

Assume now that the discrimination probabilities $\psi\left(\mathbf{x}, \mathbf{y}\right)$ on $\mathbf{E}$ (with the same meaning as in the previous subsection) can be obtained from some symmetrical intrinsic distance d on $\mathbf{E}$ by means of (4), with β being a continuous increasing function. It is sufficient to assume that (4) holds for small values of d only. Then, as proved in Dzhafarov (2002b),

$$d\left(\mathbf{a}, \mathbf{b}\right) = G_1\left(\mathbf{a}, \mathbf{b}\right) = G_2\left(\mathbf{a}, \mathbf{b}\right)$$

for all $\mathbf{a}, \mathbf{b} \in \mathbf{E}$. In other words, $\psi\left(\mathbf{x}, \mathbf{y}\right)$ cannot monotonically and continuously depend on any (symmetrical) intrinsic metric other than the Fechnerian one. The latter in this case is symmetrical, and its two kinds G_1 and G_2 coincide.[6]

The classical MDS, including its modification proposed in Shepard and Carroll (1966), falls within this category of models. In the context of continuous stimulus spaces, therefore, Fechnerian Scaling and MDS are not simply compatible, the former is in fact a necessary consequence of the latter (under the assumption of intrinsicality, and without confining the class of metrics d to Minkowski ones). Fechnerian computations, however, are applicable in a much broader class of cases, including those where the probability-distance hypothesis is false (as we know it generally to be).

It should be noted for completeness that some nonclassical versions of MDS are based on Tversky's (1977) or Krumhansl's (1978) schemes rather than on the probability-distance hypothesis, and they have the potential of handling nonconstant self-dissimilarity or asymmetry (e.g., DeSarbo, Johnson, Manrai, Manrai, & Edwards, 1992; Weeks & Bentler, 1982). We do not review these approaches here. Certain versions of MDS can be viewed as intermediate between the classical MDS and Fechnerian Scaling. Shepard and Carroll (1966) discussed MDS methods where only sufficiently small distances are monotonically related to pairwise dissimilarities. More recently, this idea was implemented in two algorithms where large distances are obtained by cumulating small distances within stimulus sets viewed as manifolds embedded in Euclidean spaces (Roweis & Saul, 2000; Tenenbaum,

---

[6]This account is somewhat simplistic: Because the probability-distance hypothesis implies Constant Self-Dissimilarity, the theorem proved in Dzhafarov (2002b) is compatible with Fechnerian distances computed with Φ other than identity function (see Footnote 5). We could avoid mentioning this by positing in the formulation of the probability-distance hypothesis that $\beta\left(h\right)$ in (4) has a nonzero finite derivative at $h = 0+$. With this assumption, psychometric increments, hence also Fechnerian distances, are unique up to multiplication by a positive constant. Equation $d \equiv G_1 \equiv G_2$, therefore, could more generally be written as $d \equiv kG_1 \equiv kG_2$ $(k > 0)$. Throughout this chapter, we ignore the trivial distinction between different multiples of Fechnerian metrics. (It should also be noted that in Dzhafarov, 2002b, intrinsic metrics are called internal, and a single distance G is used in place of G_1 and G_2.)

de Silva, & Langford, 2000). When applied to discrimination probabilities, these modifications of MDS cannot handle nonconstant self-dissimilarity, but the idea of cumulating small differences can be viewed as the essence of Fechnerian Scaling.

2.3. Overall Fechnerian Distances in Continuous Spaces

The asymmetry of the oriented Fechnerian distances creates a difficulty in interpretation. It is easy to understand that in general, $\psi(\mathbf{x}, \mathbf{y}) \neq \psi(\mathbf{y}, \mathbf{x})$: stimulus $\mathbf{x}$ in the two cases belongs to two different observation areas and can therefore be perceived differently (the same being true for y). In $G_1(\mathbf{a}, \mathbf{b})$, however, $\mathbf{a}$ and $\mathbf{b}$ belong to the same (first) observation area, and the noncoincidence of $G_1(\mathbf{a}, \mathbf{b})$ and $G_1(\mathbf{b}, \mathbf{a})$ prevents one from interpreting either of them as a reasonable measure of perceptual dissimilarity between $\mathbf{a}$ and $\mathbf{b}$ (in the first observation area, "from the point of view" of a given perceiver). The same consideration applies, of course, to G_2. In MDFS, this difficulty is resolved by taking as a measure of perceptual dissimilarity the *overall Fechnerian distances* $G_1(\mathbf{a}, \mathbf{b}) + G_1(\mathbf{b}, \mathbf{a})$ and $G_2(\mathbf{a}, \mathbf{b}) + G_2(\mathbf{b}, \mathbf{a})$. What justifies this particular choice of symmetrization is the remarkable fact that

$$G_1(\mathbf{a}, \mathbf{b}) + G_1(\mathbf{b}, \mathbf{a}) = G_2(\mathbf{a}, \mathbf{b}) + G_2(\mathbf{b}, \mathbf{a}) = G(\mathbf{a}, \mathbf{b}), \qquad (7)$$

where the overall Fechnerian distance $G(\mathbf{a}, \mathbf{b})$ (we need not now specify of which kind) can be easily checked to satisfy all properties of a metric (Dzhafarov, 2002d; Dzhafarov & Colonius, 2005a).

On a moment's reflection, (7) makes perfect sense. We wish to obtain a measure of perceptual dissimilarity between $\mathbf{a}$ and $\mathbf{b}$, and we use the procedure of pairwise presentations with same-different judgments to achieve this goal. The meaning of (7) is that in speaking of perceptual dissimilarities among stimuli, one can abstract away from this particular empirical procedure. Caution should be exercised, however: the observation-area-invariance of the overall Fechnerian distance is predicated on the *canonical form* of Regular Minimality. In a more general case, as explained in Section 3.6, $G_1(\mathbf{a}, \mathbf{b}) + G_1(\mathbf{b}, \mathbf{a})$ equals $G_2(\mathbf{a}', \mathbf{b}') + G_2(\mathbf{b}', \mathbf{a}')$ if $\mathbf{a}$ and $\mathbf{a}'$ (as well as $\mathbf{b}$ and $\mathbf{b}'$) are PSEs, not necessarily physically identical.

Equation (7) is an immediate consequence of the following proposition (Dzhafarov, 2002d; Dzhafarov & Colonius, 2005a): for any smooth arcs $\mathbf{a} \to \mathbf{x} \to \mathbf{b}$ and $\mathbf{b} \to \mathbf{y} \to \mathbf{a}$,

$$L^{(1)}[\mathbf{a} \to \mathbf{x} \to \mathbf{b}] + L^{(1)}[\mathbf{b} \to \mathbf{y} \to \mathbf{a}]$$
$$= L^{(2)}[\mathbf{a} \to \mathbf{y} \to \mathbf{b}] + L^{(1)}[\mathbf{b} \to \mathbf{x} \to \mathbf{a}]. \qquad (8)$$

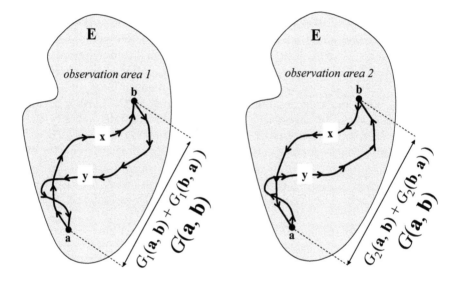

Fig. 3: Illustration for the Second Main Theorem: the psychometric length of the first kind of a closed loop from **a** to **b** and back equals the psychometric length of the second kind for the same loop traversed in the opposite direction. This leads to the equality of the overall Fechnerian distances in the two observation areas.

Put differently, the psychometric length of the first kind for any *closed loop* containing **a** and **b** equals the psychometric length of the second kind for the same closed loop but traversed in the opposite direction.

Together (8) and its corollary (7) constitute what we call the Second Main Theorem of Fechnerian Scaling (see Fig. 3). This theorem plays a critical role in extending the continuous theory to discrete and other, more complex object spaces (Dzhafarov & Colonius, 2005b).

3.   FECHNERIAN SCALING OF DISCRETE OBJECT SETS (FSDOS)

The mathematical simplicity of this special case of Fechnerian Scaling allows us to present it in a greater detail than we did MDFS.

3.1.   Discrete Object Spaces

Recall that a space of stimuli (or objects) is a set **S** of all objects of a particular kind endowed with a discrimination probability function $\psi(\mathbf{x}, \mathbf{y})$. For any $\mathbf{x}, \mathbf{y} \in \mathbf{S}$, we define *psychometric increments* of the first and second kind (or, in the first and second observation areas) as, respectively,

$$\begin{aligned} \phi^{(1)}(\mathbf{x}, \mathbf{y}) &= \psi(\mathbf{x}, \mathbf{y}) - \psi(\mathbf{x}, \mathbf{x}), \\ \phi^{(2)}(\mathbf{x}, \mathbf{y}) &= \psi(\mathbf{y}, \mathbf{x}) - \psi(\mathbf{x}, \mathbf{x}). \end{aligned} \tag{9}$$

Psychometric increments of both kinds are positive due to (a canonical form of) Regular Minimality, (3). A space **S** is called *discrete* if, for any $\mathbf{x} \in \mathbf{S}$,

$$\inf_{\mathbf{y}} \left[\phi^{(1)}(\mathbf{x}, \mathbf{y}) \right] > 0, \qquad \inf_{\mathbf{y}} \left[\phi^{(2)}(\mathbf{x}, \mathbf{y}) \right] > 0.$$

In other words, the psychometric increments of either kind from **x** to other stimuli cannot fall below some positive quantity. Intuitively, other stimuli cannot "get arbitrarily close" to **x**. Clearly, stimuli in a discrete space cannot be connected by arcs (continuous images of intervals of reals).

3.2.   Main Idea

To understand how Fechnerian computations can be made in discrete spaces, let us return for a moment to continuous spaces **E** discussed in the previous section.

Consider a smooth arc $\mathbf{x}(t)$,

$$\mathbf{x}: [\alpha, \beta] \rightarrow \mathbf{E}, \mathbf{x}(\alpha) = \mathbf{a}, \mathbf{x}(\beta) = \mathbf{b},$$

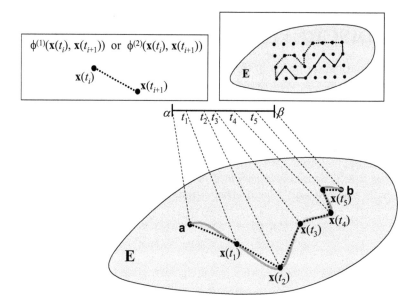

Fig. 4: The psychometric length of the first (second) kind of an arc can be approximated by the sum of psychometric increments of the first (second) kind chained along the arc. The right insert shows that if **E** is represented by a dense grid of points, the Fechnerian computations involve taking all possible chains leading from one point to another through successions of immediately neighboring points.

as shown in Fig. 4. We know that its psychometric length $L^{(\iota)}\left[\mathbf{a} \rightarrow \mathbf{x} \rightarrow \mathbf{b}\right]$ of the ιth kind ($\iota = 1, 2$) is obtained by cumulating psychometric differentials (6) of the same kind along this arc. It is also possible, however, to approximate $L^{(\iota)}\left[\mathbf{a} \rightarrow \mathbf{x} \rightarrow \mathbf{b}\right]$ by subdividing $[\alpha, \beta]$ into

$$\alpha = t_0, t_1, ..., t_k, t_{k+1} = \beta$$

and computing the sum of the chained psychometric increments

$$L^{(1)}\left[\mathbf{x}\left(t_0\right), \mathbf{x}\left(t_1\right), ..., \mathbf{x}\left(t_{k+1}\right)\right] = \sum_{i=0}^{k} \phi^{(\iota)}\left(\mathbf{x}\left(t_i\right), \mathbf{x}\left(t_{i+1}\right)\right). \quad (10)$$

As shown in Dzhafarov and Colonius (2005a), by progressively refining the partitioning, $\max_i \{t_{i+1} - t_i\} \rightarrow 0$, this sum can be made as close as one wishes to the value of $L^{(\iota)}\left[\mathbf{a} \rightarrow \mathbf{x} \rightarrow \mathbf{b}\right]$.

In practical computations, $\mathbf{E}$ (which, we recall, is an open connected region of n-dimensional vectors of reals) can be represented by a sufficiently dense discrete grid of points. In view of the result just mentioned, the oriented Fechnerian distance $G_{\iota}\left(\mathbf{a}, \mathbf{b}\right)$ ($\iota = 1, 2$) between any $\mathbf{a}$ and $\mathbf{b}$ in this case can be approximated by (a) considering all possible chains of successive neighboring points leading from $\mathbf{a}$ to $\mathbf{b}$, (b) computing sums (10) for each of these chains, and (c) taking the smallest value.

This almost immediately leads to the algorithm for Fechnerian computations in discrete spaces. The main difference is that in discrete spaces, we have no physical ordering of stimuli to rely on, and the notion of "neighboring points" is not defined. In a sense, every point in a discrete space can be viewed as a "potential neighbor" of any other point. Consequently, in place of "all possible chains of successive neighboring points leading from $\mathbf{a}$ to $\mathbf{b}$," one has to consider simply *all possible chains of points leading from* $\mathbf{a}$ *to* $\mathbf{b}$ (see Fig. 5).

3.3.   Illustration

Returning to our toy example (matrix TOY_0, reproduced here for the reader's convenience together with L_0 and G_0), let us compute the Fechnerian distance between, say, objects $\mathbf{D}$ and $\mathbf{B}$.

TOY_0	A	B	C	D
A	0.1	0.8	0.6	0.6
B	0.8	0.1	0.9	0.9
C	1	0.6	0.5	1
D	1	1	0.7	0.5

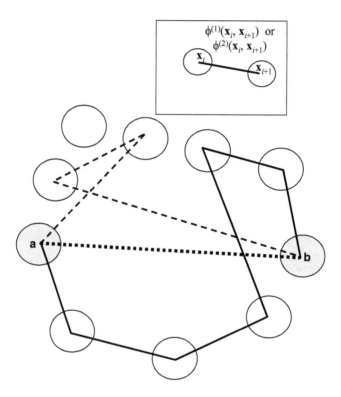

Fig. 5: In a discrete space (10 elements whereof are shown in an arbitrary spatial arrangement), Fechnerian computations are performed by taking sums of psychometric increments (of the first or second kind, as shown in the inset) for all possible chains leading from one point to another.

L_0	A	B	C	D
A	A	ACBA	ACA	ADA
B	BACB	B	BCB	BDCB
C	CAC	CBC	C	CDC
D	DAD	DCBD	DCD	D

G_0	A	B	C	D
A	0	1.3	1	1
B	1.3	0	0.9	1.1
C	1	0.9	0	0.7
D	1	1.1	0.7	0

The whole stimulus space here consists of four stimuli, $\{A, B, C, D\}$, and we have five different chains in this space which are comprised of distinct (nonrecurring) objects and lead from D to B:

$$DB, DAB, DCB, DACB, DCAB.$$

We begin by computing their psychometric lengths of the first kind, $L^{(1)}[DB]$, $L^{(1)}[DAB]$, and so forth. By analogy with (10), $L^{(1)}[DCAB]$, for example, is computed as

$$
\begin{aligned}
L^{(1)}[DCAB] &= \phi^{(1)}(D, C) + \phi^{(1)}(C, A) + \phi^{(1)}(A, B) \\
&= [\psi(D, C) - \psi(D, D)] + [\psi(C, A) - \psi(C, C)] \\
&\quad + [\psi(A, B) - \psi(A, A)] \\
&= [0.7 - 0.5] + [1.0 - 0.5] + [0.8 - 0.1] = 1.4.
\end{aligned}
$$

We have used here the definition of $\phi^{(1)}(x, y)$ given in (9). Repeating this procedure for all our five chains, we will find out that the smallest value is provided by

$$
\begin{aligned}
L^{(1)}[DCB] &= \phi^{(1)}(D, C) + \phi^{(1)}(C, B) \\
&= [\psi(D, C) - \psi(D, D)] + [\psi(C, B) - \psi(C, C)] \\
&= [0.7 - 0.5] + [0.6 - 0.5] = 0.3.
\end{aligned}
$$

Note that this value is smaller than the length of the one-link chain ("direct connection") DB:

$$L^{(1)}[DB] = \phi^{(1)}(D, B) = \psi(D, B) - \psi(D, D) = 1.0 - 0.5 = 0.5.$$

The chain DCB can be called a *geodesic chain* connecting D to B. (Generally, there can be more than one geodesic chain, of the same length, for a given pair of stimuli, but in our toy example, all geodesics are unique.) Its length is taken to be the oriented Fechnerian distance of the first kind from D to B,

$$G_1(D, B) = 0.3.$$

Consider now the same five chains but viewed in the opposite direction, that is, all chains in $\{\mathbf{A}, \mathbf{B}, \mathbf{C}, \mathbf{D}\}$ leading from $\mathbf{B}$ to $\mathbf{D}$, and compute for these chains the psychometric lengths of the first kind: $L^{(1)}\,[\mathbf{BD}]$, $L^{(1)}\,[\mathbf{BAD}]$, and so forth. Having done this, we find out that this time, the shortest chain is the one-link chain $\mathbf{BD}$, with the length

$$L^{(1)}\,[\mathbf{BD}] = \phi^{(1)}\,(\mathbf{B}, \mathbf{D}) = \psi\,(\mathbf{B}, \mathbf{D}) - \psi\,(\mathbf{B}, \mathbf{B}) = 0.9 - 0.1 = 0.8.$$

The geodesic chain from $\mathbf{B}$ to $\mathbf{D}$ therefore is $\mathbf{BD}$, and the oriented Fechnerian distance of the first kind from $\mathbf{B}$ to $\mathbf{D}$ is

$$G_1\,(\mathbf{B}, \mathbf{D}) = 0.8.$$

Using the same logic as for continuous stimulus spaces, we now compute the (symmetrical) overall Fechnerian distance between $\mathbf{D}$ and $\mathbf{B}$ by adding the two oriented distances "to and fro,"

$$G\,(\mathbf{D}, \mathbf{B}) = G\,(\mathbf{B}, \mathbf{D}) = G_1\,(\mathbf{D}, \mathbf{B}) + G_1\,(\mathbf{B}, \mathbf{D}) = 0.3 + 0.8 = 1.1.$$

This is the value we find in cells $(\mathbf{D}, \mathbf{B})$ and $(\mathbf{B}, \mathbf{D})$ of matrix G_0. The concatenation of the two geodesic chains, $\mathbf{DCB}$ and $\mathbf{BD}$, forms the *geodesic loop* between $\mathbf{D}$ and $\mathbf{B}$, which we find in cells $(\mathbf{D}, \mathbf{B})$ and $(\mathbf{B}, \mathbf{D})$ of matrix L_0. This loop, of course, can be written in three different ways depending on which of its three distinct elements we choose to begin and end with. The convention adopted in matrix L_0 is to begin and end with the row object: $\mathbf{DCBD}$ in cell $(\mathbf{D}, \mathbf{B})$ and $\mathbf{BDCB}$ in cell $(\mathbf{B}, \mathbf{D})$.

Note that the overall Fechnerian distance $G\,(\mathbf{D}, \mathbf{B})$ and the corresponding geodesic loop could also be found by computing psychometric lengths for all 25 possible closed loops containing objects $\mathbf{D}$ and $\mathbf{B}$ in space $\{\mathbf{A}, \mathbf{B}, \mathbf{C}, \mathbf{D}\}$ and finding the smallest. This, however, would be a more wasteful procedure.

The reason we do not need to add the qualification "of the first kind" to the designations of the overall Fechnerian distance $G\,(\mathbf{D}, \mathbf{B})$ and the geodesic loop $\mathbf{DCBD}$ is that precisely the same value of $G\,(\mathbf{D}, \mathbf{B})$ and the same geodesic loop (only traversed in the opposite direction) are obtained if the computations are performed with psychometric increments of the second kind.

For chain $\mathbf{DCAB}$, for example, the psychometric length of the second kind, using the definition of $\phi^{(2)}$ in (9), is computed as

$$\begin{aligned}
L^{(2)}\,[\mathbf{DCAB}] &= \phi^{(2)}\,(\mathbf{D}, \mathbf{C}) + \phi^{(2)}\,(\mathbf{C}, \mathbf{A}) + \phi^{(2)}\,(\mathbf{A}, \mathbf{B}) \\
&= [\psi\,(\mathbf{C}, \mathbf{D}) - \psi\,(\mathbf{D}, \mathbf{D})] + [\psi\,(\mathbf{A}, \mathbf{C}) - \psi\,(\mathbf{C}, \mathbf{C})] \\
&\quad + [\psi\,(\mathbf{B}, \mathbf{A}) - \psi\,(\mathbf{A}, \mathbf{A})] \\
&= [1.0 - 0.5] + [0.6 - 0.5] + [0.8 - 0.1] = 1.3.
\end{aligned}$$

Repeating this computation for all our five chains leading from **D** to **B**, the shortest chain is found to be **DB**, with the length

$$L^{(2)}\,[\mathbf{DB}] = \phi^{(2)}\,(\mathbf{D},\mathbf{B}) = \psi\,(\mathbf{B},\mathbf{D}) - \psi\,(\mathbf{D},\mathbf{D}) = 0.9 - 0.5 = 0.4,$$

taken to be the value of $G_2\,(\mathbf{D},\mathbf{B})$, the oriented Fechnerian distance form **D** to **B** of the second kind. For the same five chains but viewed as leading from **B** to **D**, the shortest chain is **BCD**, with the length

$$
\begin{aligned}
L^{(2)}\,[\mathbf{BCD}] &= \phi^{(2)}\,(\mathbf{B},\mathbf{C}) + \phi^{(2)}\,(\mathbf{C},\mathbf{D}) \\
&= [\psi\,(\mathbf{C},\mathbf{B}) - \psi\,(\mathbf{B},\mathbf{B})] + [\psi\,(\mathbf{D},\mathbf{C}) - \psi\,(\mathbf{C},\mathbf{C})] \\
&= [0.6 - 0.1] + [0.7 - 0.5] = 0.7
\end{aligned}
$$

taken to be the value of $G_2\,(\mathbf{B},\mathbf{D})$, the oriented Fechnerian distance form **B** to **D** of the second kind. Their sum is

$$G\,(\mathbf{D},\mathbf{B}) = G\,(\mathbf{B},\mathbf{D}) = G_2\,(\mathbf{D},\mathbf{B}) + G_2\,(\mathbf{B},\mathbf{D}) = 0.4 + 0.7 = 1.1,$$

precisely the same value for the overall Fechnerian distance as before (although the oriented distances are different). The geodesic loop obtained by concatenating the geodesic chains **DB** and **BCD** is also the same as we find in matrix L_0 in cells **(D, B)** and **(B, D)**, but read from right to left: **DBCD** in cell **(D, B)** and **BCDB** in cell **(B, D)**.

The complete formulation of the convention adopted in L_0 therefore is as follows: the geodesic loop in cell $(\mathbf{x}, \mathbf{y})$ begins and ends with **x** and is read from left to right for the computations of the first kind, and from right to left for the computations of the second kind (yielding one and the same result, the overall Fechnerian distance between **x** and **y**).

3.4.   Procedure of Fechnerian Scaling of Discrete Object Sets

It is clear that any finite set $S = \{\mathbf{s}_1, \mathbf{s}_2, ..., \mathbf{s}_N\}$ endowed with probabilities $p_{ij} = \psi\,(\mathbf{s}_i, \mathbf{s}_j)$ forms a discrete space in the sense of our formal definition. As this case is of the greatest interest in empirical applications, in the following we confine our discussion to finite object spaces. All our statements, however, unless specifically qualified, apply to discrete object spaces of arbitrary cardinality.

The procedure shown later is described as if one knew the probabilities p_{ij} on the population level. If sample sizes do not warrant this approximation, the procedure should ideally be repeated with a large number of matrices p_{ij} that are statistically retainable given a matrix of frequency estimates $\hat{p}_{ij}$. We return to this issue in the concluding section.

The computation of Fechnerian distances G_{ij} among $\{s_1, s_2, ..., s_N\}$ proceeds in several steps. The first step in the computation is to check for Regular Minimality: for any i and all $j \neq i$,

$$p_{ii} < \min\{p_{ij}, p_{ji}\}.$$

If Regular Minimality is violated (on the population level), FSDOS will not work. Put differently, given a matrix of frequency estimates $\hat{\psi}(s_i, s_j)$, one should use statistically retainable matrices of probabilities p_{ij} that do satisfy Regular Minimality; and if no such matrices can be found, FSDOS is not applicable. The theory of Fechnerian Scaling treats Regular Minimality as the defining property of discrimination. If it is not satisfied, something can be wrong in the procedure: for collective perceivers, for example, substantially different groups of people could be responding to different pairs of stimuli (violating thereby the requirement of having a "single perceiver"), or the semantic meaning of the responses "same" and "different" could vary from one pair of stimuli to another. (Alternatively, of course, the theory of Fechnerian Scaling may be wrong itself, which would be a preferable conclusion if regular Minimality was found to be violated systematically, or at least not very rarely.)

Having Regular Minimality verified, we compute psychometric increments of the first and second kind,

$$\phi^{(1)}(s_i, s_j) = p_{ij} - p_{ii},$$
$$\phi^{(2)}(s_i, s_j) = p_{ji} - p_{ii},$$

which are positive for all $j \neq i$.

Consider now a chain of stimuli $s_i = x_1, x_2, ..., x_k = s_j$ leading from s_i to s_j, with $k \geq 2$. The psychometric length of the first kind for this chain, $L^{(1)}[x_1, x_2, ..., x_k]$, is defined as the sum of the psychometric increments $\phi^{(1)}(x_m, x_{m+1})$ taken along this chain,

$$L^{(1)}[x_1, x_2, ..., x_k] = \sum_{m=1}^{k} \phi^{(1)}(x_m, x_{m+1}).$$

The set of different psychometric lengths across all possible chains of distinct elements connecting s_i to s_j being finite, it contains a minimum value $L_{\min}^{(1)}(s_i, s_j)$. (The consideration can always be confined to chains $(x_1, x_2, ..., x_k)$ of distinct elements, because if $x_l = x_m$ ($l < m$), the length $L^{(1)}$ cannot increase if the subchain $(x_{l+1}, ..., x_m)$ is removed.) This value is called the oriented Fechnerian distance of the first kind from object s_i to object s_j:

$$G_1(s_i, s_j) = L_{\min}^{(1)}(s_i, s_j).$$

It is easy to prove that the oriented Fechnerian distance satisfies all properties of a metric, except for symmetry: (A) $G_1 (\mathbf{s}_i, \mathbf{s}_j) \geq 0$; (B) $G_1 (\mathbf{s}_i, \mathbf{s}_j) = 0$ if and only if $i = j$; (C) $G_1 (\mathbf{s}_i, \mathbf{s}_j) \leq G_1 (\mathbf{s}_i, \mathbf{s}_m) + G_1 (\mathbf{s}_m, \mathbf{s}_j)$; but in general, $G_1 (\mathbf{s}_i, \mathbf{s}_j) \neq G_1 (\mathbf{s}_j, \mathbf{s}_i)$.[7] In according with the general logic of Fechnerian Scaling, $G_1 (\mathbf{s}_i, \mathbf{s}_j)$ is interpreted as the oriented Fechnerian distance from $\mathbf{s}_i$ to $\mathbf{s}_j$ in the first observation area.

Any chain from $\mathbf{s}_i$ to $\mathbf{s}_j$ whose elements are distinct and whose length equals $G_1 (\mathbf{s}_i, \mathbf{s}_j)$ is a geodesic chain from $\mathbf{s}_i$ to $\mathbf{s}_j$. There may be more than one geodesic chain for given $\mathbf{s}_i, \mathbf{s}_j$. (Note that in the case of infinite discrete sets mentioned in footnote 7 geodesic chains need not exist.)

The oriented Fechnerian distances $G_2 (\mathbf{s}_i, \mathbf{s}_j)$ of the second kind (in the second observation area) and the corresponding geodesic chains are computed analogously, using the chained sums of psychometric increments $\phi^{(2)}$ instead of $\phi^{(1)}$.

As argued earlier (Section 2.3), the order of two stimuli in a given observation area has no operational meaning, and we add the two oriented distances, "to and fro," to obtain the (symmetrical) overall Fechnerian distances

$$G_{ij} = G_1 (\mathbf{s}_i, \mathbf{s}_j) + G_1 (\mathbf{s}_j, \mathbf{s}_i) = G_{ji},$$
$$G_{ij} = G_2 (\mathbf{s}_i, \mathbf{s}_j) + G_2 (\mathbf{s}_j, \mathbf{s}_i) = G_{ji}.$$

G_{ij} clearly satisfies all the properties of a metric.

The validation for this procedure (and for writing G_{ij} without indicating observation area) is provided by the fact that

$$G_1 (\mathbf{s}_i, \mathbf{s}_j) + G_1 (\mathbf{s}_j, \mathbf{s}_i) = G_2 (\mathbf{s}_i, \mathbf{s}_j) + G_2 (\mathbf{s}_j, \mathbf{s}_i), \qquad (11)$$

that is, the distance G_{ij} between the ith and the jth objects does not depend on the observation area in which these objects are taken. This fact is a consequence of the following statement, which is of interest on its own sake: for any two chains $\mathbf{s}_i = \mathbf{x}_1, \mathbf{x}_2, ..., \mathbf{x}_k = \mathbf{s}_j$ and $\mathbf{s}_i = \mathbf{y}_1, \mathbf{y}_2, ..., \mathbf{y}_l = \mathbf{s}_j$

---

[7]Properties (A) and (B) trivially follow from the fact that for $i \neq j$, $G_1 (\mathbf{s}_i, \mathbf{s}_j)$ is the smallest of several positive quantities, $L^{(1)} [\mathbf{x}_1, \mathbf{x}_2, ..., \mathbf{x}_k]$. Property (C) follows from the observation that the chains leading from $\mathbf{s}_i$ to $\mathbf{s}_j$ through a fixed $\mathbf{s}_k$ form a proper subset of all chains leading from $\mathbf{s}_i$ to $\mathbf{s}_j$. For an infinite discrete $\mathbf{S}$, $L^{(1)}_{\min} (\mathbf{a}, \mathbf{b})$ $(\mathbf{a}, \mathbf{b} \in \mathbf{S})$ need not exist and should be replaced with $L^{(1)}_{\inf} (\mathbf{a}, \mathbf{b})$, the infimum of $L^{(1)} [\mathbf{x}_1, \mathbf{x}_2, ..., \mathbf{x}_k]$ for all finite chains of distinct elements with $\mathbf{a} = \mathbf{x}_1$ and $\mathbf{x}_k = \mathbf{b}$ $(\mathbf{x}_1, \mathbf{x}_2, ..., \mathbf{x}_k \in \mathbf{S})$. The argument for properties (A) and (B) then should be modified: for $\mathbf{a} \neq \mathbf{b}$, $G_1 (\mathbf{a}, \mathbf{b}) > 0$ because $L^{(1)}_{\inf} (\mathbf{a}, \mathbf{b}) \geq \inf_{\mathbf{x}} \left[\phi^{(1)} (\mathbf{a}, \mathbf{x}) \right]$, and by definition of discrete object spaces, $\inf_{\mathbf{x}} \left[\phi^{(1)} (\mathbf{a}, \mathbf{x}) \right] > 0$.

(connecting $\mathbf{s}_i$ to $\mathbf{s}_j$),

$$L^{(1)}\left[\mathbf{x}_1, \mathbf{x}_2, ..., \mathbf{x}_k\right] + L^{(1)}\left[\mathbf{y}_l, \mathbf{y}_{l-1}, ..., \mathbf{y}_1\right]$$
$$= L^{(2)}\left[\mathbf{y}_1, \mathbf{y}_2, ..., \mathbf{y}_l\right] + L^{(2)}\left[\mathbf{x}_k, \mathbf{x}_{k-1}, ..., \mathbf{x}_1\right]. \tag{12}$$

As the proof of this statement is elementary, it may be useful to present it here. Denoting $p'_{ij} = \psi\left(\mathbf{x}_i, \mathbf{x}_j\right)$ and $p''_{ij} = \psi\left(\mathbf{y}_i, \mathbf{y}_j\right)$,

$$L^{(1)}\left[\mathbf{x}_1, \mathbf{x}_2, ..., \mathbf{x}_k\right] + L^{(1)}\left[\mathbf{y}_l, \mathbf{y}_{l-1}, ..., \mathbf{y}_1\right]$$
$$= \sum_{m=1}^{k-1}\left(p'_{m,m+1} - p'_{ii}\right) + \sum_{m=1}^{l-1}\left(p''_{m+1,m} - p''_{m+1,m+1}\right),$$
$$L^{(2)}\left[\mathbf{y}_1, \mathbf{y}_2, ..., \mathbf{y}_l\right] + L^{(2)}\left[\mathbf{x}_k, \mathbf{x}_{k-1}, ..., \mathbf{x}_1\right]$$
$$= \sum_{m=1}^{l-1}\left(p''_{m+1,m} - p''_{m,m}\right) + \sum_{m=1}^{k-1}\left(p'_{m,m+1} - p'_{m+1,m+1}\right).$$

Subtracting the second equation from the first,

$$\left(L^{(1)}\left[\mathbf{x}_1, \mathbf{x}_2, ..., \mathbf{x}_k\right] - L^{(2)}\left[\mathbf{x}_k, \mathbf{x}_{k-1}, ..., \mathbf{x}_1\right]\right)$$
$$+ \left(L^{(1)}\left[\mathbf{y}_l, \mathbf{y}_{l-1}, ..., \mathbf{y}_1\right] - L^{(2)}\left[\mathbf{y}_1, \mathbf{y}_2, ..., \mathbf{y}_l\right]\right)$$
$$= \left(\sum_{m=1}^{k-1}\left(p'_{m,m+1} - p'_{ii}\right) - \sum_{m=1}^{k-1}\left(p'_{m,m+1} - p'_{m+1,m+1}\right)\right)$$
$$+ \left(\sum_{m=1}^{l-1}\left(p''_{m+1,m} - p''_{m+1,m+1}\right) - \sum_{m=1}^{l-1}\left(p''_{m+1,m} - p''_{m,m}\right)\right)$$
$$= \left(p'_{kk} - p'_{11}\right) + \left(p''_{11} - p''_{kk}\right).$$

But $p'_{11} = p''_{11} = p_{ii}$ and $p'_{kk} = p''_{kk} = p_{jj}$, where, we recall, $p_{ij} = \psi\left(\mathbf{s}_i, \mathbf{s}_j\right)$. The difference therefore is zero, and (12) is proved. Equation (11) follows as a corollary, on observing

$$G_1\left(\mathbf{s}_i, \mathbf{s}_j\right) + G_1\left(\mathbf{s}_j, \mathbf{s}_i\right) = \inf L^{(1)}\left[\mathbf{x}_1, \mathbf{x}_2, ..., \mathbf{x}_k\right] + \inf L^{(1)}\left[\mathbf{y}_l, \mathbf{y}_{l-1}, ..., \mathbf{y}_1\right]$$
$$= \inf\left\{L^{(1)}\left[\mathbf{x}_1, \mathbf{x}_2, ..., \mathbf{x}_k\right] + L^{(1)}\left[\mathbf{y}_l, \mathbf{y}_{l-1}, ..., \mathbf{y}_1\right]\right\}$$
$$= \inf\left\{L^{(2)}\left[\mathbf{y}_1, \mathbf{y}_2, ..., \mathbf{y}_l\right] + L^{(2)}\left[\mathbf{x}_k, \mathbf{x}_{k-1}, ..., \mathbf{x}_1\right]\right\}$$
$$= \inf L^{(2)}\left[\mathbf{y}_1, \mathbf{y}_2, ..., \mathbf{y}_l\right] + \inf L^{(2)}\left[\mathbf{x}_k, \mathbf{x}_{k-1}, ..., \mathbf{x}_1\right]$$
$$= G_2\left(\mathbf{s}_j, \mathbf{s}_i\right) + G_2\left(\mathbf{s}_i, \mathbf{s}_j\right).$$

Together (11) and (12) provide a simple version of the Second Main Theorem of Fechnerian Scaling, mentioned earlier, when discussing MDFS.

An equivalent way of defining the overall Fechnerian distances G_{ij} is to consider all *closed loops* $\mathbf{x}_1, \mathbf{x}_2, ..., \mathbf{x}_n, \mathbf{x}_1$ $(n \geq 2)$ containing two given stimuli $\mathbf{s}_i, \mathbf{s}_j$: G_{ij} is the shortest of the psychometric lengths computed for all such loops. Note that the psychometric length of a loop depends on the direction in which it is traversed: generally,

$$L^{(1)}\left(\mathbf{x}_1, \mathbf{x}_2, ..., \mathbf{x}_n, \mathbf{x}_1\right) \neq L^{(1)}\left(\mathbf{x}_1, \mathbf{x}_n, ..., \mathbf{x}_2, \mathbf{x}_1\right),$$
$$L^{(2)}\left(\mathbf{x}_1, \mathbf{x}_2, ..., \mathbf{x}_n, \mathbf{x}_1\right) \neq L^{(2)}\left(\mathbf{x}_1, \mathbf{x}_n, ..., \mathbf{x}_2, \mathbf{x}_1\right).$$

The result just demonstrated tells us, however, that

$$L^{(1)}\left(\mathbf{x}_1, \mathbf{x}_2, ..., \mathbf{x}_n, \mathbf{x}_1\right) = L^{(2)}\left(\mathbf{x}_1, \mathbf{x}_n, ..., \mathbf{x}_2, \mathbf{x}_1\right),$$

that is, any closed loop in the first observation area has the same length as the same closed loop traversed in the opposite direction in the second observation area. In particular, if $\mathbf{x}_1, \mathbf{x}_2, ..., \mathbf{x}_n, \mathbf{x}_1$ is a geodesic (i.e., shortest) loop containing the objects $\mathbf{s}_i, \mathbf{s}_j$ in the first observation area (obviously, the concatenation of the geodesic chains connecting $\mathbf{s}_i$ to $\mathbf{s}_j$ and $\mathbf{s}_j$ to $\mathbf{s}_i$), then the same loop is a geodesic loop in the second observation area, if traversed in the opposite direction, $\mathbf{x}_1, \mathbf{x}_n, ..., \mathbf{x}_2, \mathbf{x}_1$.

The computational procedure of FSDOS is summarized in the form of a detailed algorithm presented in the Appendix at the end of this chapter.

3.5.   Two Examples

We used the procedure just described to compute Fechnerian distances and geodesic loops among 36 Morse codes with pairwise discrimination probabilities reported in Rothkopf (1957), and among 32 Morse-code-like signals data with discrimination probabilities reported in Wish (1967). For typographic reasons only, small subsets of these stimulus sets are shown in matrices Ro and Wi in Section 1.3, chosen because they form "self-contained" *subspaces*: any two elements of such a subset can be connected by a geodesic loop lying entirely within the subset. The Fechnerian distances and geodesic loops are presented here for these subsets only: for matrix Ro, they are

G_{Ro}	B	C	0	1	2	3	4	5	6	7	8	9
B	0	95	151	142	118	95	97	16	57	77	140	157
0	151	133	0	48	105	160	150	147	127	99	61	73
1	142	114	48	0	57	132	164	147	125	128	106	121
2	118	116	105	57	0	100	123	105	129	142	158	161
3	95	143	160	132	100	0	68	95	127	145	165	169
4	97	152	150	164	123	68	0	106	138	160	171	174
5	16	109	147	147	105	95	106	0	41	61	124	143
6	57	122	127	125	129	127	138	41	0	44	92	118
7	77	107	99	128	142	145	160	61	44	0	63	83
8	140	136	61	106	158	165	171	124	92	63	0	26
9	157	156	73	121	161	169	174	143	118	83	26	0

L_{Ro}	B	0	1	2	3	4	5	6	7	8	9
B	B	B0B	B1B	BX25B	B35B	B4B	B5B	B565B	B5675B	B567875B	B975B
0	0B0	0	010	01210	030	040	050	0670	070	080	090
1	1B1	101	1	121	131	141	151	161	171	1081	10901
2	25BX2	21012	212	2	232	242	252	2562	272	21082	292
3	35B3	303	313	323	3	343	35B3	363	3673	383	393
4	4B4	404	414	424	434	4	45B4	4564	474	484	494
5	5B5	505	515	525	5B35	5B45	5	565	5675	567875	5975
6	65B56	6706	616	6256	636	6456	656	6	676	6786	678986
7	75B567	707	717	727	7367	747	7567	767	7	787	7897
8	875B5678	808	8108	82108	838	848	875678	8678	878	8	898
9	975B9	909	90109	929	939	949	9759	986789	9789	989	9

and for matrix Wi they are[8]

---

[8]In the complete 32×32 matrix reported in Wish (1967); but outside the 10×10 submatrix Wi, there are two violations of Regular Minimality, both due to a single value, $\hat{p}_{TV} = 0.03$: this value is the same as $\hat{p}_{VV}$ and smaller than $\hat{p}_{TT} = 0.06$ (using the labeling of stimuli described in Section 1.3); see also Footnote 4. As Wish's data are used here for illustration purposes only, we simply replaced $\hat{p}_{TV} = 0.03$ with $p_{TV} = 0.07$, putting $p_{ij} = \hat{p}_{ij}$ for the rest of the data. Chi-square deviation of thus defined matrix of p_{ij} from the matrix of $\hat{p}_{ij}$ is negligibly small.

G_{WI}	S	U	W	X	0	1	2	3	4	5
S	0	32	72	89	57	119	112	128	119	138
U	32	0	76	79	89	107	80	116	107	128
W	72	76	0	30	119	55	122	67	58	79
X	89	79	30	0	123	67	94	39	45	49
0	57	89	119	123	0	113	71	143	95	132
1	119	107	55	67	113	0	109	31	72	108
2	112	80	122	94	71	109	0	116	92	74
3	128	116	67	39	143	31	116	0	84	77
4	119	107	58	45	95	72	92	84	0	68
5	138	128	79	49	132	108	74	77	68	0

L_{WI}	S	U	W	X	0	1	2	3	4	5
S	s	SUS	SWS	SUXS	S0S	SU1WS	SU2US	SUX3XS	SUX4WS	SUX5XS
U	USU	u	UWU	UXWU	US0SU	U1WU	U2U	UX31WU	UX4WU	UX5XWU
W	WSW	WUW	w	WXW	WS0W	W1W	W2XW	WX31W	WX4W	WX5XW
X	XSUX	XWUX	XWX	x	X0X	X31WX	X2X	X3X	X4X	X5X
0	0S0	0SUS0	0WS0	0X0	0	010	020	0130	040	0250
1	1WSU1	1WU1	1W1	1WX31	101	1	121	131	141	135X31
2	2USU2	2U2	2XW2	2X2	202	212	2	232	242	252
3	3XSUX3	31WUX3	31WX3	3X3	3013	313	323	3	3X4X3	35X3
4	4WSUX4	4WUX4	4WX4	4X4	404	414	424	4X3X4	4	454
5	5XSUX5	5XWUX5	5XWX5	5X5	5025	5X3135	525	5X35	545	5

Recall our convention on presenting geodesic loops. Thus, in matrix L_{Ro}, the geodesic chain from letter B to digit 8 in the first observation area is $B \rightarrow 5 \rightarrow 6 \rightarrow 7 \rightarrow 8$ and that from 8 to B is $8 \rightarrow 7 \rightarrow 5 \rightarrow B$. In the second observation area, the geodesic chains should be read from right to left: $8 \leftarrow 7 \leftarrow 5 \leftarrow B$ from B to 8, and $B \leftarrow 5 \leftarrow 6 \leftarrow 7 \leftarrow 8$ from 8 to B. The oriented Fechnerian distances (lengths of the geodesic chains) are

---

A more comprehensive procedure should have involved a repeated generation of statistically retainable p_{ij} matrices subject to Regular Minimality, as discussed in the concluding section.

$G_1(B, 8) = .70$, $G_1(8, B) = .70$, $G_2(B, 8) = .77$, and $G_2(8, B) = .63$. The lengths of the closed loops in both observation areas add up to the same value, $G(8, B) = 1.40$, as they should.

Note that Fechnerian distances G_{ij} are not monotonically related to discrimination probabilities p_{ij}: there is no functional relation between the two because the computation of G_{ij} for any *given* (i, j) involves p_{ij} values for *all* (i, j). And, the oriented Fechnerian distances $G_1(s_i, s_j)$ and $G_2(s_i, s_j)$ are not monotonically related to psychometric increments $p_{ij} - p_{ii}$ and $p_{ji} - p_{ii}$, due to the existence of longer-than-one-link geodesic chains. There is, however, a strong positive correlation between p_{ij} and G_{ij}: 0.94 for Rothkopf's data and 0.89 for Wish's data (the Pearson correlation for the entire matrices, 36×36 and 32×32). This indicates that the probability-distance hypothesis, even if known to be false mathematically, may still be acceptable as a crude approximation. We may expect consequently that MDS-distances could provide crude approximations to the Fechnerian distances. That the adjective "crude" cannot be dispensed with is indicated by the relatively low values of Kendall's correlation between p_{ij} and G_{ij}: 0.76 for Rothkopf's data and 0.68 for Wish's data.

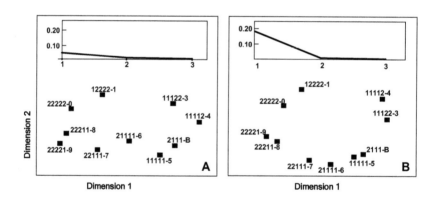

Fig. 6: Two-dimensional Euclidean representations for discrimination probabilities (nonmetric MDS, Panel A) and for Fechnerian distances in matrix G_{Ro} (metric MDS, Panel B). The MDS program used is PROXSCAL 1.0 in SPSS 11.5, minimizing raw stress. Sequence of "1"s and "2"s preceding a dash is the Morse code for the symbol following the dash. Insets are scree plots (normalized raw stress versus number of dimensions).

MDS can be used in conjunction with FSDOS, as a follow-up analysis once Fechnerian distances have been computed. A nonmetric version of MDS can be applied to Fechnerian distances (as opposed to discrimination

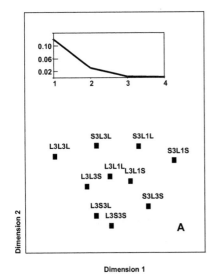 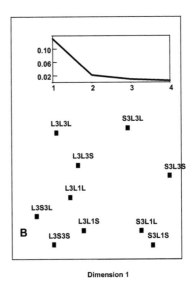

Fig. 7: Same as Fig. 6, but for discrimination probabilities (nonmetric MDS, Panel A) and for Fechnerian distances in matrix G_{Wi} (metric MDS, Panel B). L stands for long tone, S for short tone, whereas digits 1 an 3 show the lengths of the two pauses.

probabilities directly) simply to provide a rough graphical representation for matrices like Ro and Wi. More interestingly, a *metric* version of MDS can be applied to Fechnerian distances to test the hypothesis that Fechnerian distances, not restricted a priori to any particular class (except for being intrinsic), de facto belong to a class of Euclidean metrics (or, more generally, Minkowski ones), at least approximately; the degree of approximation for any given dimensionality is measured by the achieved stress value. Geometrically, metric MDS on Fechnerian distances is an attempt to *isometrically embed* the discrete object space into a low-dimensional Euclidean (or Minkowskian) space. Isometric embedment (or *immersion*) means mapping without distorting pairwise distances. Figures 6 and 7 provide a comparison of the metric MDS on Fechnerian distances (matrices Ro, Wi) with nonmetric MDS performed on discrimination probabilities directly (matrices G_{Ro}, G_{Wi}). Using the value of normalized raw stress as our criterion, the two-dimensional solution is almost equally good in both analyses. Therefore, to the extent that we consider the traditional MDS solution acceptable, we can view the Fechnerian distances in these two cases as being approximately Euclidean. The configurations of points obtained by performing the metric MDS on Fechnerian distances and nonmetric MDS on discrimination probabilities are more similar in Fig. 6 than in Fig. 7, indicating that MDS-distances provide a better approximation to Fechnerian distances in the former case. This may reflect the fact that the correlation between the probabilities and Fechnerian distances for Rothkopf's data is higher than for Wish's data (0.94 vs. 0.89). A detailed comparison of the configurations provided by the two analyses, as well as such related issues as interpretation of axes, are, however, beyond the scope of this chapter.

3.6. General Form of Regular Minimality

In continuous stimulus spaces, it often happens that Regular Minimality does not hold in a canonical form: for a fixed value of $\mathbf{x}$, $\psi(\mathbf{x}, \mathbf{y})$ achieves its minimum not at $\mathbf{y} = \mathbf{x}$ but at some other value of $\mathbf{y}$. It has been noticed since Fechner (1860), for example, that when one and the same stimulus is presented twice in a succession, the second presentation often seems larger (bigger, brighter, etc.) than the first: this is the classical phenomenon of "time error." It follows that in a successive pair of unidimensional stimuli, (x, y), the two elements maximally resemble each other when y is physically smaller than x. Other examples were discussed in Chapter 1. Although it is possible that in discrete stimulus spaces Regular Minimality always holds in a canonical form, it need not be so a priori.

Returning once again to our toy example, assume that matrix TOY_0 was the result of a canonical relabeling of matrix TOY_1,

TOY$_1$	$\mathbf{y}_a$	$\mathbf{y}_b$	$\mathbf{y}_c$	$\mathbf{y}_d$
$\mathbf{x}_a$	0.6	0.6	0.1	0.8
$\mathbf{x}_b$	0.9	0.9	0.8	0.1
$\mathbf{x}_c$	1	0.5	1	0.6
$\mathbf{x}_d$	0.5	0.7	1	1

with the correspondence table

$\mathcal{O}_1$	$\mathbf{x}_a$	$\mathbf{x}_b$	$\mathbf{x}_c$	$\mathbf{x}_d$
$\mathcal{O}_2$	$\mathbf{y}_c$	$\mathbf{y}_d$	$\mathbf{y}_b$	$\mathbf{y}_a$
common label	**A**	**B**	**C**	**D**

where $\mathcal{O}_1$ and $\mathcal{O}_2$, as usual, denote the two observation areas (row stimuli and column stimuli). Having performed the Fechnerian analysis on TOY$_0$ and having computed the matrices L_0 and G_0, it makes sense now to return to the original labeling (using the table of correspondences above) and present the Fechnerian distances and geodesic loops separately for the first and the second observation areas:

L_{11}	a	b	c	d
a	a	acba	aca	ada
b	bacb	b	bcb	bdcb
c	cac	cbc	c	cdc
d	dad	dcbd	dcd	d

G_{11}	a	b	c	d
a	0	1.3	1	1
b	1.3	0	0.9	1.1
c	1	0.9	0	0.7
d	1	1.1	0.7	0

L_{12}	c	d	b	a
c	c	cbdc	cbc	cac
d	dcbd	d	dbd	dabd
b	bcb	bdb	b	bab
a	aca	abda	aba	a

G_{12}	c	d	b	a
c	0	1.3	1	1
d	1.3	0	0.9	1.1
b	1	0.9	0	0.7
a	1	1.1	0.7	0

Denoting, as indicated in Section 1.2, the overall Fechnerian distances in the first and second observation areas by $G^{(1)}(\mathbf{a}, \mathbf{b})$ and $G^{(2)}(\mathbf{a}, \mathbf{b})$, respectively, not to be confused with the oriented Fechnerian distances $G_1(\mathbf{a}, \mathbf{b})$ and $G_2(\mathbf{a}, \mathbf{b})$,

$$G^{(1)}(\mathbf{a}, \mathbf{b}) = G_1(\mathbf{a}, \mathbf{b}) + G_1(\mathbf{b}, \mathbf{a}) = G^{(1)}(\mathbf{b}, \mathbf{a}),$$
$$G^{(2)}(\mathbf{a}, \mathbf{b}) = G_2(\mathbf{a}, \mathbf{b}) + G_2(\mathbf{b}, \mathbf{a}) = G^{(2)}(\mathbf{b}, \mathbf{a}).$$

We see, for instance, that $G^{(1)}(\mathbf{a}, \mathbf{b})$ is 1.3, whereas $G^{(2)}(\mathbf{a}, \mathbf{b})$ is 0.7, reflecting the fact that $\mathbf{a}, \mathbf{b}$ are perceived differently in the two observation areas. On the other hand, $G^{(2)}(\mathbf{c}, \mathbf{d})$ is 1.3., the same as $G^{(1)}(\mathbf{a}, \mathbf{b})$. This reflects the fact that $\mathbf{c}$ and $\mathbf{d}$ in $\mathcal{O}_2$ are the PSEs for, respectively, $\mathbf{a}$ and $\mathbf{b}$ in $\mathcal{O}_1$. Moreover, the geodesic loop containing $\mathbf{c}, \mathbf{d}$ (in $\mathcal{O}_2$) is obtained from the geodesic loop containing $\mathbf{a}, \mathbf{b}$ (in $\mathcal{O}_1$) by replacing every element of the latter loop by its PSE.

4. CONCLUDING REMARKS ON FECHNERIAN SCALING OF DISCRETE OBJECT SETS

We confine these concluding remarks to FSDOS only because this is the case of Fechnerian Scaling we presented in a relatively comprehensive way. With some technical caveats and modifications, the discussion to follow also applies to MDFS and the more general theory of continuous and "discrete-continuous" stimulus spaces presented in Dzhafarov and Colonius (2005a, 2005b).

4.1. Statistical Issues

In some applications, the number of replications from which frequency estimates of $p_{ij} = \psi(\mathbf{s}_i, \mathbf{s}_j)$ are obtained can be made sufficiently large to ignore statistical issues and treat FSDOS as being performed on essentially a population level. To a large extent, this is how the theory of FSDOS is presented in this chapter. The questions of finding the joint sampling distribution for Fechnerian distances $\hat{G}_{ij}$ $(i, j = 1, 2, ..., N)$ or joint confidence intervals for G_{ij} are beyond the scope of this chapter. We can, however, outline a general approach.

The estimators $\hat{P}_{ij}$ of the probabilities p_{ij} are obtained as

$$\hat{P}_{ij} = \frac{1}{R_{ij}} \sum_{k=1}^{R_{ij}} X_{ijk},$$

where $\{X_{ij1}, ..., X_{ijR_{ij}}\}$ are random variables representing binary responses ($1 = different$, $0 = same$). The index k may represent chronological trial numbers for $(\mathbf{s}_i, \mathbf{s}_j)$, different examples of this pair, different respondents, or some combination thereof. Random variables X_{ijk} and $X_{i'j'k'}$ can be treated as stochastically independent, provided $(i, j, k) \neq (i', j', k')$. Strictly speaking, X_{ijk} and $X_{i'j'k'}$ are *unrelated* random variables, they do not have a joint distribution (i.e., there is no pairing scheme for potential realizations of these two variables). Unrelated random variables, however (with no pairing scheme), can always be treated as independent (all-to-all pairing).[9]

Assuming that $\Pr[X_{ijk} = 1]$ does not vary too much as a function of k (i.e., ignoring such factors as fatigue, learning, and individual differences), $\hat{P}_{ij}$ may be viewed as independent normally distributed variables with means p_{ij} and variances $p_{ij}(1 - p_{ij})/R_{ij}$, from which it would follow that the joint distribution of the psychometric lengths of all chains with distinct elements is asymptotically multivariate normal, with both the means and covariances being known functions of true probabilities p_{ij}. The problem then is reduced to finding the (asymptotic) joint sampling distribution of the minima of psychometric lengths with common terminal points. Realistically, the problem is more likely to be dealt with by means of Monte Carlo simulations.

Monte Carlo is also likely to be used for constructing joint confidence intervals for G_{ij}, given a matrix of $\hat{p}_{ij}$. The procedure consists of repeatedly replacing the latter with matrices of p_{ij} that are subject to Regular Minimality and deviate from $\hat{p}_{ij}$ less than some critical value (e.g., by the conventional chi-square criterion), and computing Fechnerian distances from each of these matrices.

4.2.   Choice of Object Set

In some cases, as with Rothkopf's (1957) Morse codes, the set S of stimuli used in an experiment or computation may contain all objects of a given kind. If such a set is too large or infinite, however, one can only use a subset S' of the entire S. This gives rise to a problem: for any two

---

[9] In psychometric applications, it is customary to treat random variables obtained from one and the same group of observers responding to different treatments as being paired by the observer, that is, having a joint distribution and being potentially interdependent. This is not a mathematical necessity, however, but merely an indication of what one is interested in. Let $R_{ij} = R_{i'j'} = R$, and let K be the random variable attaining values $(1, ..., R)$ with (say) equal probabilities. The question of traditional interest then can be formulated as that of finding $\Pr[X_{ijK} = 1 \text{ and } X_{i'j'K} = 1]$ (the probability that responses randomly chosen from the two cells are 1 given that they are by one and the same observer), which need not decompose as $\Pr[X_{ijK} = 1]\Pr[X_{i'j'K} = 1]$ although X_{ijk} and $X_{i'j'k}$ are independent for every k. In this context, however, the relevant question is different: what is $\Pr[X_{ijK} = 1 \text{ and } X_{i'j'K'} = 1]$ (the probability that responses randomly chosen from the two cells are 1)? Here, K and K' are independent random variables attaining values $(1, ..., R_{ij})$ and $(1, ..., R_{i'j'})$, respectively: in this case, R_{ij} and $R_{i'j'}$ need not be the same, and all computations are invariant with respect to all possible permutations of the third index in all sets $\{X_{ij1}, ..., X_{ijR_{ij}}\}$.

stimuli $\mathbf{a}, \mathbf{b} \in S'$, the Fechnerian distance $G(\mathbf{a}, \mathbf{b})$ will generally depend on what other stimuli are included in S'. Thus, adding a new object s_{N+1} to a subset $\{\mathbf{s}_1, \mathbf{s}_2, ..., \mathbf{s}_N\}$ may change the pairwise discrimination probabilities $\psi(\mathbf{s}_i, \mathbf{s}_j)$ within the old subset $(i, j = 1, 2, ..., N)$. This generally happens in a psychophysical experiment, when pairs of stimuli are presented repeatedly to a single observer. In a group experiment with each pair presented just once, or for the "paper-and-pencil" perceivers (as in our example with statistical models), adding s_{N+1} may not change $\psi(\mathbf{s}_i, \mathbf{s}_j)$ within $\{\mathbf{s}_1, \mathbf{s}_2, ..., \mathbf{s}_N\}$, but it will still add new chains with which to connect any given stimuli $\mathbf{s}_i, \mathbf{s}_j$ $(i, j = 1, 2, ..., N)$; as a result, the minimum psychometric lengths $L_{\min}^{(\iota)}(\mathbf{s}_i, \mathbf{s}_j)$ and $L_{\min}^{(\iota)}(\mathbf{s}_j, \mathbf{s}_i)$ $(\iota = 1, 2)$ will generally decrease.[10]

A formal approach to this issue is to simply state that the Fechnerian distance between two given stimuli is a relative concept: $G(\mathbf{a}, \mathbf{b})$ shows how far apart the two stimuli are "from the point of view" of a given perceiver and *with respect to a given object set*. This approach may be sufficient in a variety of applications, especially in psychophysical experiments with repeated presentations of pairs to a single observer: one might hypothesize that the observer in such a situation gets adapted to the immediate context of the stimuli in play, effectively confining to it the subjective "universe of possibilities." A discussion of this "adaptation to subspace" hypothesis can be found in Dzhafarov and Colonius (2005a).

Like in many other situations involving sampling, however (including, for example, sampling of respondents in a group experiment), one may only be interested in a particular subset S' of stimuli to the extent that it is representative of the entire set S of stimuli of a particular kind. In this case, one faces two distinctly different questions. The first question is empirical: is S' large enough (well chosen enough) for its further enlargements not to lead to noticeable changes in discrimination probabilities within S'? This question is not FSDOS-specific, any other analysis of discrimination probabilities (e.g., MDS) will have to address it, too. The second question is computational, and it is FSDOS-specific: provided the first question is answered in the affirmative, is S' large (well chosen) enough for its further enlargements not to lead to noticeable changes in Fechnerian distances within S'? A detailed discussion being outside the scope of this chapter, we can only mention what seems to be an obvious approach: the affirmative answer to the second question can be given if one can show, by means of an

---

[10]This decrease must not be interpreted as a decrease in subjective dissimilarity. Fechnerian distances are determined up to multiplication by an arbitrary positive constant, which means that only *relative* Fechnerian distances $G(\mathbf{a}, \mathbf{b}) / G(\mathbf{c}, \mathbf{d})$ are meaningfully interpretable. Adding a new object to a subset may very well increase $G(\mathbf{a}, \mathbf{b})$ with respect to some or even all other distances.

appropriate version of subsampling, that the exclusion of a few stimuli from $\mathbf{S}'$ does not lead to changes in Fechnerian distances within the remaining subset.

4.3.   Other Empirical Procedures

The procedure of pairwise presentations with same–different judgments is the focal empirical paradigm for FSDOS. With some caution, however, FS-DOS can also be applied to other empirical paradigms, such as the *identification* paradigm: all stimuli $\{\mathbf{s}_1, \mathbf{s}_2, ..., \mathbf{s}_N\}$ are associated with rigidly fixed, normative reactions $\{R_1, R_2, ..., R_N\}$ (e.g., fixed names, if the perceiving system is a person or group of people), and the stimuli are presented one at a time. Such an experiment results in (estimates of) the stimulus-response confusion probabilities $\eta(R_j|\mathbf{s}_i)$ with which reaction R_j (normatively reserved for $\mathbf{s}_j$) is given to object $\mathbf{s}_i$. FSDOS here can be applied under the additional assumption that $\eta(R_j|\mathbf{s}_i)$ can be interpreted as $1 - \psi(\mathbf{s}_i, \mathbf{s}_j)$. The Regular Minimality property here means that each object $\mathbf{s}_i$ has a single modal reaction R_j (in the canonical form, R_i), and then any other object evokes R_j less frequently than does $\mathbf{s}_i$. Thus understood, Regular Minimality is satisfied, for example, in the data reported in Shepard (1957, 1958). We reproduce here one of the matrices from this work (matrix Sh, rows are stimuli, columns normative responses, entries conditional probabilities of responses given stimuli), together with the matrix of Fechnerian distances (G_{Sh}). Geodesic loops are not shown because the space $\{\mathbf{A}, \mathbf{B}, ..., \mathbf{I}\}$ here turns out to be a "Fechnerian simplex": a geodesic chain from $\mathbf{a}$ to $\mathbf{b}$ in this space is always the one-link chain $\mathbf{a} \rightarrow \mathbf{b}$.[11]

Sh	A	B	C	D	E	F	G	H	I
A	0.678	0.148	0.054	0.03	0.025	0.02	0.016	0.011	0.016
B	0.167	0.544	0.066	0.077	0.053	0.015	0.045	0.018	0.015
C	0.06	0.07	0.615	0.015	0.107	0.067	0.022	0.03	0.014
D	0.015	0.104	0.016	0.542	0.057	0.005	0.163	0.032	0.065
E	0.037	0.068	0.12	0.057	0.46	0.075	0.057	0.099	0.03
F	0.027	0.029	0.053	0.015	0.036	0.715	0.015	0.095	0.014
G	0.011	0.033	0.015	0.145	0.049	0.016	0.533	0.052	0.145
H	0.016	0.027	0.031	0.046	0.069	0.096	0.053	0.628	0.034
I	0.005	0.016	0.011	0.068	0.02	0.021	0.061	0.018	0.78

---

[11] For the identification paradigm the construction of sampling distributions and confidence intervals mentioned in Section 4.1 should be modified, as the probability estimators within rows are no longer stochastically independent: $\sum_{j=1}^{N} \eta(R_j|\mathbf{s}_i) = 1$.

G_{Sh}	A	B	C	D	E	F	G	H	I
A	0	0.907	1.179	1.175	1.076	1.346	1.184	1.279	1.437
B	0.907	0	1.023	0.905	0.883	1.215	0.999	1.127	1.293
C	1.179	1.023	0	1.126	0.848	1.21	1.111	1.182	1.37
D	1.175	0.905	1.126	0	0.888	1.237	0.767	1.092	1.189
E	1.076	0.883	0.848	0.888	0	1.064	0.887	0.92	1.19
F	1.346	1.215	1.21	1.237	1.064	0	1.217	1.152	1.46
G	1.184	0.999	1.111	0.767	0.887	1.217	0	1.056	1.107
H	1.279	1.127	1.182	1.092	0.92	1.152	1.056	0	1.356
I	1.437	1.293	1.37	1.189	1.19	1.46	1.107	1.356	0

In a variant of the identification procedure, the reactions may be *preference ranks* for stimuli $\{s_1, s_2, ..., s_N\}$, R_1 designating, say, the most preferred object, R_N the least preferred. Suppose that Regular Minimality holds in the following sense: each object has a modal (most frequent) rank, each rank has a modal object, and R_j is the modal rank for s_i if and only if s_i is the modal object for R_j. Then the frequency rank R_j that is assigned to stimulus s_i can be taken as an estimate of $1 - \psi(s_i, s_j)$, and the data be subjected to FSDOS. The fact that these and similar procedures are used in a variety of areas (psychophysics, neurophysiology, consumer research, educational testing, political science), combined with the great simplicity of the algorithm for FSDOS, makes one hope that its potential application sphere may be very large.

4.4.   Transformation of Discrimination Probabilities

This is probably the most difficult of the open problems remaining in Fechnerian Scaling. If $\psi(\mathbf{x}, \mathbf{y})$ satisfies Regular Minimality, then so does

$$\phi(\mathbf{x}, \mathbf{y}) = \varphi[\psi(\mathbf{x}, \mathbf{y})],$$

for any strictly increasing transformation φ. Regular Minimality is the only prerequisite for FSDOS, and the latter makes no critical use of the fact that the values of $\psi(\mathbf{x}, \mathbf{y})$ are probabilities, or even that they are confined to the interval $[0, 1]$. The question arises, therefore: Is there a principled way of choosing the "right" transformation $\varphi[\psi(\mathbf{x}, \mathbf{y})]$ of $\psi(\mathbf{x}, \mathbf{y})$? In particular, is it justifiable to use the "raw" discrimination probabilities?

One possible approach to this issue is to relate it to another issue: to that of the possibility of experimental manipulations or spontaneous changes of context that change discrimination probabilities but leave intact subjective dissimilarities among the stimuli. In other words, we may relate the issue of possible transformations of discrimination probabilities to that of *response bias*.

Suppose that according to some theory of response bias, discrimination probability functions can be presented as $\psi_B(\mathbf{x}, \mathbf{y})$, where B is value of response bias, varying within some abstract set (of reals, real-valued vectors, functions, etc.). Intuitively, this means that although $\psi_{B_1}(\mathbf{x}, \mathbf{y})$ and $\psi_{B_2}(\mathbf{x}, \mathbf{y})$ for two distinct response bias values may be different, the difference is not in "true" subjective dissimilarities but merely in the "overall readiness" of the perceiver to respond "different" rather than "same." If Fechnerian distances are to be interpreted as "true" subjective dissimilarities, one should expect then that Fechnerian metrics corresponding to $\psi_{B_1}(\mathbf{x}, \mathbf{y})$ and $\psi_{B_2}(\mathbf{x}, \mathbf{y})$ are identical (up to multiplication by positive constants). This may or may not be true for Fechnerian metrics computed directly from $\psi_B(\mathbf{x}, \mathbf{y})$, and if it is not, it may be true for Fechnerian metrics computed from some transformation $\varphi[\psi_B(\mathbf{x}, \mathbf{y})]$ thereof. The solution for the problem of what transformations of discrimination probabilities one should make use of can now be formulated as follows: choose $\phi_B(\mathbf{x}, \mathbf{y}) = \varphi[\psi_B(\mathbf{x}, \mathbf{y})]$ so that $G(\mathbf{a}, \mathbf{b})$ computed from $\phi_B(\mathbf{x}, \mathbf{y})$ is invariant (up to positive scaling) with respect to B.

The approach proposed is, of course, open-ended, as the solution now depends on one's theory of response bias, independent of Fechnerian Scaling. Thus, if one adopts Luce's (1963) or Blackwell's (1953) linear model of bias, φ is essentially the identity function and one should deal with "raw" discrimination probabilities. If one adopts the conventional d' measure of sensitivity, φ can be chosen as the inverse of the standard normal integral,

$$\psi(\mathbf{x}, \mathbf{y}) = \frac{1}{\sqrt{2\pi}} \int_{-\infty}^{\varphi[\psi(\mathbf{x}, \mathbf{y})]} e^{-z^2/2} dz.$$

We do not know which model of response bias should be preferred.

Another approach to the problem of choosing the "right" transformation φ, which we mention without elaborating, is through adopting a model for computing discrimination probabilities from Fechnerian distances (and, possibly, other functions of stimuli). Thus, in Chapter 1, we discussed a "quadrilateral dissimilarity" model and its mathematically equivalent "uncertainty blobs" counterpart. According to this model, if we assume the canonical form of Regular Minimality, $\psi(\mathbf{x}, \mathbf{y})$ (hence also $\varphi[\psi(\mathbf{x}, \mathbf{y})]$) is a strictly increasing transformation of

$$S(\mathbf{x}, \mathbf{y}) = R_1(\mathbf{x}) + 2D(\mathbf{x}, \mathbf{y}) + R_2(\mathbf{y}),$$

where $D(\mathbf{x}, \mathbf{y})$ is some intrinsic metric and R_1, R_2 some positive functions subject to certain constrains. It is easy to show that $D(\mathbf{x}, \mathbf{y})$ will generally be different from the Fechnerian metric $G(\mathbf{x}, \mathbf{y})$ computed from thus generated $\psi(\mathbf{x}, \mathbf{y})$. The two intrinsic metrics may coincide, however, if $G(\mathbf{x}, \mathbf{y})$ is computed from $\varphi[\psi(\mathbf{x}, \mathbf{y})]$ rather than $\psi(\mathbf{x}, \mathbf{y})$. This suggests the following solution for the problem of what transformations of discrimination probabilities one should make use of: choose $\phi(\mathbf{x}, \mathbf{y}) = \varphi[\psi(\mathbf{x}, \mathbf{y})]$ so that $G(\mathbf{a}, \mathbf{b})$ computed from $\phi(\mathbf{x}, \mathbf{y})$ coincide with $D(\mathbf{x}, \mathbf{y})$ in the "quadrilateral dissimilarity" model.

APPENDIX: ALGORITHM OF FECHNERIAN SCALING OF DISCRETE OBJECT SETS

Given: a set of objects $\{\mathbf{s}_1, \mathbf{s}_2, ..., \mathbf{s}_N\}$ and $N \times N$ matrix of discrimination probabilities $\psi(\mathbf{s}_i, \mathbf{s}_j)$ (referred to later as the original matrix).

1. Check the matrix for Regular Minimality: for $i = 1, ..., N$, the ith row should contain a single minimum $\psi(\mathbf{s}_i, \mathbf{s}_j)$ in cell (i, j), and this value should also be a single minimum in the jth column.

    • The row object $\mathbf{s}_i$ and the column object $\mathbf{s}_j$ forming such a cell, are points of subjective equality (PSE) for each other.

2. Form the table of mutual PSEs (row object vs. column object):

$$(\mathbf{s}_1, \mathbf{s}_{j_1}), (\mathbf{s}_2, \mathbf{s}_{j_2}), ..., (\mathbf{s}_N, \mathbf{s}_{j_N}).$$

    • $(j_1, j_2, ..., j_N)$ is a complete permutation of $(1, 2, ..., N)$.

3. Relabel the objects by assigning the same but otherwise arbitrary labels to mutual PSEs:

$$(\mathbf{s}_1, \mathbf{s}_{j_1}) \to (\mathbf{a}_1, \mathbf{a}_1), (\mathbf{s}_2, \mathbf{s}_{j_2}) \to (\mathbf{a}_2, \mathbf{a}_2), ..., (\mathbf{s}_N, \mathbf{s}_{j_N}) \to (\mathbf{a}_N, \mathbf{a}_N).$$

4. Form the matrix $\{\mathbf{a}_1, \mathbf{a}_2, ..., \mathbf{a}_N\} \times \{\mathbf{a}_1, \mathbf{a}_2, ..., \mathbf{a}_N\}$, with PSEs comprising the main diagonal.

    • Denote $\psi(\mathbf{a}_i, \mathbf{a}_j) = p_{ij}$ $(i, j = 1, ..., N)$.
    • Regular minimality now is satisfied in the canonical form: $p_{ii} < \min\{p_{ij}, p_{ji}\}$ for all $j \neq i$.

5. Compute the matrix of psychometric increments of the first kind,

$$\phi^{(1)}(\mathbf{a}_i, \mathbf{a}_j) = p_{ij} - p_{ii}.$$

6. For every ordered pair $(\mathbf{a}_i, \mathbf{a}_j)$, compute the smallest value of

$$L^{(1)}\left(\mathbf{x}_1, \mathbf{x}_2, ..., \mathbf{x}_k\right) = \sum_{m=1}^{k-1} \phi^{(1)}\left(\mathbf{x}_m, \mathbf{x}_{m+1}\right)$$

across all possible chains $\mathbf{a}_i = \mathbf{x}_1, \mathbf{x}_2, ..., \mathbf{x}_k = \mathbf{a}_j$ $(k = 1, ..., N)$ whose elements are distinct.
   - This minimum value, $L_{\min}^{(1)}\left(\mathbf{a}_i, \mathbf{a}_j\right)$, is the oriented Fechnerian distance $G_1\left(\mathbf{a}_i, \mathbf{a}_j\right)$, of the first kind.
   - Any chain at which this minimum is achieved is a Fechnerian geodesic chain from $\mathbf{a}_i$ to $\mathbf{a}_j$.
   - [Simple heuristics can significantly reduce the combinatorial search for $G_1\left(\mathbf{a}_i, \mathbf{a}_j\right)$.]
7. From the $N \times N$ matrix of $G_1\left(\mathbf{a}_i, \mathbf{a}_j\right)$, compute the overall Fechnerian distances

$$G_{ij} = G_1\left(\mathbf{a}_i, \mathbf{a}_j\right) + G_1\left(\mathbf{a}_j, \mathbf{a}_i\right) = G_{ji}.$$

   - The concatenation of a geodesic chain from $\mathbf{a}_i$ to $\mathbf{a}_j$ with that from $\mathbf{a}_j$ to $\mathbf{a}_i$ forms a geodesic loop between $\mathbf{a}_i$ and $\mathbf{a}_j$ whose length $L^{(1)}$ equals G_{ij}.

8. (Alternatively or additionally, for verification purposes.) Perform Steps 5, 6, 7 with $\phi^{(2)}\left(\mathbf{a}_i, \mathbf{a}_j\right) = p_{ji} - p_{ii}$ replacing $\phi^{(1)}\left(\mathbf{a}_i, \mathbf{a}_j\right)$ to obtain oriented Fechnerian distances $G_2\left(\mathbf{a}_i, \mathbf{a}_j\right)$, of the second kind, overall Fechnerian distances $G_{ij} = G_2\left(\mathbf{a}_i, \mathbf{a}_j\right) + G_2\left(\mathbf{a}_j, \mathbf{a}_i\right) = G_{ji}$, and the corresponding geodesic chains and loops between $\mathbf{a}_i$ and $\mathbf{a}_j$.
   - Overall Fechnerian distances should be the same,

$$G_2\left(\mathbf{a}_i, \mathbf{a}_j\right) + G_2\left(\mathbf{a}_j, \mathbf{a}_i\right) = G_1\left(\mathbf{a}_i, \mathbf{a}_j\right) + G_1\left(\mathbf{a}_j, \mathbf{a}_i\right).$$

   - Geodesic chains and loops are the same, but read in the opposite direction.
9. In the matrix of overall Fechnerian distances, relabel the objects back,

$$\{\mathbf{a}_1 \rightarrow \mathbf{s}_1, \mathbf{a}_2 \rightarrow \mathbf{s}_2, ..., \mathbf{a}_N \rightarrow \mathbf{s}_N\}$$

and

$$\{\mathbf{a}_1 \rightarrow \mathbf{s}_{j_1}, \mathbf{a}_2 \rightarrow \mathbf{s}_{j_2}, ..., \mathbf{a}_N \rightarrow \mathbf{s}_{j_N}\},$$

to obtain, separately, the matrix of Fechnerian distances $G_{ij}^{(1)}$ for the row objects of the original matrix and the matrix of Fechnerian distances $G_{ij}^{(2)}$ for the column objects of the original matrix.
   - $G_{ij}^{(1)} = G_{i'j'}^{(2)}$ if and only if $(\mathbf{s}_i, \mathbf{s}_{i'})$ and $(\mathbf{s}_j, \mathbf{s}_{j'})$ are pairs of mutual PSEs.

10. In the matrix of geodesic loops, relabel all the objects back, as in the previous step, to obtain the geodesic loops between the row objects of the original matrix, and separately, the geodesic loops between the column objects of the original matrix.

- A loop $x_1, x_2, ..., x_n, x_1$ is a geodesic loop between the row objects s_i and s_j if and only if the corresponding loop of PSEs $y_1, y_2, ..., y_n, y_1$ traversed in the opposite direction (i.e., $y_1, y_n, ..., y_2, y_1$) is a geodesic loop between the column objects $s_{i'}$ and $s_{j'}$ that are PSEs for s_i and s_j, respectively.

Remark 1. No relabeling is needed if Regular Minimality in the original matrix holds in the canonical form to begin with. The matrices of Fechnerian distances and geodesic loops for the row and column objects then coincide (except that the geodesic loops for the column objects should be read in the opposite direction).

Remark 2. The original matrix of probabilities $\psi(s_i, s_j)$ can be any matrix that satisfies Regular Minimality and whose values are statistically compatible with the empirical estimates $\hat{\psi}(s_i, s_j)$. The algorithm does not work if no such matrix can be found. With large sample sizes, $\psi(s_i, s_j)$ can be simply identified with $\hat{\psi}(s_i, s_j)$, with smaller sample sizes, one may need to try a large set of matrices, $\psi(s_i, s_j)$ statistically compatible with given $\hat{\psi}(s_i, s_j)$, and to replicate the algorithm with each of these to eventually obtain joint confidence intervals for Fechnerian distances.

Acknowledgement: This research was supported by National Science Foundation grant SES 0318010 to Purdue University.

References

Blackwell, H. R. (1953). Psychophysical thresholds: experimental studies of methods of measurement. *Engineering Research Bulletin*, No. 36. Ann Arbor: University of Michgan Press.

Borg, I., & Groenen, P. (1997). *Modern multidimensional scaling*. New York: Springer-Verlag.

Corter, J. E. (1996). *Tree models of similarity and association*. Beverly Hills, CA: Sage.

DeSarbo, W. S., Johnson, M. D., Manrai, A. K., Manrai, L. A., & Edwards, E. A. (1992) TSCALE: A new multidimensional scaling procedure based on Tversky's contrast model. *Psychometrika*, 57, 43–70.

Dzhafarov, E. N. (2002a). Multidimensional Fechnerian scaling: Regular variation version. *Journal of Mathematical Psychology*, 46, 226–244.

Dzhafarov, E. N. (2002b). Multidimensional Fechnerian scaling: Probability-distance hypothesis. *Journal of Mathematical Psychology*, 46, 352–374.

Dzhafarov, E. N. (2002c). Multidimensional Fechnerian scaling: Perceptual separability. *Journal of Mathematical Psychology*, 46, 564–582.

Dzhafarov, E. N. (2002d). Multidimensional Fechnerian scaling: Pairwise comparisons, regular minimality, and nonconstant self-similarity. *Journal of Mathematical Psychology*, 46, 583–608.

Dzhafarov, E. N. (2003a). Thurstonian-type representations for "same–different" discriminations: Deterministic decisions and independent images. *Journal of Mathematical Psychology*, 47, 208–228.

Dzhafarov, E. N. (2003b). Thurstonian-type representations for "same–different" discriminations: Probabilistic decisions and interdependent images. *Journal of Mathematical Psychology*, 47, 229–243.

Dzhafarov, E. N., & Colonius, H. (1999). Fechnerian metrics in unidimensional and multidimensional stimulus spaces. *Psychonomic Bulletin and Review*, 6, 239–268.

Dzhafarov, E. N., & Colonius, H. (2001). Multidimensional Fechnerian scaling: Basics. *Journal of Mathematical Psychology*, 45, 670–719.

Dzhafarov, E. N., & Colonius, H. (2005a). Psychophysics without physics: A purely psychological theory of Fechnerian Scaling in continuous stimulus spaces. *Journal of Mathematical Psychology*, 49, 1–50.

Dzhafarov, E. N., & Colonius, H. (2005b). Psychophysics without physics: Extension of Fechnerian Scaling from continuous to discrete and discrete-continuous stimulus spaces. *Journal of Mathematical Psychology*, 49, 125–141.

Everitt, B. S., & Rabe-Hesketh, S. (1997). *The analysis of proximity data.* New York: Wiley.

Fechner, G. T. (1860). *Elemente der Psychophysik* [Elements of psychophysics]. Leipzig, Germany: Breitkopf & Härtel.

Hartigan, J. A. (1975). *Clustering algorithms.* New York:Wiley.

Krumhansl, C. L. (1978). Concerning the applicability of geometric models to similarity data: The interrelationship between similarity and spatial density. *Psychological Review*, 85, 445–463.

Kruskal, J. B., & Wish, M. (1978). *Multidimensional scaling.* Beverly Hills, CA: Sage.

Luce, R. D. (1963). A threshold theory for simple detection experiments. *Psychological Review*, 70, 61–79.

Rothkopf, E. Z. (1957). A measure of stimulus similarity and errors in some paired-associate learning tasks. *Journal of Experimental Psychology*, 53, 94–102.

Roweis, S. T., & Saul, L. K. (2000). Nonlinear dimensionality reduction by locally linear embedding. *Science*, 290, 2323-2326.

Sankoff, D. & Kruskal, J. (1999). *Time warps, string edits, and macromolecules.* Stanford, CA: CSLI Publications.

Semple, C., & Steele, M. (2003). *Phylogenetics.* Oxford, England: Oxford University Press.

Shepard, R. N. (1957). Stimulus and response generalization: A stochastic model relating generalization to distance in psychological space. *Psychometrika*, 22, 325–345.

Shepard, R. N. (1958). Stimulus and response generalization: Tests of a model relating generalization to distance in psychological space. *Journal of Experimental Psychology*, 55, 509–523.

Shepard, R. N., and Carroll, J. D. (1966). Parametric representation of nonlinear data structures. In P. R. Krishnaiah (Ed.), *Multivariate analysis* (pp. 561–592). New York, NY: Academic Press.

Suppes, P., Krantz, D. H., Luce, R. D., & Tversky, A. (1989). *Foundations of Measurement*, vol. 2. San Diego, CA: Academic Press.

Tenenbaum, J. B., de Silva, V., & Langford, J. C. (2000). A global geometric framework for nonlinear dimensionality reduction. *Science*, 290, 2319–2323.

Tversky, A. (1977). Features of similarity. *Psychological Review*, 84, 327–352.

Weeks, D. G., & Bentler, P. M. (1982). Restricted multidimensional scaling models for asymmetric proximities. *Psychometrika*, 47, 201–208.

Wish, M. (1967). A model for the perception of Morse code-like signals. *Human Factors*, 9, 529–540.

3

Global Psychophysical Judgments of Intensity: Summary of a Theory and Experiments

R. Duncan Luce[1] and Ragnar Steingrimsson[2]

[1] University of California, Irvine
[2] New York University

This chapter has three thrusts: (a) It formulates in a common framework mathematical representations of two global sensory procedures: summation of intensity and the method of ratio production (Luce, 2002, 2004). Until recently, these two topics have not been treated together in the literature. (b) Although the psychophysical representations we arrive at include both free parameters and free functions, a message of this work, especially illustrated in Steingrimsson and Luce (2005a, 2005b),[3] is that one can evaluate the adequacy of the representations without ever estimating either the parameters or the functions, but rather by just evaluating parameter-free behavioral properties that give rise to the representations. (c) A closely related message is that, to the degree that the theory holds, no individual differences arise in the defining behavioral properties except, of course, for the fact that each person has his or her own sense of the relative intensities of two stimuli, that is, the subjective intensity ordering. At the same time, the potential exists for substantial individual differences in the representations in the following sense: there is a strictly increasing psychophysical function and a strictly increasing function that distorts numerical responses but that is not otherwise constrained without additional axioms. The work on the forms of these functions, although quite well developed, is not yet in final manuscript form. Nonetheless, we cover it in some detail in Sections 5 and 6. A number of interesting open problems are listed.

---

[3] In the remainder of the chapter, the four collaborative articles by Steingrimsson and Luce are identified as SL-I, SL-II, and so forth.

The chapter describes, without proof, the theory and discusses our joint experimental program to test that theory. As of November 2005, some of this work, SL-I and SL-II (see footnote 1), is published, whereas SL-III on the forms of the psychophysical function revision is in press, and SL-IV, on the forms of the weighting function, is nearing completion. Portions of all of these, including much of the experimental work, derive in part from Steingrimsson's (2002) University of California, Irvine dissertation. The network of results and the results of experimental testing reported are summarized in Fig. 4 later in Section 7.2.

We formulate the exposition in terms of loudness judgments about pure tones of the same frequency and phase. However, many other interpretations of the primitives are possible and each one has to be evaluated empirically in a separate experimental program of some magnitude. Some work on brightness summation across the two eyes is currently underway by the second author.

1.   Primitives and Representations

1.1.   Ordering of Joint Presentations

Let x denote the signal intensity less the threshold intensity of a pure tone presented to the left ear. We stress that we mean an intensity difference, not the more usual intensity ratio that leads to differences in dB. Let u denote an intensity less the threshold of a pure tone of the same frequency and phase presented to the right ear. Thus, 0 is the threshold intensity in each ear; intensities below threshold are set to 0. The notation (x, u) means the simultaneous presentation of x in the left ear and u in the right ear. This part of the model is, of course, an idealization—in reality, the threshold is a random variable which we idealize as a single number. In this connection and elsewhere, we rely on the position articulated shortly before his death by the youthful philosopher Frank Ramsey (1931/1964) in talking about decision making under uncertainty:

> Even in physics we cannot maintain that things that are equal to the same thing are equal to one another unless we take "equal" not as meaning "sensibly equal" but a fictitious or hypothetical relation. I do not want to discuss the metaphysics or epistemology of this process, but merely to remark that if it is allowable in physics it is allowable in psychology also. The logical simplicity characteristic of the relations dealt within a science is never attained by nature alone without any admixture of fiction. (p. 168/p. 70)

In the task we used, respondents were asked to judge if (x, u) is at least as loud as (y, v), which is denoted $(x, u) \succsim (y, v)$. The results we report show conditions such that this loudness ordering is reflected by a numerical mapping, called a psychophysical function, $\Psi : \mathbb{R}_+ \times \mathbb{R}_+ \xrightarrow{onto} \mathbb{R}_+$, where[4] $\mathbb{R}_+ := [0, \infty[$, that is strictly increasing in each variable and is order preserving, that is,

$$(x, u) \succsim (y, v) \Leftrightarrow \Psi(x, u) \geq \Psi(y, v), \tag{1}$$
$$\Psi(0, 0) = 0. \tag{2}$$

And we assume that loudness and intensity agree to the extent that

$$(x, 0) \succsim (y, 0) \Leftrightarrow x \geq y,$$
$$(0, u) \succsim (0, v) \Leftrightarrow u \geq v.$$

Thus, $\Psi(x, 0)$ and $\Psi(0, u)$ are each strictly increasing.

We assume that the respondent can always establish matches of three types to each stimulus:

$$(x, u) \sim (z_l, 0), \ (x, u) \sim (0, z_r), \ (x, u) \sim (z_s, z_s), \tag{3}$$

where $\sim$ means equally loud. The left and right matches z_l and z_r are called asymmetric and z_s is called a symmetric match. Symmetric matches have the decided advantage of reducing the degree of localization change between (x, u) and the matching pair. The asymmetric matches encounter some difficulties, which we discuss in Section 5.1, and overcome in Section 5.2.

Note that each of the z's is a function of both x and u. To make that explicit and suggestive, we use an operator notation:

$$x \oplus_i u := z_i \quad (i = l, r, s). \tag{4}$$

It is not difficult to show that each of the $\oplus_i$ defined by (4) is, indeed, a binary operation that is defined for each pair (x, u) of intensities. The operator $\oplus_i$ may be referred to as a summation operator; however, one must not confuse $\oplus_i$ with $+$, that is, the addition of physical intensities. Some readers of our work have expressed discomfort over the fact that we can explore, for example, whether the operation is associative, that is,

$$x \oplus_i (y \oplus_i z) = (x \oplus_i y) \oplus_i z \quad (i = l, r, s), \tag{5}$$

despite the fact that the notation

$$(x, (y, z)) \sim ((x, y), z)$$

---

[4] The notation $A := B$ means that A is defined to be B.

is, itself, meaningless. Such a defined operator is, however, a familiar and commonly used trick in the theory of measurement to map something with two or more dimensions into a structure on a single dimension. See, for example, the treatment of conjoint measurement in Section 6.2.4 of Krantz, Luce, Suppes, and Tversky (1971) and in Section 19.6 of Luce, Krantz, Suppes, and Tversky (1990).

One can show under weak assumptions (see Proposition 1 of Luce, 2002) that $\succsim$ is a weak order (that is, transitive and connected), that (x, u) is strictly increasing in each variable, and that 0 is a right identity of $\oplus_l$, that is,

$$x = x \oplus_l 0, \tag{6}$$

and 0 is a left identity of $\oplus_r$, that is,

$$u = 0 \oplus_r u, \tag{7}$$

whereas 0 is not an identity of $\oplus_s$ at all. However, the symmetric operation is idempotent in the sense that

$$x \oplus_s x = x. \tag{8}$$

These properties play important roles in some of the proofs.

We assume that the function $\Psi(x, u)$ is decomposable in the sense that it depends just on its components $\Psi(x, 0)$ and $\Psi(0, u)$,

$$\Psi(x, u) = F[\Psi(x, 0), \Psi(0, u)]. \tag{9}$$

One natural question is the following: What is the nature of that dependence, that is, what is the mathematical form of F? A second natural question is the following: How do $\Psi(x, 0)$ and $\Psi(0, u)$ depend on the physical intensities x and u, respectively? These are ancient problems with very large literatures which we make no attempt to summarize here. Some references appear later. Neither question, it should be mentioned, is resolved in any fully satisfactory manner if one restricts attention just to the primitive ordering $\succsim$ of the conjoint structure of intensities, $\langle \mathbb{R}_+ \times \mathbb{R}_+, \succsim \rangle$. To have a well constrained theory that arrives at specific answers seems to require some structure beyond the ordering so far introduced. Later, in Section 4, we encounter two examples of such additional linking structures, which, in these cases, are two forms of a distribution law. This important point, which is familiar from physics, does not seem to have been as widely recognized by psychologists as we think that it should be.

Two points should be stressed. The first is that the theory is not domain specific, which means that it has many potential interpretations in addition to our auditory one. For example, also in audition, Karin Zimmer and

Wolfgang Ellermeier,[5] interpreted (x, u) to mean a brief signal of intensity x followed almost immediately by a another brief signal of intensity u. Other interpretations, using visual stimuli, are brightness summation of hemifields or across the two eyes. Each conceivable interpretation will, of course, require separate experimental verification, although drawing on our experience with the two ear experiments should be beneficial.

The second point is that the approach taken here is entirely behavioral and so is independent of any particular biological account of the behavior. Consequently, we do not attempt to draw any such conclusions from our results.

1.2. Ratio Productions

To the ordering of signal pairs, we add the independent structure of a generalized form of ratio production. This entails the presentation to a respondent of a positive number p and the stimuli (x, x) and (y, y), where $y < x$, and asking the respondent to produce the stimulus (z, z) for which the loudness "interval" from (y, y) to (z, z) is perceived to stand in the ratio p to the "interval" from (y, y) to (x, x). Because the z chosen by the respondent is a function of p, x, and y, we may again represent that functional dependence in the operational form

$$(x, x) \circ_p (y, y) := (z, z). \tag{10}$$

This operation, which we call (subjective) ratio production, is somewhat like Stevens's magnitude production[6] (for a summary, see Stevens, 1975) which is usually described as finding the signal (z, z) that stands in proportion p to stimulus (x, x). Thus, his method is the special case of ours but with $(y, y) = (0, 0)$—the threshold intensity or below. Thus, $(x, x) \circ_p (0, 0) = (z, z)$.

We assume two things about $\circ_p$: (a) it is strictly increasing in the first variable and nonconstant and continuous in the second one, and (b) that Ψ over $\circ_p$ is also decomposable in the sense that

$$\Psi[(x, x) \circ_p (y, y)] = G_p[\Psi(x, x), \Psi(y, y)]. \tag{11}$$

---

[5] As reported at the 2001 meeting of the European Mathematical Psychology Group in Lisbon, Portugal.

[6] In a generalized ratio estimation, the respondent is presented with two pairs of stimuli, (y, y) to (z, z) and (y, y) to (x, x), where $y < x, z$, and is asked to state the ratio $p = p(x, y, z)$ of the interval between the first two to the interval between the second two. This is discussed in SL-III and is summarized later in Sec. 6.1. This procedure is, of course, conceptually related to S. S. Stevens's magnitude estimation where no standard is provided [see after (10)].

1.3.   The Representations

Building on the assumptions given earlier, Luce (2002, 2004) presented necessary and sufficient qualitative conditions the following representations, which are discussed later in Sections 3 and 4.[7]

$$\Psi(x, u) = \Psi(x, 0) + \Psi(0, u) + \delta\Psi(x, 0)\Psi(0, u) \quad (\delta \geq 0), \tag{12}$$

$$W(p) = \frac{\Psi\left[(x, x) \circ_p (y, y)\right] - \Psi(y, y)}{\Psi(x, x) - \Psi(y, y)} \quad (x > y \geq 0), \tag{13}$$

where δ is a (non-negative) constant and the function $W : [0, \infty[\xrightarrow{onto} [0, \infty[$ is strictly increasing. The "summation" formula (12) has been dubbed p-additive because it is the unique polynomial function of $\Psi(x, 0)$ and $\Psi(0, u)$ with $\Psi(0, 0) = 0$ that can be transformed into additive form (see Section 3.2).

Under certain assumptions, one can also show that, for some $\gamma > 0$,

$$\Psi(x, 0) = \gamma\Psi(0, x), \tag{14}$$

which we call constant bias; however, for other assumptions, constant bias is not forced. More specifically, if the properties stated later in Sections 3 and 4 hold for asymmetric matches, then constant bias, (14), holds in addition to the two representations (12) and (13) (Luce, 2002, 2004). In contrast, if the properties hold using symmetric matches, then one can prove that (12) holds with $\delta = 0$, that (13) holds, but that constant bias, (14), need not hold. Because constant bias seems intuitively unlikely—the ears often do not seem to be identical—we are probably going to be best off with the symmetric theory. We discuss data on whether our young respondents satisfy the assumption of having symmetric ears above threshold. We also investigate empirically whether $\delta = 0$ (Section 3.3), which has to hold if symmetric matches satisfy the conditions. If $\delta = 0$, empirical testing of the theory is simplified considerably.

Nothing in the theory giving rise to (12) and (13) dictates explicit mathematical forms for $\Psi(x, 0)$ as a function of the physical intensity x, for $\Psi(0, u)$ as a function of u, or for $W(p)$ as a function of p. One attempt to work out the form of Ψ based just on the summation operation is summarized later in Section 5.4. It leads to a sum of power functions. Another condition, also leading to a power function form, which is based on ratio

---

[7]In Luce (2002), all of the results are presented in terms of psychophysical functions on each signal dimension, as was also the first submitted version of Luce (2004). As a reviewer, Ehtibar Dzhafarov saw how they could be neatly brought together as a psychophysical function over the signal pairs, and Luce adopted that formulation.

productions, is provided in Section 6.3. The experimental data make clear that our endeavors are incomplete. Our attempts to find out something about W, which currently also are incomplete, are summarized in Section 6.

Where do the representations (12) and (13) come from, and how do we test them? Various testable conditions that are necessary and sufficient for the representations are outlined and the results of several experimental tests are summarized. Note that we make no attempt to fit the representations themselves directly to data. In particular, no parametric assumptions are imposed about the nature of the functions Ψ and W. Later, in Section 5.4, we see how to test for the power function form of Ψ using parameter-free properties, and then in Section 6, again using parameter-free properties, we arrive at two possible forms for W.

2.   Methods of Testing

The many experiments discussed employ empirical interpretations of the two operations. One is $x \oplus_i u := z_i$ $(i = l, r, s)$, (4), which involves estimating a value z_i that is experienced as equal in loudness to the joint-presentation (x, u). The other is $(x, x) \circ_p (y, y) := (z, z)$ $(y < x)$, (10), which involves estimating a value z that makes the loudness "interval" between (y, y) and (x, x) be a proportion p of the interval between (y, y) and (z, z). The first procedure is referred to as matching and the second as ratio production.

The stimuli used were, in all cases, 1,000 Hz, in phase pure tones of 100 ms duration that included 10 ms on and off ramps. Throughout, signals are described as dB relative to sound pressure level (SPL).

2.1.   Matching Procedure

To describe the testing, we employ the notation $\langle A, B \rangle$ to mean the presentation of stimulus A followed after 450 ms by stimulus B, where A and B are joint presentations. Then the three matches of (3) are obtained using whichever is relevant of the following three trial forms:

$$\langle (x, u), (z_l, 0) \rangle, \tag{15}$$

$$\langle (x, u), (0, z_r) \rangle, \tag{16}$$

$$\langle (x, u), (z_s, z_s) \rangle. \tag{17}$$

In practice, respondents heard a stimulus followed 450 ms later by another tone pair in the left, right, or both ears, as the case might be. Respondents used key presses either to adjust the sound pressure level of z_i, $i = l, r, s$ (one of four differently sized steps), to repeat the previous trial, or to indicate satisfaction with the loudness match. Following each adjustment, the altered tone sequence was played. This process was repeated until respondents were satisfied that the second tone matched the first tone in loudness.

2.2. Ratio Production Procedures

The basic trial form is $\langle\langle A, B\rangle, \langle A, C\rangle\rangle$ where $\langle A, B\rangle$ and $\langle A, C\rangle$ represent the first and the second intensity interval respectively. The $\langle A, B\rangle$ and $\langle A, C\rangle$ were separated by 750 ms, and between A and B (and A and C), the delay was 450 ms.

An estimate of $x \circ_{p,i} y = v_i$, in the case of $i = s$, was obtained using the trial type

$$\langle\langle(y, y), (x, x)\rangle, \langle(y, y), (v_s, v_s)\rangle\rangle, \tag{18}$$

where the value of v_s was under the respondents' control. In practice, respondents heard two tones separated by 450 ms (the first interval) then 750 ms later, another such set of tones was heard (the second interval). The tone in the first pair in both intervals is the same and less intense than the second tone. Respondents continued to alter the sound pressure level of v_s until they experienced the second loudness interval as being a proportion p of the first one.

As mentioned earlier, the special case of $y = 0$ is an operation akin to Stevens's magnitude production, which involves finding the signal (z, z) that stands in proportion p to stimulus (x, x). With $i = s$, this was estimated using the trial type

$$\langle(x, x), (v_s, v_s)\rangle. \tag{19}$$

In practice, respondents heard two tones, separated by 450 ms, and they adjusted the second tone to be a proportion p of the first tone.

Trial forms in the case of $i = r, l$ are constructed in a manner analogous to (18) and (19).

2.3. Statistics

The four SL articles examined parameter-free null hypotheses of the form $L = R$, where L means the signal equivalent on the left side of the condition and R is the parallel equivalent for the right side. Not having any a priori idea concerning the distribution of empirical estimates, we used the nonparametric Mann-Whitney U test at the 0.05 level. To improve our statistical evaluation, we checked, using Monte Carlo simulations based on the bootstrap technique (Efron & Tibshirani, 1993), whether L and R could, at the 0.05 level, be argued to come from the same underlying distribution. This was our criterion for accepting the null hypothesis as supporting the behavioral property.

Recently there has been a flurry of activity concerned with Bayesian approaches to axiom testing. The first published reference is Karabatsos (2005). These methods have not been applied to our data.

2.4.   Additional Methodological Observations

During the course of doing these studies, we encountered and overcame or attenuated some methodological issues (details in SL-I).

The well-known time-order error—that is, the impact of (x, u) depends on whether it occurs before or after (y, v)—means that it is important to use some counterbalancing of stimulus presentations or to ensure that the errors are balanced on the two sides of a behavioral indifference.

Some experiments require us to use an estimate from one step as input to a second one. If a median or other average from the first step is used as the input in a second step, then whatever error it contains is necessarily carried over into that second one, but all information about the variance is lost. After some experience we concluded that the results are more satisfactory if we used each individual estimate from the first step as an input to the second one. Then the errors of the first estimate are carried into the second step and average out there, while preserving the variance information.

Variability for ratio productions tends to be higher than for matching. This fact means that, in evaluating our conclusions, some attention needs to be paid to the number of observations made by each respondent.

3.   Summations and Productions Separately

Much of the mathematical formulation of the theory was first developed for utility theory (summarized[8] in Luce, 2000) under the assumption that the following property, called joint-presentation symmetry (jp-symmetry), holds:

$$(x, u) \sim (u, x). \tag{20}$$

Under the current psychophysical interpretation, this means that the ears are identical in dealing with intensities above their respective thresholds. We know this need not always hold (e.g., single-ear deafness resulting from exposure of one ear, usually the left, to percussive rifle shots), but at first we thought that it might be approximately true for young people with no known hearing defects. Note that jp-symmetry, (20), is equivalent to $\oplus_l \equiv \oplus_r$ and $\oplus_s$, all being commutative operators, that is,

$$x \oplus_i y = y \oplus_i x \quad (i = l, r, s).$$

---

[8] Errata: see Luce's web page at http:www.socsci.uci.edu.

3.1. Evidence Against Symmetric Hearing Using Symmetric Matching

Using symmetric matching, we obtained

$$z = x \oplus_s y \text{ and } z' = y \oplus_s x,$$

using the trial form (17). Each respondent made from 34-50 matches per stimulus. We used tones with intensities $a = 58$ dB, $b = 64$ dB, $c = 70$ dB SPL, which gave rise to six ordered stimulus pairs: (a, b), (a, c), (b, c) and (b, a), (c, a), (b, c). For each (x, u) pair, we tested statistically whether the null hypothesis $z = z'$ held. With 15 respondents there were 45 tests of which 23 rejected the null hypothesis. The pattern of results suggests that jp-symmetry fails for at least 12 of the 15 respondents.

The negative outcome of this experiment motivated the developments in Luce (2004) where jp-symmetry is not assumed to hold.

Later, in Section 5.1, we turn to the use of asymmetric matches to study the properties underlying the representation. They sometimes exhibit an undesirable phenomenon for which we suggest an explanation in terms of filtering, and after the fact, show that the properties, described later using asymmetric matches, are unaffected by the filter. However, some of the arguments rest on a property that corresponds to the psychophysical function being sums of power functions, and that may not always be sustained.

3.2. Thomsen Condition

The representation (12) with $\delta = 0$,

$$\Psi(x, u) = \Psi(x, 0) + \Psi(0, u), \tag{21}$$

is nothing but an additive conjoint representation (Krantz et al., 1971, Ch. 6). And, for $\delta > 0$, the p-additive representation, (12), can be rewritten as

$$1 + \delta\Psi(x, u) = [1 + \delta\Psi(x, 0)] [1 + \delta\Psi(0, u)],$$

so under the transformation

$$\Theta(x, u) = \ln[1 + \delta\Psi(x, u)], \tag{22}$$

the conjoint structure again has an additive representation. So data bearing on the existence of an additive presentation is of interest whether or not $\delta = 0$.

With our background assumptions—weak ordering, strict monotonicity, solvability, and that intensity changes in either ear affect loudness—we can formulate a property that is analogous to the numerical Archimedean property that for any two positive numbers a and b, one can find an integer n such that $na > b$. Thus, by Krantz et al. (1971) we need only the following condition, called the Thomsen condition, in order to construct an additive representation Θ.

$$\left.\begin{array}{c}(x,t) \sim (z,v) \\ (z,u) \sim (y,t)\end{array}\right\} \implies (x,u) \sim (y,v) \qquad (23)$$

This notation is used in the conjoint measurement literature. It can, of course, be rewritten in operator form, but that is both less familiar and appears to be more complex. If all of the $\sim$ are replaced by $\succsim$, the resulting condition is called double cancellation. The reason for that term is that the condition can be paraphrased as involving the two "cancellations" t and z, each of which appears on each side of the hypotheses, to arrive at the conclusion.

We know of no empirical literature in audition, other than our study described later, that tests the Thomsen condition, per se. What has been published concerning conjoint additivity all examined double cancellation, which we feel is a somewhat less sensitive challenge than is the Thomsen condition. Of the double cancellation studies, three support it: Falmagne, Iverson, and Marcovici (1979), Levelt, Riemersma, and Bunt (1972), and Schneider (1988), where the latter differed from the other studies in having frequencies varying by more than a critical band in the two ears. Rejecting it were Falmagne (1976) with but one respondent, and Gigerenzer and Strube (1983) with 12 respondents. Because of this inconsistency, we felt it necessary to test the Thomsen condition within our own experimental context. Our experimental design was closest to that of Gigerenzer and Strube (1983).

The Thomsen condition was tested by successively obtaining the estimates, z', y', and y'',

$$(x,t) \sim (z',v)$$
$$(z',u) \sim (y',t)$$
$$(x,u) \sim (y'',v)$$

using the trial form in (17), where the first of the two tones in the second joint-presentation is varied. The property is said to hold if we do not reject the hypothesis that the observations y' and y'' all come from a single distribution.

We used two stimulus sets, **A** and **B**, in our test of the Thomsen condition:

$$\mathbf{A} : x = 66, t = 62, v = 58, \text{ and } u = 70 \text{ dB},$$
$$\mathbf{B} : x = 62, t = 59, v = 47, \text{ and } u = 74 \text{ dB}.$$

Stimulus set **B** consisted of stimuli having the same relative intensity relations as those used by Gigerenzer and Strube (1983), although we used 1,000 Hz whereas they used both 200 Hz and 2,000 Hz, a difference that may be relevant.

We initially ran the respondents on **A**, after which we decided to add **B** to have a more direct comparison with their study.

With 12 respondents, there were 24 tests of which 5 rejected the null hypothesis. Of the five failures, four occurred in set **A** and one in **B**. This fact suggests that a good deal of practice may regularize the behavior. (See SL-I for details.) In summary, we feel that the Thomsen condition has been adequately sustained.

3.3.   Bisymmetry

On the assumption that we have a p-additive representation, (12), we next turn to the question of whether $\delta = 0$. All of the experimental testing is a good deal simpler when $\delta = 0$ than it would be otherwise—an example is the testing of the property called joint-presentation decomposition (Section 4.1).

Given the p-additive representation, one can show (Luce, 2004, Corollary 2 to Theorem 1, p. 450) that for a person who violates jp-symmetry, (20), $\delta = 0$ is equivalent to the following property, called bisymmetry:

$$(x \oplus_i y) \oplus_i (u \oplus_i v) = (x \oplus_i u) \oplus_i (y \oplus_i v) \quad (i = l, r, s). \qquad (24)$$

Note that the two sides of bisymmetry simply involve the interchange of y and u. Bisymmetry is not predicted when $\delta \neq 0$ except for constant bias with $\gamma = 1$. Because we have considerable evidence against $\gamma = 1$ (Section 3.1), we know that bisymmetry holds if, and only if, $\delta = 0$.

Testing involved obtaining the estimates

$$w_i = x \oplus_i y \text{ and } w_i' = u \oplus_i v, \quad [\text{right side of (24)}],$$
$$z_i = x \oplus_i u \text{ and } z_i' = y \oplus_i v \quad [\text{left side of (24)}],$$

and then in a second step obtaining

$$t_i = w_i \oplus_i w_i' \text{ and } t_i' = z_i \oplus_i z_i'.$$

The property is said to hold if t_i and t_i' are found to be statistically equivalent. The property was tested, for both symmetric and left-ear matches, using trials of the form (17) and (15), respectively, and intensities $x = 58$ dB, $y = 64$ dB, $u = 70$ dB, and $v = 76$ dB. With six respondents there were no rejections of bisymmetry. So we assume $\delta = 0$ in what follows (SL-I).

3.4.   Production commutativity

If we rewrite $(13)^9$ as

$$\Psi\left[(x, x) \circ_p (y, y)\right] = W(p)[\Psi(x, x) - \Psi(y, y)] + \Psi(y, y),$$

then by direct substitution the following behavioral property, called production commutativity, readily follows. For $p > 0, q > 0$,

$$[(x, x) \circ_p (y, y)] \circ_q (y, y) \sim [(x, x) \circ_q (y, y)] \circ_p (y, y). \qquad (25)$$

Observe that the two sides differ only in the order of applying p and q, which is the reason for the term commutativity. This property also arose in Narens's (1996) theory of magnitude estimation. Ellermeier and Faulhammer (2000) tested that prediction in the special case where $y = 0$ for $p, q > 1$ and Zimmer (2005) did so for $p, q < 1$. Both studies found it sustained. The general form of production commutativity has yet to be tested with $p < 1 < q$.

In the presence of our other assumptions, production commutativity turns out to be sufficient as well as necessary for (13) to hold.

Production commutativity was tested using symmetric ratio productions requiring four estimates in two steps. The first involved obtaining estimates of v and w satisfying

$$(x, x) \circ_p (y, y) \sim (v, v),$$
$$(v, v) \circ_q (y, y) \sim (w, w),$$

and the second of obtaining estimates of v' and w' satisfying

$$(x, x) \circ_q (y, y) \sim (v', v'),$$
$$(v', v') \circ_p (y, y) \sim (w', w').$$

The property is considered to hold if w and w' are found to be statistically equivalent. Trials were of the form in (18). The intensities used were $x = 64$ dB and $u = 70$ dB and the proportions used were $p = 2$ and $q = 3$, giving rise to four trial conditions in each step. Four respondents yielded four tests, and the null hypothesis of production commutativity was not rejected in any of them (SL-I).

3.5.   Discussion

The results of the experiments on the Thomsen condition and on production commutativity support the existence of a $\Psi_\oplus$ as in (12) and $\Psi_{\circ_p}$ as in (13)

---

[9] To those familiar with utility theory, the following form is basically subjective weighted utility (Luce & Marley, 2005).

separately. However, from these data alone we cannot conclude that the same function Ψ applies both to summations and productions, that is, $\Psi_\oplus = \Psi_{\circ_p}$. Although we have no evidence at this point to assume that, we do know that both are strictly increasing with $\succsim$, and so there is a strictly increasing, real-valued function connecting them: $\Psi_{\circ_p}(x, u) = f(\Psi_\oplus(x, u))$.

So our next task is to ask for conditions necessary and sufficient for the function f to be the identity function. Such conditions involve some interlocking of the two structures $\langle \mathbb{R}_+ \times \mathbb{R}_+, \succsim \rangle$ and $\langle \mathbb{R}_+ \times \mathbb{R}_+, \succsim, \circ_p \rangle$, which can be reduced to the one dimensional structures of the form $\langle \mathbb{R}_+, \geq, \oplus_i \rangle$ and $\langle \mathbb{R}_+, \geq, \circ_{p,i} \rangle$, respectively. We turn to that interlocking issue.

4.   Links Between Summation and Production

It turns out that two necessary properties of the representations establish the needed interlock or linkage between the primitives, and these properties along with those discussed earlier are sufficient to yield a common representation, $\Psi = \Psi_\oplus = \Psi_{\circ_p}$ (Theorem 2 of Luce, 2004). In a sense, the novelty of this theory lies in formulating their interlock purely behaviorally.

The links that we impose are analogous to the familiar "distribution" properties such as those in set theory, namely,

$$(A \cup B) \cap C = (A \cap C) \cup (B \cap C), \tag{26}$$
$$(A \cap B) \cup C = (A \cup C) \cap (B \cup C). \tag{27}$$

If we replace $\cup$ by $\oplus$ and $\cap$ by $\circ_p$ we get, respectively, what are called later simple joint-presentation decomposition, (Section 4.1), and segregation, (4.2). Some of the significance of such an interlock is discussed by Luce (2005).

To help formulate these properties, we define the following induced production operators $\circ_{p,i}$, $i = l, r, s$, which are special cases of the general operation $\circ_p$ defined by (10):

$$(x \circ_{p,l} y, 0) := (x, 0) \circ_p (y, 0), \tag{28}$$
$$(0, u \circ_{p,r} v) := (0, u) \circ_p (0, v), \tag{29}$$
$$(x \circ_{p,s} y, x \circ_{p,s} y) := (x, x) \circ_p (y, y). \tag{30}$$

4.1.   Simple Joint-Presentation Decomposition

As suggested above, the analogue of (26), linking the two operations $\oplus_i$ and $\circ_{p,i}$ is a property that is called simple joint-presentation (SJP-) decomposition: For all signals x, u and any number $p > 0$,

$$(x \oplus_i u) \circ_{p,i} 0 = (x \circ_{p,i} 0) \oplus_i (u \circ_{p,i} 0) \quad (i = l, r, s). \tag{31}$$

When $\delta \neq 0$, the corresponding property becomes vastly more difficult to test because the term $u\circ_{p,i}0$ is replaced by $u\circ_{q,i}0$ where $q = q(x,p)$. Thus, one must first determine $q(x,p)$ empirically and then check the condition corresponding to (31) with q replacing the second p on right.

SJP-decomposition has two levels of estimation which were done in two steps. First, the estimates

$$t_s = (x \oplus_s u) \circ_{p,s} 0,$$
$$w_s = x \circ_{p,s} 0,$$
$$s_s = u \circ_{p,s} 0,$$

were obtained using trials of the form in (18). We computed the means[10] of the empirical estimates of w_s and s_s and used them in the second step, which consisted of the match

$$t'_s = w_s \oplus_s s_s,$$

using trials of the form in (16). The property is considered to hold if t_s and t'_s are found to be statistically equivalent. We used one pair of intensities, $x = 64$ dB and $u = 70$ dB and the two values of p, namely $p = 2/3$ and $p = 2$. With four respondents there were eight tests and SJP-decomposition was not rejected in six of the eight (SL-II).

4.2. Segregation

The second property linking the two operations, the analogue of (27) but taking into account the noncommutativity of $\oplus_i$, is what is called segregation:

For all $x, u, p \in \mathbb{R}_+$, left segregation holds if

$$u \oplus_i (x \circ_{p,i} 0) \sim (u \oplus_i x) \circ_{p,i} (u \oplus_i 0) \quad (i = l, r, s). \tag{32}$$

And right segregation holds if

$$(x \circ_{p,i} 0) \oplus_i u \sim (x \oplus_i u) \circ_{p,i} (0 \oplus_i u) \quad (i = l, r, s). \tag{33}$$

If jp-symmetry, (20), holds, then right and left segregation are equivalent. Otherwise they are distinct.

---

[10] At the time this experiment was run, we did not fully understand the advantages of using sequential estimates.

Note that because 0 is a right identity of $\oplus_l$, (7), testing left segregation is easier for $i = l$, and similarly, right segregation is easier for $i = r$. For $i = s$ both need to be tested.

For each respondent (except one), we studied only one form of segregation, either left or right (see SL-II for details).

In the case of right segregation, four estimates must be made:

$$w_r = x \circ_{p,r} 0,$$
$$t_r = w_r \oplus_r u,$$
$$z_r = x \oplus_r u,$$
$$t'_r = z_r \circ_{p,r} u.$$

The property is said to hold if t_r and t'_r are not found to be statistically different.

Note that the intensities w_r and z_r are first estimated in the right ear but then they must be presented in the left ear for the case $(w_r, u) \sim (0, w_r \oplus_r u)$. The converse is true for left segregation. The trials used for matching were of the forms in (15) to (17) depending on the matching ear; the ratio productions used were (18) and (19), or their equivalents for asymmetric productions.

We used one intensity pair, $x = 72$ dB and $u = 68$ dB, except for one respondent where each was decreased by 4 dB to avoid productions limited by a 85 dB safety bound. A theoretical predication is that the property holds for both $p < 1$ and $p \geq 1$, hence $p = 2/3$ and $p = 2$ were used.

Four respondents produced 10 tests and the null hypothesis was accepted in eight of them (SL-II).

4.3. Discussion

Given the complexity of testing these two properties of the model and given the potential for artifacts, we feel that the support found for the model leading to the additive representation, (12) with $\delta = 0$, and the subjective proportion representation, (13), is not too bad.

Assuming that there is a common Ψ underlying the representation, an interesting theoretical challenge exists. Taken by itself, the p-additive representation of $\oplus_i$ could have $\delta \lesseqgtr 0$. For $\delta < 0$, it is not difficult to see that Ψ is bounded by $1/|\delta|$ and so $\Psi : \mathbb{R}_+ \times \mathbb{R}_+ \xrightarrow{onto} I = [0, 1/|\delta|]$. Of course, we have given data on bisymmetry that suggests $\delta = 0$. However, we cannot really rule out that δ may be slightly different from 0, as we discuss later in Section 5.8. On the face of it, boundedness seems quite plausible. Psychophysical scales of intensity seem to have upper bounds tied in with potential sensory damage and so infinite ones are decidedly an idealization.

However, within the theory as currently formulated, bounded Ψ is definitely not possible[11] because one can iterate the operator as, for example, in the second step: $(x \circ_{p,i} 0) \circ_{p,i} 0$, and this forces Ψ to be unbounded.[12] So the challenge is to discover a suitable modification of (13) that is bounded and work out its properties.

5.   Sensory Filtering, Multiplicative Invariance, and Forms for Ψ

5.1.   Asymmetric matching and jp-symmetry

Earlier (see the beginning of Section 3) we discussed the use of symmetric matches in checking jp-symmetry. Now we discuss the use of asymmetric left and right matches. The latter sometimes exhibited the following phenomenon which at first seemed disturbing but, in fact, seems to have rather mild consequences. Consider the following asymmetric matches:

$$(x, u) \sim (x \oplus_l u, 0), \ (u, x) \sim (u \oplus_l x, 0),$$
$$(x, u) \sim (0, x \oplus_r u), \ (u, x) \sim (0, u \oplus_r x).$$

Suppose that jp-symmetry fails, as it often seems to, and suppose that $(x, u) \succ (u, x)$. Then one expects to observe that both $x \oplus_l u > u \oplus_l x$ and $x \oplus_r u > u \oplus_r x$—that is, that left and right matches will agree in what they say about jp-symmetry. We carried out such an experiment, obtaining the asymmetric matches above using the trials forms in (15) and (16), and the same stimuli as used earlier (Section 3.1). Although the expected agreement held for four respondents, it did not hold for two, even after considerable experience in the experimental situation. Moreover, for those who were qualitatively consistent, the magnitude of the differences $x \oplus_l u - u \oplus_l x$ and $x \oplus_r u - u \oplus_r x$ varied considerably. Evidently, matching in a single ear had some significant impact. Of course, one impact is manifest in a sharp change of localization, which at first concerned some readers of our work.

---

[11] This fact was pointed out by Ehtibar Dzhafarov in a referee report, dated October 8, 2000, of Luce (2002).

[12] Set $y = 0$ in (13) and consider a sequence x_n with $x_0 > 0$ such that

$$W(p) = \Psi(x_n, x_n)/\Psi(x_{n-1}, x_{n-1}).$$

A simple induction yields

$$\Psi(x_n, x_n) = W(p)^n \Psi(x_0, x_0) > 0.$$

For $W(p) > 1$, this is unbounded.

But the inconsistency just described is more worrisome as it means that an experimental procedure that relies on the assumption of bias independent of the matching ear will not be reliable. In practice, this has not proven to be an obstacle in our other experiments. We offer a possible account of this effect in the next two subsections.

5.2.   Sensory Filtering in the Asymmetric Cases

Suppose that asymmetric matching has the effect of either enhancing (in the auditory system) all signals in the matching ear or attenuating those in the other ear. If these effects entail a simple multiplicative factor on intensity, that is, a constant dB shift, then the two ideas are equivalent. If we assume that there is an attenuation or intensity filter factor η on the non-matched ear, then for the left matching case, the experimental stimulus (x, u) becomes, effectively, $(x, \eta u)$. And when matching in the right ear, (x, u) becomes effectively $(\eta x, u)$, where $0 < \eta \leq 1$. Thus, when we ask the respondents to solve the three indifferences of (3) what they actually do, according to this theory, is set

$$z_l = x \oplus_l \eta u \Leftrightarrow (z_l, 0) \sim (x, \eta u),$$
$$z_r = \eta x \oplus_r u \Leftrightarrow (0, z_r) \sim (\eta x, u),$$
$$z_s = x \oplus_s u \Leftrightarrow (z_s, z_s) \sim (x, u).$$

Note that the filter plays no role in the symmetric matches.

Under a further condition that is called multiplicative invariance (Section 5.3), which is equivalent to $\delta = 0$ and that $\Psi(x, 0)$ and $\Psi(0, x)$ are each a power function of x, but with different powers, one can show that the filtering concept does indeed accommodate the aforementioned phenomenon of asymmetric matching in connection with checking jp-symmetry.

5.3.   Multiplicative invariance

Fortunately, we were able to show that filtering does not distort any of the experimental tests of the properties discussed earlier (Sections 3 and 4), where asymmetric matching is used, provided that the operations $\oplus_i$ have an additive representation shown earlier (Sections 3.2 and 3.3), and that the following property of σ−Multiplicative Invariance (σ−MI) holds: For all signals $x \geq 0, u \geq 0$, for any factor $\lambda \geq 0$, and for $\oplus_i$, $i = l, r$, defined by (3) and (4), there is some constant $\sigma > 0$ such that

$$\lambda x \oplus_l \lambda^\sigma u = \lambda(x \oplus_l u), \tag{34}$$

and

$$\lambda x \oplus_r \lambda^\sigma u = \lambda^\sigma(x \oplus_r u). \tag{35}$$

We observe that this property is, itself, invariant under sensory filtering because with filtering that expression becomes

$$\lambda x \oplus_l \eta \lambda^\sigma u = \lambda(x \oplus_l \eta u), \tag{36}$$

$$\eta \lambda x \oplus_r \lambda^\sigma u = \lambda^\sigma(\eta x \oplus_r u). \tag{37}$$

Because $\eta \lambda^\sigma = \lambda^\sigma \eta$, setting $v = \eta u$ in (36) shows that it is of the form (34) and setting $y = \eta x$ (37) shows it is of the form (35). Thus, filtering does not affect the use of $\sigma-$MI when discussing other properties.

Turning to our other necessary properties discussed earlier (Sections 3 and 4), elementary calculations show that they are invariant under filtering either with no further assumption or assuming multiplicative invariance (see Table 1).

Table 1: Effect of filtering on properties.

Property	Assumption None	$\sigma-$MI
Thomsen	X	
Bisymmetry		X
Production Commutativity	X	
SJP-Decomposition	X	
Segregation		X
SJP = Simple Joint-Presentation		
MI = Multiplicative Invariance		

We examine one important implication of $\sigma-$MI in the next subsection and report some relevant data.

5.4. Ψ a Sum of Power Functions

So far, we have arrived at a representation with two free parameters, δ and γ, and two free increasing functions, Ψ and W, and we have shown that, most likely, $\delta = 0$. It is clear that one further goal of our project is to develop behavioral characterizations under which each of the functions belong to a specific family with very few free parameters. In this section we take up one argument for the bivariate Ψ being a sum of power functions and later (Section 6.1) we give a different argument for the power function form of Ψ and also consider two possible forms for W, rejecting one and possibly keeping the other.

Assuming that the representation (12) holds (see Sections 1.3 and 3.2) and that $\delta = 0$ (see Section 3.3), then one can show that $\sigma-$MI is equivalent to Ψ being a sum of power functions, (51), with exponents β_l and β_r such that $\sigma = \beta_l/\beta_r$, that is,

$$\Psi(x, u) = \alpha_l x^{\beta_l} + \alpha_r u^{\beta_r} = \alpha_l x^{\beta_l} + \alpha_r u^{\beta_l/\sigma}. \tag{38}$$

The proof, which is in SL-III, is a minor modification of that given by Aczél, Falmagne, and Luce (2000) for $\sigma = 1$. Thus, $\sigma-$MI is a behavioral test for the power function form (38).

Note that

$$\frac{\Psi(x, 0)}{\Psi(0, x)} = \frac{\alpha_l}{\alpha_r} x^{\beta_l - \beta_r}.$$

Thus the constant bias property (14) holds iff $\gamma = \frac{\alpha_l}{\alpha_r}$ and $\sigma = \frac{\beta_l}{\beta_r} = 1$.

Recall that x and u in (34) and (35) are intensity differences between the signal intensity actually presented and the threshold intensity for that ear. However, the experimental design and results are typically reported in dB terms. In the current situation, this practice represents a notational difficulty because, for example, λx in dB terms is

$$10\log(\lambda x) = 10\log\lambda + 10\log x.$$

Thus, the multiplicative factor becomes additive when written in dBs. In the following, the intensity notation will be maintained in equations but actual experimental quantities are reported in dBs SPL where $\lambda_{dB} = 10\log\lambda$ stands for the additive factor.

5.5. Tests of $1-$MI

We did this experiment before we had developed the general result about $\sigma-$MI. The test was carried out in two steps: The first is an experimental one in which the respondents estimate

$$t_i = (\lambda x) \oplus_i (\lambda u) \quad \text{and} \quad z_i = x \oplus_i u,$$

obtained using trial-form (15) or (16) as the case might be. This is followed by a purely "arithmetic" step in which the multiplication $t_i' = \lambda \times z_i$ is performed by the experimenter. $1-$MI is said to hold if the hypothesis $t_i = t_i'$ is not statistically rejected.

For the experiment, we used $x = 64$ dB and $u = 70$ dB and two values for λ_{dB}, 4 and -4 dB ($\lambda = 2.5$ and 0.4, respectively).

Of 22 respondents, 12 satisfied $1-$MI in both tests, three failed both, and seven failed one. So we have a crude estimate of about half of the respondents satisfying multiplicative invariance with $\sigma = 1$. The fact of so many failures led us to explore how to estimate σ and then to estimate whether or not the 1-MI results were likely to change by doing the σ−MI experiment using that estimate.

5.6. Estimating σ and η

To test multiplicative invariance, it is most desirable to estimate σ and not to have to run a parametric experiment. To that end, using the representation (38), one can show that there exist constants c_1 and c_2 such that

$$(0 \oplus_l x)_{dB} = c_1 + \frac{1}{\sigma} x_{dB}, \tag{39}$$

$$(x \oplus_r 0)_{dB} = c_2 + \sigma x_{dB}, \tag{40}$$

from which it follows that there is a constant c_3 such that

$$(x \oplus_r 0)_{dB} = c_3 + \sigma^2 (0 \oplus_l x)_{dB} \tag{41}$$

follows. One can regress as shown and also in the other direction. Each gives an estimate of σ and we used the geometric mean of the two estimates of σ. This appears to be a suitable way to estimate σ—suitable in the sense that if (38) holds, then this is what it must be.

In terms of the power function representation itself one can show that the constants c_1 in (39), c_2 in (40), and c_3 in (41) are explicit functions of γ and η and, solving for these parameters, one can show that

$$\log \eta = \frac{\sigma c_1 + c_2}{10(1 + \sigma)}, \tag{42}$$

$$\log \gamma = \frac{\beta_r c_3}{10(1 + \sigma)}. \tag{43}$$

5.7. Estimates of σ

For seven of the respondents for whom we tested 1−MI, we also collected the estimates $z_r = (x \oplus_r 0)$ and $z_l = (0 \oplus_l x)$ using trial-forms (15) and (16), and the three instantiations of x, 58, 66, and 74 dB SPL. Then, we estimated σ using (41) and linear regression. The estimates were obtained by regressing both on $(0 \oplus_l x)_{dB}$ and $(x \oplus_r 0)_{dB}$, separately, and the final estimate was taken as the geometric mean of the two and we tested statistically whether $\sigma = 1$. These results, including the numerical direction of the estimated σs, are summarized in the left portion of Table 2. To evaluate whether or not it would be worthwhile to do the σ−MI experiment, we asked the following: In which direction would σ have to deviate from 1 in order to alter the

Table 2: Summary of numerical direction of σ needed to fit data and obtained estimates.

| | | Test of 1-MI | | | | Estimates of σ | |
| | | Needed | | | | Numerical | |
1−MI	Total	$\sigma < 1$	$\sigma > 1$	Contradictory	Total	$\hat{\sigma} < 1$	$\hat{\sigma} > 1$
Passed	12	2	7	3	5	1	4
Failed	10	2	7	1	2	0	2
Total	22	4	14	4	7	1	6

Note: MI = Multiplicative Invariance.

previous data testing 1−MI (22 respondents) toward equality of the two sides? These results are summarized in the right portion of Table 2.

From the last row of Table 2, we see that for four of the 22 respondents we need a value of $\sigma < 1$ to fit the data, for 14 of them a value of $\sigma < 1$, and for four the data suggest contradictory directions. In the subset of seven respondents for whom we estimated σ (Left portion of Table 2), one respondent had an estimate of $\sigma > 1$, and for six an estimate of $\sigma > 1$ was obtained.

For these 7 respondents, the needed and obtained numerical direction of σ is the same for 4 and different for 2. In 1 case, the needed direction of σ is inconclusive, which is well reflected in the obtained σ being close to one. This means the pattern of results appears reasonable for 5 and inappropriate for 2 of 7 respondents.

For those who passed 1−MI, a sum of power functions is already a reasonable description of behavior. The interesting cases are for those who either failed 1−MI or yielded σ estimates suggesting material deviations from 1. Of the two who failed 1−MI, the direction of the estimated σ was the same as the expected for one, and for those who passed 1−MI, σ was estimated different from 1 for one respondent. In the former case, a correction factor would add 0.02 dB to δ and in the latter it is 0.70 dB. The smaller factor is insignificant but the latter could well affect the results. Based on this sample, running the σ−MI experiment appears only worthwhile for one respondent. Here a correction factor would add 1.1 dB to δ. Testing led to an estimate of σ insufficiently large for the respondent to pass σ−MI.

In conclusion, the σ estimates are reasonably in line with expectations but in this current sample not much seems to be gained from them. Specifically, the results of the σ estimation do not seem to provide a correction factor that explains the respondent's deviations from 1−MI. Thus, we have evidence that about half of the respondents are well described by the sum of power functions, but that we do not know what forms fit the other half.

5.8. Ψ a p-Additive Sum of Power Functions

There is another possible reason for failures of $\sigma-$MI. Recall that, based on the empirical fact that we did not reject the property of bisymmetry, (24), we concluded that $\delta = 0$ could not be rejected. Nonetheless, our results for $1-$MI seem to be consistent with that property for only about 50% of the respondents and we concluded on the basis of our estimates of σ that going to $\sigma-$MI would not improve the picture. But we cannot ignore the possibility that our test of bisymmetry simply was not sufficiently sensitive to catch the fact that, really, for some respondents $\delta \neq 0$. Assuming that the function for each ear individually, $\Psi(x, 0)$ and $\Psi(0, u)$ are each a power function, as discussed later (Section 6.2), then this line of argument suggests that instead of Ψ being the sum of power functions, (38), it possibly is the more general p-additive form:

$$\begin{aligned}\Psi(x, u) &= \alpha_l x^{\beta_l} + \alpha_r u^{\beta_r} + \delta \alpha_l \alpha_r x^{\beta_l} u^{\beta_r} \\ &= \alpha_l x^{\beta_l} + \alpha_r u^{\beta_l/\sigma} + \delta \alpha_l \alpha_r x^{\beta_l} u^{\beta_l/\sigma}.\end{aligned} \qquad (44)$$

Note that the formulas (39) and (40) are unchanged by this generalization because when one signal is 0, the δ term vanishes. Thus, the formulas for estimating σ and η, (41) and (42), are also unchanged. So, the important question becomes the following: What property replaces $\sigma-$MI in characterizing the p-additive form with $\delta \neq 0$, rather than additive sum, of power functions, (44)? This theoretical question has yet to be answered. If and when we find that property, clearly it should be tested empirically.

6.   Ratio Estimation and the Forms for W

To those familiar with the empirical literature on "direct scaling" methods, our discussion may seem unusual because so far it has focused exclusively on ratio production and not at all on ratio estimation and its close relative magnitude estimation. Magnitude estimation is far more emphasized in the empirical and applications literatures than is magnitude production. We remedy this lacuna in the theory now.

Here it is useful to define the following:

$$\psi_l(x) := \Psi(x, 0), \qquad (45)$$
$$\psi_r(u) := \Psi(0, u), \qquad (46)$$
$$\psi_s(x) := \Psi(x, x). \qquad (47)$$

We work with the generic ψ_i.

6.1.   Ratio Estimation Interpreted Within This Theory

A fairly natural interpretation of ratio estimations can be given in terms of (13) with $y = 0$. Instead of producing $z_i(x,p) = x \circ_{p,i} 0$, $i = l, r, s$, such that $z_i(x,p)$ stands in the ratio p to x, the respondent is asked to state the value of p_i that corresponds to the subjective ratio of z to x. This value may be called the *perceived ratio* of intensity z to intensity x. If we change variables by setting $t = z/x$, then p_i is a function of both t and x, that is, $p_i = p_i(t, x)$. Note that p_i is a dimensionless number. According to (13) and using the definition of ψ_i,

$$W\left(p_i(t,x)\right) = \frac{\psi_i(tx)}{\psi_i(x)}. \tag{48}$$

This relation among the three unknown functions, ψ_i, p_i, W, is fundamental to what follows.

The empirical literature on magnitude estimates has sometimes involved giving a standard x and in other experiments it was left up to the respondent to set his or her own standard. Stevens (1975, pp. 26-30) argued for the latter procedure. From our perspective, this means that it is very unclear what a person is trying to do when responding—comparing the present stimulus to some fixed internal standard or to the previous signal or to what? And, therefore, it means that averaging over respondents, who may be doing different things, is even less satisfactory than it usually is.

The literature seems to have assumed implicitly that the ratio estimate $p_i(t, x)$ depends only on t, not on x, that is,

$$p_i(t, x) = p_i(t). \tag{49}$$

The only auditory data we have uncovered on this are Beck and Shaw (1965) and Hellman and Zwislocki (1961). The latter article had nine respondents provide ratio estimates to five different standard pairs $(x_0, 10)$ where $x_0 = 40, 60, 70, 80, 90$ dB SPL. The geometric-mean results for the respondents are shown in their Fig. 6. If one shifts the intensity scale (in dB) so that all the standard pairs are at the same point of the graph, we get the plot shown in Fig. 1a. For values above the standard, there does not seem to be any differences in the curves, in agreement with (49). But things are not so favorable for values below the standard. Of course, there are possible artifacts. Experience in this area suggests that many people are uneasy about the lower end of the numerical scale, especially below 1. They seem to feel "crowded" in the region of fractions, and such crowding should only increase as one lowers the standard. It therefore seems reasonable to do the study with moduli of, say, 100 or larger.

This is exactly what Beck and Shaw (1965) did: they collected magnitude estimates of loudness as a function of four standards, 25, 77, 81, and 101 dB SPL, and two moduli, 100 and 500 (incomplete factorial design), and reported the median magnitude estimates, shown in their Fig. 1. They collected data for both even and irregularly spaced stimuli, but concluded that the results were the same. Hence, we have averaged over the stimulus spacing conditions. In our Fig. 1b, we have replotted their data by shifting them to a common standard (s) and modulus (m) and on the same scale as those of Hellman and Zwislocki (1961). Note, only their 77/81 dB conditions extends both below and above the standard. Here we find, contrary to the data of Hellman and Zwislocki (1961), for values below the standard, there seems to be a very small if any difference in the slope of the curves, which agrees with (49). However, for at least two of the four graphs, the slope is shallower for values above as compared to below the standard. The shallower slopes above the standard are both for graphs generated by the lowest standard (25 dB), where as for the moderate standards (77, 81 dB), the slopes appear unchanged on either side of the standard. It almost appears that respondents had established an upper bound to the response scale, and so exhibited response attenuation to achieve that.

Also, in our theory one should treat the abscissa as the intensity less the threshold intensity, which these authors had no reason to do. This has the potential of changing the slopes closest to threshold, that is, for Hellman and Zwislocki's (1961) data below the standard ($p < 1$) but not for intensities well above threshold ($p > 1$). They reported an average threshold of 6 dB SPL, which is clearly too small to alter the results in a material way. Nevertheless, were these experiments repeated, we would favor the data be plotted in terms of the intensity less the threshold intensity for individual respondents.

We conducted an analysis of the apparent effect of standards and moduli on slope value and concluded, first, that the data are consistent with slopes below the standard decreasing with increasing standards and above it to increase with decrease in standard. Second, by overlaying the graphs of the two studies, the data are consistent with slopes both below and above the standard to increase with decreasing moduli.

Poulton (1968), who examined the same data sets, came to a conclusion similar to ours. He modeled these effects in his Fig. 1C, according to which there is a range of standards and moduli for which $p(z, t) = p(z)$ is true in magnitude estimation. Although we do not test this hypothesis, the assertion that pairs of standards and moduli can be chosen such that magnitude estimates above and below the standard are the same, does accord with the available data. That is, ratio independence, (49), is satisfied in at least some cases.

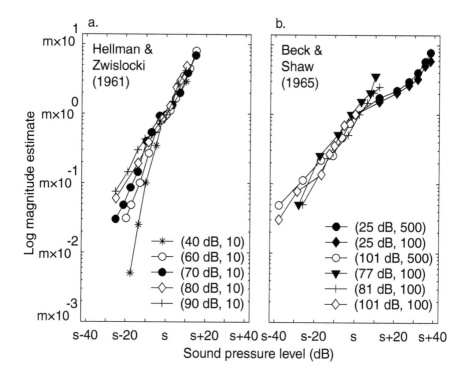

Fig. 1: Panel a. contains auditory data adapted from Fig. 6 of Hellman and Zwislocki (1961). Plotted in panel b. are data adapted from Fig. 1 of Beck and Shaw (1965). Each graph shows results of magnitude estimates as a function of stimuli in dB SPL and with respect to a common standard (s) and modulus (m), indicated as (s, m).

6.2.   Psychophysical Power Functions

Anyhow, assuming that (48) holds, then (49) immediately yields

$$W(p_i(t)) = \frac{\psi_i(tx)}{\psi_i(x)}, \tag{50}$$

which is a Pexider functional equation (Aczél, 1966, p. 144) whose solutions with $\psi_i(0) = 0$ are, for some constants, $\alpha_i > 0, \beta_i > 0$,

$$\psi_i(t) = \alpha_i t^{\beta_i} \quad (t \geq 0), \tag{51}$$

$$W(p_i(t)) = t^{\beta_i} \quad (t \geq 0). \tag{52}$$

Recall that the ψ_i are the production psychophysical functions all defined in terms of Ψ by (45) for $i = l$ and by (46) for $i = r$. So (51) agrees with our earlier result about sums of power functions being implied when multiplicative invariance is satisfied (Section 5.4). And, of course, (49) holds if the psychophysical function is a power function.

6.3.   Do Ratio Estimates Also Form Power Functions?

The conclusion (52) tells us that, when we observe empirically the estimation function $p_i(t)$, it is a power function, but it is seen through the distortion W^{-1}. Stevens (1975) claimed that the magnitude estimation psychophysical functions are, themselves, power functions, which was approximately true for geometric means over respondents; however this is not really the case for data collected on individuals (see Fig. 2). This fact is again a caution about averaging over respondents.

Moreover, Stevens (1975) attempted to defend the position that both the magnitude and production functions are power functions, although he was quite aware that empirically they do not prove to be simple inverses of one another (p. 31). Indeed, he spoke of an unexplained "regression" effect which has never really been fully illuminated (Stevens, 1975, p. 32).

So let us consider the possibility that, as Stevens claimed,

$$p_i(t) = \rho_i t^{\nu_i} \quad (t > 0, \rho_i > 0, \nu_i > 0). \tag{53}$$

Note that because p_i is dimensionless, the parameter ρ_i is a constant, not a free parameter. It is quite easy to see that if (52) holds, then p_i is a power function, (53), if, and only if, $W(p)$ is also a power function with exponent $\omega_i := \beta_i/\nu_i$, that is,

$$W_i(p) = \left(\frac{p}{\rho_i}\right)^{\omega_i}$$

$$= W_i(1)p^{\omega_i} \quad (p \geq 0). \tag{54}$$

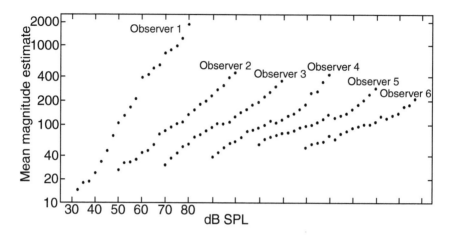

Fig. 2: Reproduction of Fig. 1 of Green and Luce (1974)

This form has different implications depending on whether the constant $\rho_i = 1$ or $\neq 1$. Note that $\rho_i = 1$ holds if, and only if, $W_i(1) = 1$. From here on we assume that W_i, being a cognitive function, is independent of $i = l, r$ and so can be denoted W. Both cases rest on an exploration of the property of threshold production commutativity:

$$(x \circ_{p,i} 0) \circ_{q,i} 0 = (x \circ_{q,i} 0) \circ_{p,i} 0 = x \circ_{t,i} 0, \tag{55}$$

which by (13), is equivalent to

$$W(p)W(q) = W(t). \tag{56}$$

To increase generality, we suppose that (56) holds for $p > 1, q > 1$, and separately, for $p < 1, q < 1$, but not necessarily for the crossed cases: $p > 1 > q$ or $q > 1 > p$. Assuming the continuity of $W(p)$ at $p = 1$, it is easy to show that if this obtains, then the following statements are equivalent: (1) There exist constants ω and ω^* such that

$$W(p) = W(1) \begin{cases} p^{\omega}, & p \geq 1 \\ p^{\omega^*}, & p < 1 \end{cases}. \tag{57}$$

(2) The relation among p, q, and t is given by:

$$t = kpq \text{ where } k = \begin{cases} W(1)^{1/\omega}, & p \geq 1 \\ W(1)^{1/\omega^*}, & p < 1 \end{cases}. \tag{58}$$

We call (58) k−multiplicative. If we also assume that (56) holds for $p > 1 > q$ or $p < 1 < q$, then $\omega = \omega^*$. Some pilot data we have collected strongly suggests that (58) does not hold for the crossed cases $p > 1 > q$ and $p < 1 < q$ and that $W(1) < 1$. Further empirical work is reported in SL-IV.

The only published data concerning (55), of which we are aware, are those of Ellermeier and Faulhammer (2000) and Zimmer (2005). They restricted their attention to the case of $\rho_i = 1$, which is equivalent to $W(1) = 1$, because Narens (1996) arrived at (58) with $k = 1$ as a consequence of his formalization of what he believed Stevens (1975) might have meant theoretically when invoking magnitude methods. Ellermeier and Faulhammer (2000) and Zimmer (2005) tested it experimentally and unambiguously rejected it. To our knowledge no one that we know, other than us, has attempted to collect sufficient data to see how well (58) fits the data with $\rho_i \neq 1$ in (53). Our preliminary data are promising, but incomplete.

So the answer to the question of the heading—"Do ratio estimates form power functions?"—is that at this point we do not know. The key prediction (58) has yet to be fully checked. If, however, the general power function form is rejected, then the task of finding the form of W remains open. We discuss next an interesting, but ultimately unsuccessful, attempt: the Prelec function.

6.4. If Ratio Estimation Is Not a Power Function, What Is W?

Prelec's Function

Within the context of utility theory for risky gambles and for $0 < p \leq 1$, a weighting function was proposed and axiomatized by Prelec (1998) that had the desirable feature that, depending on the combinations of the parameters, the function can be concave, convex, S-shaped, or inverse S-shaped. Empirical data on preferences among gambles seemed to suggest that the inverse S-shaped form holds (Luce, 2000, especially Fig. 3.10 on p. 99). The Prelec form for the weighting function, generalized from the unit interval to all positive numbers is

$$W(p) = \begin{cases} \exp\left[-\lambda\left(-\ln p\right)^{\mu}\right] & (0 < p \leq 1) \\ \exp\left[-\lambda'\left(\ln p\right)^{\mu}\right] & (1 < p) \end{cases} , \qquad (59)$$

where $\lambda > 0$, $\lambda' > 0$, and $\mu > 0$. The special case of $\mu = 1$ is a power function with $W(1) = 1$, which we know is wrong.

Reduction Invariance: A Behavioral Equivalent of Prelec's W

Prelec gave one axiomatization of the form (59) and Luce (2001) gave the following simpler one, called reduction invariance, defined as follows: Suppose that positive $p, q, t = t(p, q)$ are such that (55) is satisfied for all $x > 0$. Then for any natural number N,

$$(x \circ_{p^N, i} 0) \circ_{q^N, i} 0 = x \circ_{t^N, i} 0. \tag{60}$$

In words, if the compounding of p and q in magnitude productions is the same as the single production of t, then the compounding of p^N and q^N is the same as the single production of t^N. On the assumptions that (56) holds for p^N, q^N, and t^N, and that W is strictly increasing function on the interval $]0, 1]$, Luce (2001) showed that reduction invariance, (60), is equivalent to the Prelec function (59) holding in the unit interval. Indeed, it turns out that its holding for two values of N such as $N = 2, 3$ are sufficient to get the result. Another pair that works equally well is $N = 2/3, 2$. One can also show that it works for N any positive real number; however, any two values without a common factor suffice. It is not difficult to see how to extend the proof to deal with the interval $]1, \infty[$

Zimmer (2005) was the first to test this hypothesis and she rejected it. Her method entailed working with bounds and showing that the observed data fall outside them. In SL-IV, we also tested it using our ratio-production procedure. We too found that it failed. The fact that W is a cognitive distortion of numbers may mean that it will also fail empirically in other domains, such as utility theory, when reduction invariance is studied directly.

Testing was done using two-ear $(i = s)$ productions. First, the two successive estimates

$$v_s = x \circ_{p,s} 0, \tag{61}$$

$$t_s = z_s \circ_{p,s} 0, \tag{62}$$

were obtained. Then, using the simple Up-Down method (Levitt, 1971), a t was estimated such that $x \circ_{t,i} 0 \sim t_s$. With the estimate of t and our choice for N, the following estimates were obtained:

$$t'_s = (x \circ_{p^N, i} 0) \circ_{q^N, i} 0$$

$$w'_s = x \circ_{s^N, i} 0.$$

The property is said to hold if the hypothesis $t'_s = w'_s$ is not statistically rejected.

We used the two instantiations, $x = 64$ dB and $x = 70$ dB, and the proportions, presented as percentages, $p = 160\%$ and $q = 80\%$, except for one respondent where $q = 40\%$ and another where $p = 140\%$. The power

N was chosen as close to 2 as would provide numbers close to a multiple of five for each of p^N, q^N, and t^N.

The property was rejected for six of six respondents. For three, the failure was beyond much question. But taking into account the complexity of the testing procedure and the multiple levels of estimation, the failure for the other three was not dramatic. Indeed, had our data been as variable as Zimmer's (2005), we almost certainly would have accepted the property of reduction invariance in those three cases.

When we tested reduction invariance, we did not know about the potential problems outlined earlier (Section 6.3) of testing this property using the mixed case of $p > 1$, $q < 1$. Without further testing, the failure we observed is potentially related to this issue; however Zimmer's (2005) data are not based on mixed cases; she used $p < 1$, $q < 1$. This further suggests that the property should be tested with $p > 1$, $q > 1$; we aim to report such data in SL-IV.

No one has yet explored what happens to reduction invariance if it is assumed that the right side of (59) is multiplied by $W(1) \neq 1$.

6.5. Predictions About Covariation and Sequential Effects

When ψ_i is assumed to be a power function, we have the following inverse relations between ratio productions and ratio estimates:

$$r_i(p) = W(p)^{1/\beta_i} \quad (p \text{ given}), \tag{63}$$

$$p_i(r) = W^{-1}(r^{\beta_i}) \quad (r \text{ given}). \tag{64}$$

In the usual dB form in which data are plotted these are

$$r_{i,dB}(p) = \frac{1}{\beta_i} W_{dB}(p), \tag{65}$$

$$p_{i,dB}(r) = W_{dB}^{-1}(r^{\beta_i}) = W_{dB}^{-1}\left(\exp \frac{1}{10}(\beta_i r_{dB})\right). \tag{66}$$

What Happens When W Is a Power Function?

If we suppose that W is a power function of the form (54), then a routine calculation yields

$$W^{-1}(r^{\beta_i}) = \rho_i r^{\nu_i},$$

and so

$$r_{i,dB}(p) = \frac{1}{\nu_i}\left(p_{dB} - \rho_{i,dB}\right),$$

$$p_{i,dB}(r) = \nu_i r_{dB} + \rho_{i,dB}.$$

In response to overwhelmingly clear empirical evidence, several authors have formulated sequential models in which the response in dB on trial n, $10 \log R_n$, depends linearly on the present signal in dB, $10 \log S_n$, the previous one, $10 \log S_{n-1}$, the previous response $10 \log R_{n-1}$, and in some cases, $10 \log S_{n-2}$ (DeCarlo, 2003; DeCarlo & Cross, 1990; Jesteadt, Luce, & Green, 1977; Lacouture, 1997; Lockhead, 2004; Luce & Steingrimsson, 2003; Marley & Cook, 1986; Mori, 1998; Petrov & Anderson, 2005)[13]. Both Lockhead (2004) and Petrov and Anderson (2005) provided many other references to the literature.

Setting

$$r_{s,n} = \frac{S_n}{S_{n-1}}, p_{s,n} = \frac{R_n}{R_{n-1}},$$

then each weighting function yields a sequential model for estimation. With symmetric stimuli (x, x), we see that for power functions

$$R_{n,dB} = R_{n-1,dB} + \nu_s \left(S_{n,dB} - S_{n-1,dB} \right) + \rho_{i,dB}.$$

What Happens When W Is a Prelec Function

If we assume that W is given by (59), then putting that form into the expressions for (65) and (66), doing a bit of algebra, and defining $\tau_i := \frac{1}{\beta_i} \left(\frac{\log 10}{10} \right)^{\mu-1}$, yields the following forms for $r_i(p)_{dB}$ and $p_i(r)_{dB}$, respectively:

$$r_i(p)_{dB} = \tau_i \begin{cases} -\lambda \left(-p_{dB} \right)^{\mu} & 0 < p \le 1 \\ \lambda' \left(p_{dB} \right)^{\mu_i} & 1 < p \end{cases}, \qquad (67)$$

$$p_i(r)_{dB} = \frac{1}{\tau_i^{1/\mu}} \begin{cases} -\left(-\frac{\beta_i}{\lambda} r_{dB} \right)^{1/\mu} & 0 < r \le 1 \\ \left(\frac{\beta_i}{\lambda'} r_{dB} \right)^{1/\mu} & 1 < r \end{cases}. \qquad (68)$$

When μ is approximately 1, then $r_i(p)$ and $p_i(r)$ are approximately power functions, that is, $r_i(p)_{dB}$ and $p_i(r)_{dB}$ are approximately linear, but with a change of the power at $p = 1$ and $r = 1$, respectively. Of course, it cannot be exactly a power function without contradicting the data of Ellermeier and Faulhammer (2000) and Zimmer (2005). Some examples of (67) are shown in Fig. 3. Such functions seem consistent with the data reported in Fig. 1.

---

[13] We thank A. A. J. Marley for supplying some of these references.

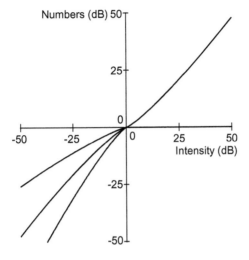

$$\text{Fig. 3:} \quad \psi(x) = \begin{cases} (.5x)^{1.2} & \text{if} \quad 0 \le x < 50 \\ -(-.cx)^{1.2} & \text{if} \quad -50 < x < 0, \end{cases}$$
were $c = 0.3, 0.5, 0.7$ from top to bottom.

Proceeding as with the power function but using Prelec's function, we get the following predicted sequential effects:

$$R_{n,dB} = R_{n-1,dB} + \tau_s^{1/\mu} \begin{cases} -\left[-\frac{\beta_s}{\lambda}\left(S_{n,dB} - S_{n-1,dB}\right)\right]^{1/\mu} & S_{n,dB} \le S_{n-1,dB} \\ \left[\frac{\beta_s}{\lambda'}\left(S_{n,dB} - S_{n-1,dB}\right)\right]^{1/\mu} & S_{n,dB} > S_{n-1,dB} \end{cases}.$$

In commenting on an earlier draft of this chapter, A. A. J. Marley raised the following issue: " ... An important phenomenon related to sequential effects (especially in absolute identification) is *assimilation* of responses to the value of the immediately previous stimulus (with smaller *contrast* effects for earlier stimuli)." (Personal communication, December 11, 2004.) For W a power function with $W(1) = 1$, they are not predicted. No one yet has investigated these phenomena when $W(1) \ne 1$. What happens in the Prelec case is not yet clear. The rank order of signal intensities seems to matter substantially.

Some aspects of Stevens's magnitude estimation and production functions may be illuminated by these results. Let us assume that when the experimenter provides no reference signal x, each respondent selects his or her own. Thus, the usual data, which are averaged over the respondents, is the average of approximately piece-wise linear functions with the break occurring in different places. Although (63) and (64) are perfect inverses, it is no surprise that under such averaging, the results are not strict inverses of one another. Something like this may provide an account of Stevens's "regression" phenomenon.

7.   Summary and Conclusions

7.1.   Summary of the Theory

The theory has three primitives:

1. The (loudness) ordering $\succsim$ on $\mathbb{R}_+ \times \mathbb{R}_+$, where $\mathbb{R}_+$ is the set of non-negative numbers corresponding to signals which are intensities less threshold intensity (intensities less than the threshold are set to 0).
2. The presentation of signal pairs, (x, u), to (e.g., the two ears of) the respondent with the defined matching operations $\oplus_i$.
3. Judgments of "interval" proportions, $\circ_p$.

Within the fairly weak structural assumptions of the theory, necessary and sufficient properties were stated that yield the representations: There exist a constant $\delta \geq 0$ and two strictly increasing functions Ψ and W such that

$$\Psi(x, u) = \Psi(x, 0) + \Psi(0, u) + \delta\Psi(x, 0)\Psi(0, u) \quad (\delta \geq 0),$$

$$W(p) = \frac{\Psi\left[(x, x) \circ_p (y, y)\right] - \Psi(y, y)}{\Psi(x, x) - \Psi(y, y)} \quad (x > y \geq 0),$$

and, under some conditions, there is a constant $\gamma > 0$ such that

$$\Psi(x, 0) = \gamma\Psi(0, x),$$

which is quite restrictive.

The property characterizing the form of $\Psi(x, u)$ is the Thomsen condition, (23). We showed next that for most people, the ears are not symmetric in the sense that $(x, u) \sim (u, x)$, in which case $\delta = 0$ is equivalent to bisymmetry of the operation $\oplus_s$. The property underlying the second expression, the one involving $\circ_p$, is production commutativity, (25). Axiomatized by themselves, these representations really are $\Psi_\oplus$ and $\Psi_{\circ_p}$ and they are not automatically the same function. To establish that equality requires two linking expressions, SJP-decomposition, (31), and one of two forms of segregation, either (32) or (33). These are two types of distribution conditions.

Next we took up the form of $\Psi(x, u)$ in terms of the intensities x and u. The property of $\sigma-$MI, (34) and (35), turns out to be equivalent to Ψ

being a sum of two power functions with the ratio of the exponents being σ. A predicted linear regression permits one to estimate σ. We also explored a simple filtering model to allow one to account for the, to us, unexpected phenomena connected with asymmetric matching. If the filter takes the form of an attenuation factor η, one can show that none of the tests of properties that we used with asymmetric matching are invalidated by the filtering. We gave formulae for estimating η and γ, respectively (42) and (43).

Our final topic was the form of the ratio estimation predicted by the theory. The results depend heavily on the assumed form of $W(p)$ as a function of p. We explored two cases: one where ratio estimates are power functions and $W(1) \neq 1$; and one where $W(1) = 1$ and W is a Prelec function, which has the nice properties of being either concave, convex, S-shaped, or inverse S-shaped depending on the parameter pairs. Both cases offered accounts of magnitude methods without a standard and of the ubiquitous sequential effects. Just how viable they are relative to data remains to be examined.

The case when W is a power function and $W(1) \neq 1$ leads to a prediction that has not been explored. That of the Prelec function for W has been shown to be equivalent to a behavioral property called reduction invariance, (60), with two studies, one of them ours, that both show that this condition fails. Thus, the problem of the form of W remains open but with a clear experiment to test the power function assumption.

7.2. Summary of Experimental Results

The theory discussed implies that properties Thomsen, 2, proportion commutativity, 4, JP-decomposition, 5, and segregation, 6, in Table 3 should hold. This is summarized in the top portion of the flow diagram of Fig. 4. Although the results are not perfect, we are reasonably satisfied. Issues concerning the forms of Ψ and W as functions are summarized at the bottom of the Fig. 4; they are clearly in much less satisfactory form at this point.

Had property jp-symmetry, that is, $(x, u) \sim (u, x)$, been sustained, which it was not, we could have used a somewhat simpler theoretical development formulated for utility theory. Given that it was not sustained, we know that bisymmetry, Property 3, corresponds to $\delta = 0$ in the representation

$$\Psi(x, u) = \Psi(x, 0) + \Psi(0, u) + \delta\Psi(x, 0)\Psi(0, u).$$

The data sustained bisymmetry, so we accepted that $\delta = 0$. Three implications follow: First, the peculiarities that we observed with asymmetric matching are predicted by a simple filtering model. Second, if $\sigma-$MI holds, various properties, 2 to 6, are not altered by the filtering model (see Table 1). Third, $\sigma-$MI is equivalent to $\Psi(x, u)$ being a sum of power functions.

Table 3: Summary of experimental results.

Property	Number of Respondents	Number of Tests	Number of Failures
Joint–Presentation Symmetry	15	45	23
Thomsen	12	24	5
Bisymmetry	6	6	0
Production Commutativity	4	4	0
Joint–Presentation Decomposition	4	8	2
Segregation	4	10	2
1–Multiplicative Invariance	22	44	13[a]
Reduction Invariance	6	12	12

[a] 12 Respondents passed both tests.

The special case of $\sigma = 1$ has been tested and was sustained for about 50% of respondents. For σ–MI we have developed a regression model for estimating σ and for seven respondents from the 1–MI experiment the estimated σ moved things in the correct direction for five of them. Mostly, however, the correction does not seem to be sufficiently large to expect that σ–MI will improve matters much.

Given the potential for experimental artifacts, we conclude that sufficient initial support for the general theory has been received to warrant further investigation—both for auditory intensity and for other interpretations of the primitives. However, questions about the forms of Ψ as a function of physical intensity and about W as a function of its argument remain unsettled.

7.3.   Conclusions

The studies summarized here seem to establish the following points:

1. As in classical physics, one does a lot better by having two or more interlocked primitive structures rather than just one in arriving at constrained representations. Our structures were $\langle \mathbb{R}_+ \times \mathbb{R}_+, \succsim \rangle$, which we reduced to the one dimensional structures $\langle \mathbb{R}_+, \geq, \oplus_i \rangle$, and $\langle \mathbb{R}_+ \times \mathbb{R}_+, \succsim , \circ_p \rangle$, which , in turn, we reduced to the one dimensional $\langle \mathbb{R}_+, \geq, \circ_{p,i} \rangle$.
2. The adequacy of such a representation theory that has both free functions and free parameters can be judged entirely in terms of parameter-free properties without, at any point, trying to fit the representations themselves to data. Again, this is familiar from classical physics.
3. As usual, more needs to be done. Among the most obvious things are:
   - Collect more data. Several specific experiments were mentioned.
   - Continue to try to improve the experimental methodology.

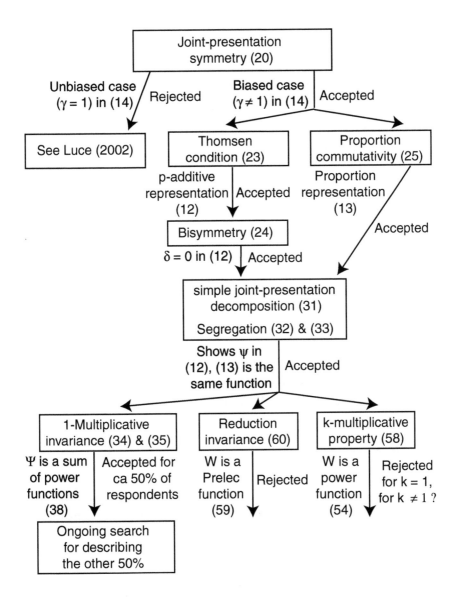

Fig. 4: The diagram shows the main testable properties discussed in this chapter and their inter-relation. A testable property is listed in each box. An arrow leads from that box to another listing the property whose testing logically follows. On the left side of the arrows is the main consequence of accepting the property and the testing result is indicated on the right side of the arrow.

- Statistical evaluation of behavioral indifferences is always an issue in testing theories of this type. We used the Mann-Whitney U test. Recently, an apparently very effective Bayesian method has been proposed for this task (Ho, Regenwetter, Niederée, & Heyer, 2005; Karabatsos, 2005; Myung, Karabatsos, & Iverson, 2005). It should be tried on our data.
- Work out the behavioral condition, presumably corresponding somewhat to $\sigma-$MI, that characterizes the p-additive form of power functions, and then test that empirically.
- Find a form for $W(p)$ as a function of p with $W(1) \neq 1$ that is characterized by a behavioral property that is sustained empirically. Open issues here are both an experiment about the form kpq, (58), and a behavioral condition corresponding to the Prelec function with $W(1) \neq 1$.
- Extend the theory to encompass auditory frequency as well as intensity.
- Study interpretations of the primitives other than auditory intensity. Currently the second author is collecting brightness data which, so far, seems comparable to the auditory data.

4. We are the first to admit, however, that the approach taken is no panacea:

- We do not have the slightest idea how to axiomatize response times in a comparable fashion.
- What about probabilistic versions of the theory? Everyone knows that when stimuli are close together, they are not perfectly discriminated and so not really algebraically ordered. Certainly this was true of our data, especially for our data involving ratio productions. Recognition of this fact has, over the years, led to probabilistic versions of various one dimensional ordered structures. But the important goal of blending probabilities with two interacting structures, $\oplus$ and $\circ_p$, in an interesting way has proved to be quite elusive.
- Also we do not know how to extend the approach to dynamic processes that, at a minimum, seem to underlie both the learning that goes on in psychophysical experiments and the ever-present sequential effects. One thing to recall about dynamic processes in physics is that they are typically formulated in terms of conservation laws (mass, momentum, angular momentum, energy, spin, etc.) that state that certain quantities, definable within the dynamic system, remain invariant over time. Nothing really comparable seems to exist in psychology. Should we be seeking such invariants? We should mention that such invariants always correspond to a form of symmetry. In some systems, the symmetry is captured by the set of

automorphisms, and in others, by more general groups of transformations. For further detail, see Luce et al. (1990), Narens (2002), and Suppes (2002).

Acknowledgements: Many of the experiments discussed here were carried out in Dr. Bruce Berg's auditory laboratory at University of California, Irvine, and his guidance is appreciated. Others were conducted at New York University and we thank the Center for Neural Science and Dr. Malcolm Semple for making resources and laboratory space available to us. We appreciate detailed comments by A. A. J. Marley and J. Gobell on earlier drafts. Some of the experimental work was supported by University of California, Irvine, and some earlier National Science Foundation grants.

References

Aczél, J. (1966). *Lectures on functional equations and their applications*. New York: Academic.

Aczél, J., Falmagne, J.-C., & Luce, R. D. (2000). Functional equations in the behavioral sciences. *Mathematica Japonica, 52*, 469-512.

Beck, J., & Shaw, W. A. (1965). Magnitude of the standard, numerical value of the standard, and stimulus spacing in the estimation of loudness. *Perceptual and Motor Skills, 21*, 151–156.

DeCarlo, L. T. (2003). An application of a dynamic model of judgment to magnitude estimation. *Perception & Psychophysics, 65*, 152-162.

DeCarlo, L. T., & Cross, D. V. (1990). Sequential effects in magnitude scaling: Models and theory. *Journal of Experimental Psychology: General, 119*, 375-396.

Efron, B., & Tibshirani, R. J. (1993). *An introduction to the bootstrap*. New York: Chapman and Hall.

Ellermeier, W., & Faulhammer, G. (2000). Empirical evaluation of axioms fundamental to Stevens' ratio-scaling approach. I. Loudness production. *Perception & Psychophysics, 62*, 1505-1511.

Falmagne, J.-C. (1976). Random conjoint measurement and loudness summation. *Psychological Review, 83*, 65-79.

Falmagne, J.-C., Iverson, G., & Marcovici, S. (1979). Binaural "loudness" summation: Probabilistic theory and data, *Psychological Review, 86*, 25-43.

Gigerenzer, G., & Strube, G. (1983). Are there limits to binaural additivity of loudness? *Journal of Experimental Psychology: Human Perception and Performance, 9*, 126-136.

Green, D. M., & Luce, R. D. (1974). Variability of magnitude estimates: a timing theory analysis. *Perception & Psychophysics, 15*, 291-300.

Hellman, R. P., & Zwislocki, J. (1961). Some factors affecting the estimation of loudness. *Journal of the Acoustical Society of America, 33*, 687-694.

Ho, M.-H, Regenwetter, M, Niederée, R., & Heyer, D (2005). Observation: An alternative perspective on van Winterfeldt et al's consequence monotonicity. *Journal of Experimental Psychology: Learning, Memory, and Cognition, 31*, 365-373.

Jesteadt, W., Luce, R. D., & Green, D. M. (1977). Sequential effects in judgments of loudness. *Journal of Experimental Psychology: Human Perception and Performance, 3*, 92-104.

Karabatsos, G. (2005). An exchangeable multinomial model for testing deterministic axioms of decision and measurement, *Journal of Mathematical Psychology, 49*, 51-69.

Krantz, D. H., Luce, R. D, Suppes, P., & Tversky, A. (1971). *Foundations of measurement, I.* New York: Academic Press.

Lacouture, Y. (1997). Bow, range, and sequential effects in absolute identification: A response-time analysis. *Psychological Research, 60*, 121-133.

Levelt, W. J. M., Riemersma, J. B., & Bunt, A. A. (1972). Binaural additivity of loudness. *British Journal of Mathematical and Statistical Psychology, 25*, 51-68.

Levitt, H. (1971). Transformed up-down methods in psychoacoustics. *Journal of the Acoustical Society of America, 49*, 467-477.

Lockhead, G. R. (2004). Absolute judgments are relative: A reinterpretation of some psychophysical data. *Review of General Psychology, 8*, 265-272.

Luce, R. D. (2000). *Utility of gains and losses: Measurement-Theoretical and experimental approaches.* Mahwah, NJ: Lawrence Erlbaum Associates, Inc.

Luce, R. D. (2001). Reduction invariance and Prelec's weighting functions. *Journal of Mathematical Psychology, 45*, 167-179.

Luce, R. D. (2002). A psychophysical theory of intensity proportions, joint presentations, and matches. *Psychological Review, 109*, 520-532.

Luce, R. D. (2004). Symmetric and asymmetric matching of joint presentations. *Psychological Review, 111*, 446-454.

Luce, R. D. (2005). Measurement analogies: Comparisons of behavioral and physical measures. *Psychometrika, 70*, 227-251.

Luce, R. D., Krantz, D. H., Suppes, P., & Tversky, A. (1990). *Foundations of measurement, III.* San Diego, CA: Academic.

Luce, R. D., & Marley, A. A. J. (2005). Ranked additive utility representations of gambles: Old and new axiomatizations. *Journal of Risk and Uncertainty, 30*, 21-62.

Luce, R. D., & Steingrimsson, R. (2003). A model of ratio production and estimation and some behavioral predictions. Berglund, B., & Borg, E. (Eds) *Fechner day 2003: Proceedings of the Nineteenth Annual Meeting of the International Society for Psychophysics,* Stockholm: International Society for Psychophysics (pp. 157-162).

Marley, A. A. J., & Cook, V. T. (1986). A limited capacity rehearsal model to psychophysical judgements applied to magnitude estimation. *Journal of Mathematical Psychology, 30*, 339-390.

Mori, S. (1998). Effects of stimulus information and number of stimuli on sequential dependencies in absolute identification. *Canadian Journal of Psychology, 52*, 72-83.

Myung, J. I., Karabatsos, G, & Iverson, G. J. (2005). A Bayesian approach to testing decision making axioms. *Journal of Mathematical Psychology, 49*, 205-225.

Narens, L. (1996). A theory of ratio magnitude estimation. *Journal of Mathematical Psychology, 40*, 109-129.

Narens, L. (2002). *Theories of meaningfulness.* Mahwah, NJ: Lawrence Erlbaum Associates, Inc.

Petrov, A. A., & Anderson, J. R. (2005). The dynamics of scaling: A memory-based anchor model of category rating and absolute identification. *Psychological Review, 112*, 383-416.

Poulton, E. C. (1968). The new psychophysics: six models for magnitude estimation. *Psychological Bulletin, 69*,1–19.

Prelec, D. (1998). The probability weighting function. *Econometrica,* 66, 497-527.

Ramsey, F. P. (1931). *The foundations of mathematics and other logical essays.* New York: Harcourt, Brace. (Ch. VII, reprinted in *Studies in Subjective Probability.* H. E. Kyburg, & H. E. Smokler, Eds., 1964. New York: Wiley, pp. 61-92.)

Schneider, B. (1988). The additivity of loudness across critical bands: A conjoint measurement approach. *Perception & Psychophysics, 43*, 211-222.

Steingrimsson, R. (2002). *Contributions to measuring three psychophysical attributes: Testing behavioral axioms for loudness, response time as an independent variable, and attentional intensity.* Unpublished dissertation, University of California, Irvine.

Steingrimsson, R., & Luce, R. D. (2005a). Empirical evaluation of a model of global psychophysical judgments: I. Behavioral properties of summations and productions. *Journal of Mathematical Psychology, 49*, 290-307.

Steingrimsson, R., & Luce, R. D. (2005b). Empirical evaluation of a model of global psychophysical judgments: II. Behavioral properties linking summations and productions. *Journal of Mathematical Psychology, 49*, 308-319.

Steingrimsson, R., & Luce, R. D. (in press). Empirical Evaluation of a Model of Global Psychophysical Judgments: III. A Form for the Psychophysical Function and Intensity Filtering. *Journal of Mathematical Psychology*

Steingrimsson, R., & Luce, R. D. (in preparation). Empirical evaluation of a model of global psychophysical judgments: IV. Forms for the weighting function.

Stevens, S. S. (1975). *Psychophysics: Introduction to its perceptual, neural, and social prospects.* New York: Wiley.

Suppes, P. (2002). *Representation and invariance of scientific structures.* Stanford, CA: CLSI Publications.

Zimmer, K. (2005). Examining the validity of numerical ratios in loudness fractionation. *Perception & Psychophysics,* 67, 569–579.

4

Referential Duality and Representational Duality in the Scaling of Multidimensional and Infinite-Dimensional Stimulus Space

Jun Zhang

University of Michigan

1. INTRODUCTION

Traditional theories of geometric representations for stimulus spaces (see, e.g., Shepard, 1962a, 1962b) rely on the notion of a "distance" in some multidimensional vector space $\mathbb{R}^n$ to describe the subjective proximity between various stimuli whose features are represented by the axes of the space. Such a distance is often viewed as induced by a "norm" of the vector space, defined as a real-valued function $\mathbb{R}^n \to \mathbb{R}$ and denoted $|| \cdot ||$, that satisfies the following conditions for all $x, y \in \mathbb{R}^n$ and $\alpha \in \mathbb{R}$: (i) $||x|| \geq 0$ with equality holding if and only if $x = 0$; (ii) $||\alpha x|| = |\alpha| \cdot ||x||$; (iii) $||x+y|| \leq ||x|| + ||y||$. The distance measure or "metric" induced by such a norm is defined as

$$\Delta(x, x') = ||x - x'|| \ .$$

Such a metric is continuous with respect to (x, x') and it satisfies the axioms of (i) non-negativity: $\Delta(x, x') \geq 0$, with 0 attained if and only if $x = x'$; (ii) symmetry: $\Delta(x, x') = \Delta(x', x)$; and (iii) triangle inequality: $\Delta(x, x') + \Delta(x', x'') \geq \Delta(x, x'')$, for any triplet x, x', x''. The norm $|| \cdot ||$ may also be used to define an inner product $\langle \cdot, \cdot \rangle$:

$$\langle x, x' \rangle = \frac{1}{2}(||x + x'||^2 - ||x||^2 - ||x'||^2) \ .$$

The inner product operation on the vector space allows one to define the angle between two vectors (and hence orthogonality), which allows one to project one vector onto another (and hence onto a subspace).

However, such a norm-based approach in defining a metric (distance) is fundamentally dissatisfying because it cannot capture the asymmetry intrinsic to comparative judgments that give rise to our sense of similarity/dissimilarity of stimuli. This asymmetry arises from the different status of a fixed reference stimulus (a *referent*, for short) and a variable comparison stimulus (a *probe*, for short), for example, between a stimulus in perception and one in memory during categorization, between the current state and a goal state during planning, between the status quo payoff and the uncertainty about possible gains or losses during decision making, and so forth. A well-cited example of such asymmetry is Tversky's (1977) demonstration that Red China was judged to be more similar to North Korea than was North Korea to Red China, making the norm-based metric Δ highly questionable. As an alternative to the norm-based approach mentioned earlier, Dzhafarov and Colonius (1999, 2001) introduced instead (a generalized version of) Finslerian metric functions defined on the tangent space of a stimulus manifold. Asymmetric or "oriented" Fechnerian distances are constructed from these metric functions which are derived from the (not necessarily symmetric) discrimination probabilities. However, in recent developments (Dzhafarov & Colonius, 2005a, 2005b), the oriented Fechnerian distances are not interpreted as subjective dissimilarities and serve only as an intermediate step in computing a symmetrized "overall Fechnerian distance," which is taken to be a measure of subjective similarity (for explanations, see Chapter 2 of this volume). Therefore, the output of Dzhafarov and Colonius's framework is still a symmetric measure of subjective similarity, though its input (discrimination probability) is generally asymmetric.

In this chapter, we discuss mathematical notions that are specifically aimed at expressing the asymmetric status of a referent and a probe in a direct and natural way. One such notion is "duality," intuitively, the quality or character of being dichotomous or twofold. A related notion is "conjugacy," referring to objects that are, in some sense, inversely or oppositely related to each other. The referent and probe in a comparative judgment are dual to each other in an obvious way: dialectically speaking, neither of them can exist without the other coexisting. The referent and probe are also conjugate to each other, because the two stimuli can switch their roles if we change our frame of reference (all these notions are given precise mathematical meanings later).

The experimental paradigm to which our analysis applies can be described as follows. Two types of stimuli, one assigned the role of a comparison stimulus (probe) and the other the role of a reference stimulus (referent), are presented to the participants, who are to make some judgment about their similarity. As an example, suppose a participant is to make a same-different judgment on the "value" of two gambles, one involving a guaranteed payoff of x utility units and the other involving a probabilistic payoff in which the participant will receive either y units or 0 with fixed probability known to the participant. In the literature on gambles, x is called the "certainty equivalent" (CE) value of a probabilistic 0/y outcome (with given probabilities).

In the experimental paradigm on which we are focusing, the value of the referent is fixed whereas that of the probe is varied within a block of trials; the variation across trials for the latter can be either random or in an ascending/descending (including "staircase") order. In our example with gambles, for a given probability of receiving y units in the second gamble, the experimenter can either hold that y value fixed and have the value of certainty equivalent x change over a series of trials (which we call the *forward procedure*), or conversely, hold x fixed and have the value of y change (which we call the *reverse procedure*). Because these two procedures are conjugate to each other, the forward/reverse terminology can itself be reversed, in which case the assignment of reference and comparison status to x and y will be exchanged as well. To fix the notation and terminology, and for this purpose only, we pick one stimulus as a referent and call this the forward procedure, and we refer to the reverse procedure as the *conjugate* one.

Two stimuli, one assigned as a referent and the other as a probe, generally would invoke substantively different mental representations; the two mutually conjugate procedures which assign the referent and probe roles to the two stimuli differently, generally would invoke distinct psychological processes. Thus, in our example with gambles, it is natural to assume that the comparative process where a fixed value of x is used as a reference for the evaluation of a series of probabilistic gambles with variable payoffs y is different from the process where one gamble with probabilistic payoff y is used as a fixed reference for the evaluation of the varied values of x — the asymmetry in this scenario may reveal some fundamental difference in the participant's mental representations of risky and risk-free outcomes as well as in the underlying psychological processes dependent on their actual assigned role as a referent or a probe.

The goal of this chapter is to investigate the duality that arises from the distinct roles played by a referent and a probe in a comparative judgment, and to formulate some basic measures related to the asymmetry (dual symmetry, to be precise) in comparing a pair of stimuli. In Section 2, we investigate the principle of "regular cross-minimality" along with the property of "nonconstant self-similarity," the notions analogous to "regular minimality" and "nonconstant self-similarity" proposed by Dzhafarov (2002) in a somewhat different context (see Chapters 1 and 2 of this volume, where the latter is called "nonconstant self-dissimilarity"). A particular representation for psychometric functions is proposed, capturing the dual nature of the status of a referent and of a probe, in both forward and reverse procedures, through the use of a conjugate pair of strictly convex functions. The resulting "psychometric differentials" (a terminology borrowed from Dzhafarov and Colonius's Fechnerian scaling theory) are *bidualistic*, namely, they exhibit both the duality of assigning the referent-probe status to stimuli (*referential duality*) and the duality of selecting one of the two mutually conjugate representations (*representational duality*); we consider this to be a distinct improvement over the symmetric distance induced by a norm. In Section 3 we construct a family of dually symmetric psychometric differentials characterized as "divergence functions" indexed by real numbers; this is done both in the multidimensional setting and in the infinite-dimensional setting. Section 4 deals with the differential geometric structure induced by these divergence functions. It is demonstrated, in particular, that the referential duality and the representational duality are reflected in the family of affine connections defined on a stimulus manifold, together with one and the same Riemannian metric. The chapter closes with a brief discussion of the implications of this formulation of duality and conjugacy that combines the mathematical tools of convex analysis, function space, and differential geometry. The materials presented in this chapter, including detailed proofs for most propositions and corollaries stated herein, have previously been published elsewhere (Zhang, 2004a, 2004b).

2. DUAL SCALING BETWEEN REFERENCE AND COMPARISON STIMULUS SPACES

We consider a comparison task in which two types of stimuli are being compared with each other, one serving as a referent and the other as a probe. Let $\Psi_y(x)$ denote, in (an arbitrarily defined) *forward procedure*, a quantity monotonically related to the discrimination probability with which x, as a comparison stimulus, is judged to be dissimilar in magnitude to y, a reference stimulus. By abuse of language, we refer to $\Psi_y(x)$ as a psychometric function, although it need not be a probability function. Similarly, $\Phi_x(y)$ denotes, in the *reverse procedure*, a quantity monotonically related to the discrimination probability describing the value of y, now a comparison stimulus, is judged to be dissimilar in magnitude to the value of x, now a reference stimulus. Here and later, $x = [x^1, \cdots, x^n]$ and $y = [y_1, \cdots, y_n]$ are assumed to be (contravariant and covariant forms of) vectors comprising certain subsets $\mathcal{X} \subseteq \mathbb{R}^n$ and $\mathcal{Y} \subseteq (\mathbb{R}^n)^*$ of some multidimensional vector space $\mathbb{R}^n$ and its dual $(\mathbb{R}^n)^*$, respectively. In this context, the dualistic assignment of the reference and comparison stimulus status to x and to y (and hence the dualism of two psychometric procedures, forward and reverse) is referred to as the *referential duality*.

2.1. Regular cross-minimality and positive diffeomorphism in stimulus mappings

By analogy with Dzhafarov's (2002) regular minimality principle, proposed in a different context, we require that $\Psi_y(x)$ and $\Phi_x(y)$ satisfy the principle of *regular cross-minimality*. The essence of this principle is as follows — *if*, corresponding to a particular value of the reference stimulus $\hat{y}$, there exists a unique value of the comparison stimulus $x = \hat{x}$ such that

$$\hat{x} = \mathrm{argmin}_x \Psi_{\hat{y}}(x) \ ,$$

then when the entire procedure is reversed, that is, when $\hat{x}$ is being held fixed and y varies, the psychometric function $\Phi_{\hat{x}}(y)$ thus obtained would have its unique minimum value at $y = \hat{y}$:

$$\hat{y} = \mathrm{argmin}_y \Phi_{\hat{x}}(y) \ .$$

In other words, when the reference stimulus ($\hat{y}$ for the forward procedure, $\hat{x}$ for the reverse procedure) is fixed and the comparison stimulus is varied (x in $\Psi_{\hat{y}}(x)$, y in $\Phi_{\hat{x}}(y)$), the corresponding psychometric functions index-psychometric!function achieve their global minima at values $x = \hat{x}, y = \hat{y}$ such that

$$\Psi_{\hat{y}}(x) \geq \min_x \Psi_{\hat{y}}(x) = \Psi_{\hat{y}}(\hat{x}) \ ,$$
$$\Phi_{\hat{x}}(y) \geq \min_y \Phi_{\hat{x}}(y) = \Phi_{\hat{x}}(\hat{y}) \ .$$

A precise statement of the principle of regular cross-minimality is with reference to the existence of a pair of mutually inverse functions (see Dzhafarov & Colonius, 2005a, and Chapter 1 in this volume):

AXIOM 1 (REGULAR CROSS-MINIMALITY). *There exist functions $\psi :$ $\mathcal{X} \to \mathcal{Y}$ and $\phi : \mathcal{Y} \to \mathcal{X}$ ($\mathcal{X} \subseteq \mathbb{R}^n$, $\mathcal{Y} \subseteq (\mathbb{R}^n)^*$) such that*

(i) $\Psi_{\hat{y}}(x) > \Psi_{\hat{y}}(\phi(\hat{y}))$, $\forall x \neq \phi(\hat{y})$;
(ii) $\Phi_{\hat{x}}(y) > \Phi_{\hat{x}}(\psi(\hat{x}))$, $\forall y \neq \psi(\hat{x})$;
(iii) $\phi = \psi^{-1}$.

It follows that ϕ and ψ must be bijective (one-to-one and onto). Below, we further assume they are sufficiently smooth and are "curl-less," therefore allowing a pair of convex functions ("potentials") to induce them.

AXIOM 2 (POSITIVE DIFFEOMORPHISM). *The mappings ψ and ϕ have symmetric and positive-definite Jacobians, with*

$$\frac{\partial \psi_i}{\partial x^j} = \frac{\partial \psi_j}{\partial x^i} , \qquad \frac{\partial \phi^i}{\partial y_j} = \frac{\partial \phi^j}{\partial y_i} , \tag{1}$$

where the subscript (or superscripts) i, j attached to the vector-valued map ψ (or ϕ) denote its i-th and j-th components.

An immediate consequence of Axiom 1 (which says that ψ, ϕ are mutually inverse functions) and Axiom 2 (which says that ψ, ϕ have symmetric, positive-definite Jacobians) is as follows:

COROLLARY 1. *There exists a pair of strictly convex functions $\Psi : \mathcal{X} \rightarrow \mathbb{R}$ and $\Phi : \mathcal{Y} \rightarrow \mathbb{R}$ such that*

(i) *they are conjugate to each other*[1]

$$\Phi^* = \Psi \longleftrightarrow \Phi = \Psi^*, \tag{2}$$

where $*$ denotes convex conjugation operation (to be explained later);

(ii) *they induce ψ, ϕ via*

$$\psi = \nabla \Psi \longleftrightarrow \phi = \nabla \Phi , \tag{3}$$

where $(\nabla \Psi)(x) = [\partial \Psi / \partial x^1, \cdots, \partial \Psi / \partial x^n]$, $(\nabla \Phi)(y) = [\partial \Phi / \partial y_1, \cdots, \partial \Phi / \partial y_n]$ denote the gradient of the functions Ψ and Φ, respectively.

Proof. Symmetry of the derivatives of ψ, ϕ, (1), allows us to write them in the form of (3) using some functions Ψ, Φ. Positive-definiteness further implies that Ψ, Φ are strictly convex. That $\phi = \psi^{-1}$ (from Axiom 1), or equivalently $(\nabla \Phi) = (\nabla \Psi)^{-1}$, implies (2) (apart from a constant). $\diamond$

Note that in the unidimensional case, ψ, ϕ are simply mappings of reals to reals and hence (1) is naturally satisfied for strictly increasing (that is, order-preserving) functions ψ and ϕ.

When the mappings $\psi = \phi^{-1} \leftrightarrow \phi = \psi^{-1}$ between the two stimulus spaces $\mathcal{X}$ and $\mathcal{Y}$ are associated with a pair of conjugate convex functions $\Psi = \Phi^*$ and $\Phi = \Psi^*$, we say that the comparison stimulus and the reference stimulus are *conjugate-scaled*. The Jacobians of the mappings ψ and ϕ between two conjugate-scaled stimulus spaces are simply

$$\frac{\partial^2 \Psi}{\partial x^i \partial x^j} \quad \text{and} \quad \frac{\partial^2 \Phi}{\partial y_i \partial y_j} ,$$

---

[1] Here and throughout this chapter, the $\leftrightarrow$ sign (or $\longleftrightarrow$ if in a displayed equation) is to be read as "and equivalently," so that "equality A $\leftrightarrow$ equality B" means that "equality A holds and equivalently equality B holds as well."

which can be shown to be matrix inverses of each other. Two conjugate-scaled representations are dual to each other; we call this *representational duality*.

Now we explain the meaning of the conjugation operation in convex analysis (see, e.g., Roberts & Varberg, 1973). A function $\Psi : \mathcal{X} \subseteq \mathbb{R}^n \to \mathbb{R}$ is called strictly convex if for $x \neq x'$ and any $\lambda \in (0,1)$,

$$(1-\lambda)\Psi(x) + \lambda\Psi(x') > \Psi((1-\lambda)x + \lambda x') . \tag{4}$$

An equality sign replaces the inequality sign shown earlier if and only if $x = x'$ when $\lambda \in (0,1)$, or if $\lambda \in \{0,1\}$. For a strictly convex function Ψ, its conjugate $\Psi^* : \mathcal{Y} \subseteq (\mathbb{R}^n)^* \to \mathbb{R}$ is defined as

$$\Psi^*(y) \equiv \langle (\nabla\Psi)^{-1}(y), y \rangle - \Psi((\nabla\Psi)^{-1}(y)) , \tag{5}$$

where $\langle x, y \rangle$ is the (Euclidean) inner product of two vectors $x \in \mathcal{X}$, $y \in \mathcal{Y}$ defined as

$$\langle x, y \rangle = \sum_{i=1}^{n} x^i y_i ,$$

which is a bilinear form mapping $\mathcal{X} \times \mathcal{Y} \to \mathbb{R}$. It can be shown that Ψ^* is also a strictly convex function, with

$$\nabla\Psi^* = (\nabla\Psi)^{-1}$$

and

$$(\Psi^*)^* = \Psi .$$

The convex conjugation operation is associated with a pair of dual vector spaces $\mathcal{X}$ and $\mathcal{Y}$. Substituting $y = (\nabla\Psi)(x) \leftrightarrow x = (\nabla\Psi^*)(y)$ into (5) yields the relationship

$$\Psi(x) + \Psi^*(\nabla\Psi(x)) - \langle x, \nabla\Psi(x) \rangle = 0 \tag{6}$$

between a convex function $\Psi(\cdot)$ and its convex conjugate $\Psi^*(\cdot)$, called the *Fenchel* duality in convex analysis (see Rockafellar, 1970).

2.2.   Psychometric differential and reference-representation biduality

Axiom 1 allows us to introduce a non-negative quantity, called the "psychometric differential." For each of the two psychometric functions, let $\mathcal{A}_\Psi(\cdot,\cdot) : \mathcal{X} \times \mathcal{Y} \to \mathbb{R}_+$ and $\mathcal{A}_\Phi(\cdot,\cdot) : \mathcal{Y} \times \mathcal{X} \to \mathbb{R}_+$ (where $\mathbb{R}_+ = \mathbb{R}^+ \cup \{0\}$) denote:

$$\mathcal{A}_\Psi(x, \hat{y}) = \Psi_{\hat{y}}(x) - \Psi_{\hat{y}}(\phi(\hat{y})) , \tag{7}$$
$$\mathcal{A}_\Phi(y, \hat{x}) = \Phi_{\hat{x}}(y) - \Phi_{\hat{x}}(\psi(\hat{x})) . \tag{8}$$

Psychometric differential is a more interesting quantity to study than the psychometric functions themselves. This is because the two psychometric functions $\Psi_{\hat{y}}(x)$ and $\Phi_{\hat{x}}(y)$, for the forward and reverse procedures respectively, being only monotonically related to the discrimination probabilities, can always contain an additive function of the reference stimulus value (denoted with the "hat"), say, $P(\hat{y})$ in the former case and $Q(\hat{x})$ in the latter case, so that their self-similarity, that is, $\Psi_{\hat{y}}(\phi(\hat{y}))$ and $\Phi_{\hat{x}}(\psi(\hat{x}))$, need not be constant but may be a function of the reference stimulus value. Stated in another way, the property of "nonconstant self-similarity" does not impose any additional constraints on the possible forms of the two psychometric functions; in this respect, the situation is very different from that in Dzhafarov and Colonius's theory, where the combination of regular minimality and nonconstant self-(dis)similarity is shown to greatly restrict the possible forms of the (single) discrimination probability function. However, not to be too unconstrained, we impose a further restriction on the psychometric differential (and indirectly on the psychometric functions).

AXIOM 3 (REFERENCE-REPRESENTATION BIDUALITY). *The two psychometric differentials as defined in (7) and (8) satisfy*

$$\mathcal{A}_\Psi(x, y) = \mathcal{A}_\Phi(y, x) .$$

Axiom 3 postulates that the referential duality and representational duality themselves are "dual," that is, when one switches the referent-probe role assignment between two stimuli as well as the conjugate-scaled representations of these stimuli, the psychometric differential remains unchanged. In other words, the asymmetry embodied in the referent-probe status of the two stimuli is linked to the asymmetry in the scaling of these stimuli by a pair of conjugate convex functions. Axiom 3 is essential to our theory; it restricts the possible forms of psychometric differentials (and hence psychometric functions).

PROPOSITION 2. *The following form of the psychometric differentials* [2],

$$\mathcal{A}_\Psi(x, y) = \Psi(x) - \langle x, y \rangle + \Psi^*(y) \ = \ \mathcal{A}_{\Psi^*}(y, x) , \qquad (9)$$
$$\mathcal{A}_\Phi(y, x) = \Phi(y) - \langle x, y \rangle + \Phi^*(x) \ = \ \mathcal{A}_{\Phi^*}(x, y) ,$$

where Ψ and Φ are conjugate convex functions, satisfies Axioms 1, 2 and 3.
Proof. Clearly

$$\mathcal{A}_\Phi(y, x) = \mathcal{A}_{\Psi^*}(y, x) = \Psi^*(y) - \langle x, y \rangle + (\Psi^*)^*(x) = \mathcal{A}_\Psi(x, y) ,$$

---

[2]Note that the subscripts Ψ and Φ when A was first introduced in (7) and (8) refer to the psychometric functions $\Psi_y(x)$ and $\Phi_x(y)$. In the statement of this proposition, $\Psi(\cdot)$ and $\Phi(\cdot)$ are single-variable convex functions, not to be confused with the two-variable psychometric functions. As a result of Proposition 2, we can subsequently treat the Ψ, Φ in the subscripts of A as $\Psi(\cdot), \Phi(\cdot)$.

because $(\Psi^*)^* = \Psi$. Axiom 3 is therefore satisfied. Regular cross-minimality (Axiom 1) is satisfied because

$$\hat{x} = \operatorname{argmin}_x \Psi_{\hat{y}}(x) = \operatorname{argmin}_x \mathcal{A}_\Psi(x, \hat{y}) = (\nabla\Psi)^{-1}(\hat{y}) = (\nabla\Phi)(\hat{y})$$

and

$$\hat{y} = \operatorname{argmin}_y \Phi_{\hat{x}}(y) = \operatorname{argmin}_y \mathcal{A}_\Phi(y, \hat{x}) = (\nabla\Phi)^{-1}(\hat{x}) = (\nabla\Psi)(\hat{x})$$

mutually imply each other. Because of the strict convexity of Φ and Ψ, the Jacobians of the mappings $\phi = \nabla\Phi, \psi = \nabla\Psi$ are symmetric and positive-definite (Axiom 2). $\diamond$

Throughout the rest of the chapter, we assume that psychometric differentials $\mathcal{A}_\Psi(x, y)$ are representable in form (9). As such $\mathcal{A}_\Psi(x, y) = \mathcal{A}_\Phi(y, x)$ measures the difference between x, y assigned to a reference stimulus and a comparison in the forward procedure and scaled by Ψ and vice versa in the reverse procedure and scaled by Φ (the term *differential* is really a misnomer in our usage because its value need not be infinitesimally small). Because the mapping between the two spaces is homeomorphic, we can express the psychometric differential $\mathcal{A}$ in an alternative way, using functions of which both arguments are defined either in $\mathcal{X}$ alone or in $\mathcal{Y}$ alone:

$$\mathcal{D}_\Psi(x, \hat{x}) = \mathcal{A}_\Psi(x, (\nabla\Psi)(\hat{x})) \ ,$$
$$\mathcal{D}_{\Psi^*}(y, \hat{y}) = \mathcal{A}_{\Psi^*}(y, (\nabla\Psi^*)(\hat{y})) \ .$$

This is an analogue of the "canonical transformation" used in Dzhafarov and Colonius's theory (see Chapter 1). Writing them out explicitly,

$$\mathcal{D}_\Psi(x, \hat{x}) = \Psi(x) - \Psi(\hat{x}) - \langle x - \hat{x}, (\nabla\Psi)(\hat{x})\rangle \ , \tag{10}$$
$$\mathcal{D}_{\Psi^*}(y, \hat{y}) = \Psi^*(y) - \Psi^*(\hat{y}) - \langle (\nabla\Psi^*)(\hat{y}), y - \hat{y}\rangle \ . \tag{11}$$

$\mathcal{D}_\Psi$ (or $\mathcal{D}_{\Psi^*}$), which is the psychometric differential in an alternative form, is a measure of dissimilarity between a probe x (respectively, y) and a referent represented by $\hat{x}$ (respectively, $\hat{y}$). Loosely speaking, we say that $\mathcal{D}_\Psi$ (or $\mathcal{D}_{\Psi^*}$) provides a "scaling" of stimuli in $\mathcal{X}$ (or $\mathcal{Y}$).

COROLLARY 3. *The two psychometric differentials $\mathcal{D}_\Psi$ and $\mathcal{D}_{\Psi^*}$ satisfy the reference-representation biduality*

$$\mathcal{D}_\Psi(x, \hat{x}) = \mathcal{D}_{\Psi^*}((\nabla\Psi)(\hat{x}), (\nabla\Psi)(x)) \ ,$$
$$\mathcal{D}_{\Psi^*}(y, \hat{y}) = \mathcal{D}_\Psi((\nabla\Psi^*)(\hat{y}), (\nabla\Psi^*)(y)) \ .$$

Proof. By straightforward application of (6) to the definition of $\mathcal{D}_\Psi$ (or $\mathcal{D}_{\Psi^*}$). $\diamond$

Expressions (10) and (11) are formally identical because $(\Psi^*)^* = \Psi$. Hence, either Ψ or Ψ^* can be viewed as the "original" convex function with the other being derived by means of conjugation. Similarly, either $\mathbb{R}^n$ or $(\mathbb{R}^n)^*$ can be viewed as the "original" vector space with the other being its dual space, because $((\mathbb{R}^n)^*)^* = \mathbb{R}^n$. The function subscript in $\mathcal{D}$ specifies the stimulus space ($\mathcal{X}$ or $\mathcal{Y}$) whereas the two function arguments of $\mathcal{D}(\cdot, \cdot)$ are always occupied by (comparison stimulus, reference stimulus), in that order.

2.3.   Properties of psychometric differentials

PROPOSITION 4. *The psychometric differential $\mathcal{D}_\Psi(x, x')$ satisfies the following properties:*

(i) *Non-negativity: For all $x, x' \in \mathcal{X}$,*

$$\mathcal{D}_\Psi(x, x') \geq 0$$

with equality holding if and only if $x = x'$.

(ii) *Conjugacy: For all $x, x' \in \mathcal{X}$,*

$$\mathcal{D}_\Psi(x, x') = \mathcal{D}_{\Psi^*}((\nabla\Psi)(x'), (\nabla\Psi)(x)) .$$

(iii) *Triangle (or generalized cosine) relation: For any three points $x, x', x'' \in \mathcal{X}$,*

$$\mathcal{D}_\Psi(x, x') + \mathcal{D}_\Psi(x', x'') - \mathcal{D}_\Psi(x, x'') = \langle x - x', (\nabla\Psi)(x'') - \nabla\Psi(x') \rangle .$$

(iv) *Quadrilateral relation: For any four points $x, x', x'', x''' \in \mathcal{X}$,*

$$\mathcal{D}_\Psi(x, x') + \mathcal{D}_\Psi(x''', x'') - \mathcal{D}_\Psi(x, x'') - \mathcal{D}_\Psi(x''', x')$$
$$= \langle x - x''', (\nabla\Psi)(x'') - (\nabla\Psi)(x') \rangle .$$

As a special case, when $x''' = x'$ so that $\mathcal{D}_\Psi(x''', x') = 0$, the aforementioned equality reduces to the triangle relation (iii).

(v) *Dual representability: For any two points $x, x' \in \mathcal{X}$,*

$$\mathcal{D}_\Psi(x, x') = \mathcal{A}_\Psi(x, (\nabla\Psi)(x')) = \mathcal{A}_{\Psi^*}((\nabla\Psi^*)^{-1}(x'), x) .$$

This is another statement of the conjugacy relation (ii).

Proof. Parts (ii) and (v) are simply Corollary 3. The proof for parts (iii) and (iv) is through direct substitution. Part (i) is a well-known property of a strictly convex function Ψ. ◇

Note that Proposition 4 can be reformulated and proved for psychometric differentials presented in the $\mathcal{A}$-form, (9). These properties of a psychometric differential make it very different from a norm-induced metric Δ

traditionally used to model dissimilarity between two stimuli (see the Introduction). The non-negativity property for Δ is retained: $\mathcal{D}_\Psi(x, x') \geq 0$ with 0 attained if and only if $x = x'$. However, the symmetry property for Δ is replaced by the bidualistic relation $\mathcal{D}_\Psi(x, x') = \mathcal{D}_{\Psi^*}((\nabla\Psi)(x'), (\nabla\Psi)(x))$ with Ψ^* satisfying $(\Psi^*)^* = \Psi$. In lieu of the triangle inequality for Δ, we have the triangle (generalized cosine) relation for $\mathcal{D}_\Psi$; in this sense $\mathcal{D}_\Psi$ can be viewed as generalizing the notion of a squared distance.

2.4.   Extending to the infinite-dimensional case with conjugate scaling

Let us consider now how to extend the psychometric differentials (10) and (11) that are defined for stimuli in multidimensional vector spaces to stimuli in infinite-dimensional function spaces. A stimulus sometimes may be represented as a function, that is, a point in an infinite-dimensional space of functions. An example is the representation of a human face by means of a function relating grey-level or elevation above a plane of pixels to the two-dimensional coordinates of these pixels (Townsend, Solomon, & Smith, 2001). There, all grey-level or elevation image functions satisfying certain regularity conditions form a function space, and the set X of pixels on which the image functions are defined form a support of the function space on X, which is always measurable. Here we denote functions on X by $p(\zeta), q(\zeta)$ where $p, q : X \to \mathbb{R}$. In the infinite-dimensional space of face-representing functions, p and q are just two different faces defined on the pixel grid X.

To construct psychometric differentials on infinite-dimensional function spaces, we first look at a special case in the multidimensional setting when the stimulus dimensions are "noninteracting," in the following sense:

$$\Psi(x) = \sum_{i=1}^{n} f(x^i) \ .$$

Here f is a smooth, strictly convex function $\mathbb{R} \to \mathbb{R}$. In this case,

$$\nabla\Psi = [f'(x^1), \cdots, f'(x^n)] \ ,$$

where f' is the ordinary derivative. The psychometric differential then becomes

$$\mathcal{D}_\Psi(x, \hat{x}) = \sum_{i=1}^{n} \mathcal{D}_f(\hat{x}^i, x^i) \ ,$$

where

$$\mathcal{D}_f(x^i, \hat{x}^i) = f(x^i) - f(\hat{x}^i) - (x^i - \hat{x}^i)f'(\hat{x}^i)$$

is defined for each individual dimension $i = 1, ..., n$.

Recall that the convex conjugate $f^* : \mathbb{R} \to \mathbb{R}$ of f is defined as

$$f^*(t) = t\,(f')^{-1}(t) - f((f')^{-1}(t)) \,,$$

with $(f^*)^* = f$ and $(f^*)' = (f')^{-1}$. So $\mathcal{D}_f$ possesses all of the properties stated in Proposition 4. In particular,

$$\mathcal{D}_f(x^i, \hat{x}^i) = \mathcal{D}_{f^*}(f'(\hat{x}^i), f'(x^i)) \,.$$

This excursion to the psychometric differential in the noninteracting multidimensional case suggests a way of constructing the psychometric differential in the infinite-dimensional case, that is, by replacing the summation across dimensions with integration over the support X,

$$\mathcal{D}_f(p, q) = \int_X \{f(p(\zeta)) - f(q(\zeta)) - (p(\zeta) - q(\zeta))f'(q(\zeta))\}\,d\mu \,, \qquad (12)$$

where $d\mu \equiv \mu(d\zeta)$ is some measure imposed on X. (Here and later, when dealing with an integral $\int_X (\cdot)d\mu$, we assume that it is finite.) Just like its multidimensional counterpart, $\mathcal{D}_f$ satisfies the bidualistic relation

$$\mathcal{D}_f(p, q) = \mathcal{D}_{f^*}(f'(q), f'(p)) \longleftrightarrow \mathcal{D}_{f^*}(p, q) = \mathcal{D}_f((f')^{-1}(q), (f')^{-1}(p)) \,.$$
$$(13)$$

In its original ($\mathcal{A}$) form (see Section 2.2), the psychometric differential for the infinite-dimensional function space is

$$\mathcal{A}_f(p, q) = \mathcal{D}_f(p, (f')^{-1}(q)) = \mathcal{D}_{f^*}(q, f'(p)) \,,$$

or written explicitly,

$$\mathcal{A}_f(p, q) = \int_X \{f(p(\zeta)) + f^*(q(\zeta)) - p(\zeta)\,q(\zeta)\}\,d\mu \,. \qquad (14)$$

It satisfies

$$\mathcal{A}_f(p, q) = \mathcal{A}_{f^*}(q, p) \,.$$

In the infinite-dimensional case, we have the additional freedom of "scaling" the p, q functions. To be concrete, we need to introduce the notion of *conjugate scaling* of functions $p(\zeta), q(\zeta)$. For a strictly increasing function $\rho : \mathbb{R} \to \mathbb{R}$, we call $\rho(\alpha)$ the *ρ-scaled representation* (of a real number α here). Clearly, a ρ-scaled representation is order invariant. For a smooth, strictly convex function f (with its conjugate f^*), we call the τ-scaled representation (of α) *conjugate* to its ρ-scaled representation with respect to f if

$$\tau(\alpha) = f'(\rho(\alpha)) = ((f^*)')^{-1}(\rho(\alpha)) \longleftrightarrow \rho(\alpha) = (f')^{-1}(\tau(\alpha)) = (f^*)'(\tau(\alpha)) \,.$$
$$(15)$$

In this case, we also say that (ρ, τ) form an *ordered pair* of conjugate scales (with respect to f). Note that any two strictly increasing functions ρ, τ form an ordered pair of conjugate scales for some f. This is because the composite functions $\tau(\rho^{-1}(\cdot))$ and $\rho(\tau^{-1}(\cdot))$, which are mutually inverse, are always strictly increasing, so we may construct a pair of strictly convex and mutually conjugate functions (for some constants c and c^*)

$$f(t) = \int_c^t \tau(\rho^{-1}(s))\, ds$$

and

$$f^*(t) = \int_{c^*}^t \rho(\tau^{-1}(s))\, ds ,$$

to be associated with the (ρ, τ) scale by satisfying (15).

For a function $p(\zeta)$, we can construct a ρ-scaled representation $\rho(p(\zeta))$ and a τ-scaled representation $\tau(p(\zeta))$, denoted for brevity $\rho_p = \rho(p(\zeta))$ and $\tau_p = \tau(p(\zeta))$, respectively; they are both defined on the same support X as is $p(\zeta)$. Similar notations apply to ρ_q, τ_q with respect to the function $q(\zeta)$. With the notion of conjugate scaling, the reference-representation biduality of psychometric differential acquires the form (compare this with (13))

$$\mathcal{D}_f(\rho_p, \rho_q) = \mathcal{D}_{f^*}(\tau_q, \tau_p) .$$

2.5. The psychometric differential as a divergence function

Mathematically, the notion of a psychometric differential on a multidimensional vector space coincides with the so-called "divergence function," also known under various other names, such as "objective function," "loss function," and "contrast function," encountered in contexts entirely different from ours: in the fields of convex optimization, machine learning, and information geometry. In the form $\mathcal{D}_\Psi(x, x')$, the psychometric differential is known as the "Bregman divergence" (Bregman, 1967), an essential quantity in the area of convex optimization (Bauschke, 2003; Bauschke, Borwein, & Combettes, 2003; Bauschke & Combettes, 2003a, 2003b). This form of divergence is also referred to as the "geometric divergence" (Kurose, 1994), due to its significance in the hypersurface realization in affine differential geometric study of statistical manifolds. In its $\mathcal{A}$-form, the psychometric differential coincides with the "canonical divergence" first encountered in the analysis of the exponential family of probability distributions using information-theoretic methods (Amari, 1982, 1985). Henceforth, we will refer to $\mathcal{A}$ as such.[3]

---

[3] In information geometry, $\mathcal{A}$ is called "canonical" because its form is uniquely given in a dually flat space using a pair of biorthogonal coordinates (see Amari &

In the infinite-dimensional case, the psychometric differential in the form (12) is essentially the "U-divergence" recently proposed in the machine learning context (Murata, Takenouchi, Kanamori, & Eguchi, 2004). If we put $f(t) = t \log t - t$ $(t > 0)$, which is strictly convex, then $\mathcal{D}_f(p, q)$ acquires the form of the familiar Kullback-Leibler divergence between two probability densities p and q:

$$K(p,q) = \int_X \left\{ q - p - p \log \frac{q}{p} \right\} d\mu = K^*(q, p) \ . \tag{16}$$

As another example, consider the so-called "α-embedding" (here parameterized with $\lambda = (1 + \alpha)/2$),

$$l^{(\lambda)} = \frac{1}{1 - \lambda} p^{1 - \lambda} \ ,$$

for $\lambda \in (0, 1)$. In this case, one can put

$$f(t) = \frac{1}{\lambda}((1 - \lambda)t)^{\frac{1}{1-\lambda}} \ , \quad f^*(t) = \frac{1}{1 - \lambda}(\lambda t)^{\frac{1}{\lambda}} \ ,$$

so that $\rho(p) = l^{(\lambda)}(p)$ and $\tau(p) = l^{(1-\lambda)}(p)$ form an ordered pair of conjugate scales with respect to f. Under α-embedding, the canonical divergence (14) becomes

$$A^{(\lambda)}(p, q) = \frac{1}{\lambda(1 - \lambda)} \int_X \left\{ (1 - \lambda)p + \lambda q - p^{1-\lambda} q^{\lambda} \right\} d\mu \ . \tag{17}$$

This is an important form of divergence, called "α-divergence" $(\alpha = 2\lambda - 1)$. It is known that the α-divergence reduces to the Kullback-Leibler divergence, (16), when $\lambda \in \{0, 1\}$ as a limiting case.

3. SCALING STIMULUS SPACE BY A FAMILY OF DIVERGENCE FUNCTIONS

The asymmetric divergence functions $\mathcal{D}_\Psi$ (for multidimensional spaces) and $\mathcal{D}_f$ (for infinite-dimensional spaces) investigated in the previous section are induced by smooth and strictly convex (but otherwise arbitrary) functions $\Psi : \mathbb{R}^n \to \mathbb{R}$ in the former case and $f : \mathbb{R} \to \mathbb{R}$ in the latter case. In this

---

Nagaoka, 2000, p. 61). On the other hand, $\mathcal{D}$ is the analogue of the "canonically transformed" psychometric function in the theory of Dzhafarov and Colonius (see Chapter 1 of this volume). One should not confuse these two usages of "canonical."

section, we show that any such Ψ (or f) induces a family of divergence functions that include $\mathcal{D}_\Psi$ (respectively, $\mathcal{D}_f$) as a special case. Although stimuli as vectors in a multidimensional space and stimuli as functions in an infinite-dimensional space are different, when there exists a parametric representation of a function, the divergence functional on the infinite-dimensional function space becomes, through a pullback to the parameter space, a divergence function on the multidimensional vector space.

3.1. Divergence on multidimensional vector space

Consider the vector space $\mathbb{R}^n$ where each point represents a stimulus. Recall that a function Ψ defined on a nonempty, convex set $\mathcal{X} \subseteq \mathbb{R}^n$ is called "strictly convex" if the inequality (4) is satisfied for any two distinct points $x, x' \in \mathcal{X}$ and any real number $\lambda \in (0, 1)$. Also recall that the inequality sign is replaced by equality when (i) $x = x'$, for any $\lambda \in \mathbb{R}$; or (ii) $\lambda \in \{0, 1\}$ for all $x, x' \in \mathcal{X}$.

PROPOSITION 5. *For any smooth, strictly convex function Ψ and any real number λ, the expression*

$$\mathcal{D}_\Psi^{(\lambda)}(x, x') = \frac{1}{\lambda(1-\lambda)} \left((1-\lambda)\Psi(x) + \lambda\Psi(x') - \Psi((1-\lambda)x + \lambda x') \right)$$

defines a parametric family (indexed by $\lambda \in \mathbb{R}$) of divergence functions.

Proof. See Proposition 1 of Zhang (2004a). $\diamond$

Note the asymmetry of each divergence function, $\mathcal{D}_\Psi^{(\lambda)}(x, x') \neq \mathcal{D}_\Psi^{(\lambda)}(x', x)$. At the same time,

$$\mathcal{D}_\Psi^{(\lambda)}(x, x') = \mathcal{D}_\Psi^{(1-\lambda)}(x', x) , \tag{18}$$

indicating that the referential duality (in assigning to x or x' the referent or probe status) is reflected in the $\lambda \leftrightarrow 1 - \lambda$ duality.

Two important special cases are as follows:

$$\lim_{\lambda \to 1} \mathcal{D}_\Psi^{(\lambda)}(x, x') = \mathcal{D}_\Psi(x, x') ,$$

$$\lim_{\lambda \to 0} \mathcal{D}_\Psi^{(\lambda)}(x, x') = \mathcal{D}_\Psi(x', x) .$$

Therefore

$$\mathcal{D}_\Psi^{(1)}(x, x') = \mathcal{D}_{\Psi^*}^{(1)}(\nabla\Psi(x'), \nabla\Psi(x)) = \mathcal{D}_{\Psi^*}^{(0)}(\nabla\Psi(x), \nabla\Psi(x')) = \mathcal{D}_\Psi^{(0)}(x', x) . \tag{19}$$

Here the (convex) conjugate scaled mappings $y = (\nabla\Psi)(x) \leftrightarrow x = (\nabla\Psi^*)(y)$ reflect the representational duality, in the choice of representing the stimulus as a vector in the original vector space $\mathcal{X}$, versus in the dual vector space $\mathcal{Y}$ (the gradient space). The aforementioned equation (19) states very concisely that when $\lambda \in \{0, 1\}$, the referential duality and the representational duality are themselves dualistic — in other words, the canonical divergence functions exhibit the reference-representation biduality.

Note that $\mathcal{D}_\Psi^{(\lambda)}$, as a parametric family of divergence functions that reduces to $\mathcal{D}_\Psi$ as its special case, is not the only family capable of doing so. For instance, we may introduce

$$\tilde{D}_\Psi^{(\lambda)}(x, x') = (1-\lambda)\, \mathcal{D}_\Psi^{(0)}(x, x') + \lambda\, \mathcal{D}_\Psi^{(1)}(x, x') = (1-\lambda)\, \mathcal{D}_\Psi(x', x) + \lambda\, \mathcal{D}_\Psi(x, x') \ .$$

It turns out that these two families of divergence functions $\mathcal{D}_\Psi^{(\lambda)}$ and $\tilde{D}_\Psi^{(\lambda)}$ agree with each other up to the third order in their Taylor expansions in terms of x and y. However, $\mathcal{D}_\Psi^{(\lambda)} \neq \tilde{D}_\Psi^{(\lambda)}$ unless $\lambda \in \{0, 1\}$; the reason lies in the fact that their Taylor expansions differ in the fourth and higher order terms. In particular, the self-dual elements ($\lambda = 1/2$) of those two families differ:

$$\mathcal{D}_\Psi^{(1/2)}(x, x') = 2\left(\Psi(x) + \Psi(x') - 2\Psi\left(\frac{x + x'}{2}\right)\right) ,$$

$$\tilde{D}_\Psi^{(1/2)}(x, x') = \frac{1}{2}\,\langle x - x', (\nabla\Psi)(x) - (\nabla\Psi)(x')\rangle \ .$$

In Section 4 it will be shown that divergence functions induce a Riemannian metric and a pair of conjugate connections. The Riemannian structure induced by $\mathcal{D}_\Psi^{(\lambda)}$ and $\tilde{D}_\Psi^{(\lambda)}$ turns out to be identical.

3.2. Divergence on infinite-dimensional function space

By analogy with (4), in function spaces, we introduce a strictly convex function $f : \mathbb{R} \to \mathbb{R}$, which satisfies

$$(1 - \lambda)f(\alpha) + \lambda f(\beta) > f((1 - \lambda)\,\alpha + \lambda\,\beta)$$

for all $\alpha \neq \beta$. This convex function f allows us to introduce a family of divergence functionals on a function space whose elements are all functions $X \to \mathbb{R}$.

PROPOSITION 6. *Let $p(\zeta), q(\zeta)$ denote two functions on X, $f : \mathbb{R} \to \mathbb{R}$ a smooth, strictly convex function, and $\lambda \in \mathbb{R}$. Then the following expression gives a family of divergence functionals under ρ-scaling*

$$\mathcal{D}_f^{(\lambda)}(\rho_p, \rho_q) = \frac{1}{\lambda(1 - \lambda)} \int_X \{(1-\lambda)\, f(\rho_p) + \lambda\, f(\rho_q) - f((1-\lambda)\,\rho_p + \lambda\rho_q)\}\, d\mu$$

$$\tag{20}$$

where $\rho : \mathbb{R} \to \mathbb{R}$ is a strictly increasing function, $d\mu(\zeta) \equiv \mu(d\zeta)$ is a measure on X.

Proof. This is analogous to Proposition 5, after integration with respect to the support X. ◇

As special cases,

$$\lim_{\lambda \to 1} \mathcal{D}_f^{(\lambda)}(\rho_p, \rho_q) = \mathcal{D}_f(\rho_p, \rho_q) = \mathcal{D}_{f^*}(\tau_q, \tau_p) ,$$

$$\lim_{\lambda \to 0} \mathcal{D}_f^{(\lambda)}(\rho_p, \rho_q) = \mathcal{D}_f(\rho_q, \rho_p) = \mathcal{D}_{f^*}(\tau_p, \tau_q) ,$$

where $\mathcal{D}_f$ is given in (12). The reference-representation biduality here can be presented as

$$\mathcal{D}_f^{(1)}(\rho_p, \rho_q) = \mathcal{D}_f^{(0)}(\rho_q, \rho_p) = \mathcal{D}_{f^*}^{(1)}(\tau_q, \tau_p)$$
$$= \mathcal{D}_{f^*}^{(0)}(\tau_p, \tau_q) = \mathcal{A}_f(\rho_p, \tau_q) = \mathcal{A}_{f^*}(\tau_q, \rho_p) .$$

An example of $\mathcal{D}_f^{(\lambda)}$ is the α-divergence (17), $\lambda = (1 + \alpha)/2$. Putting $\rho(t) = \log t$, $f(t) = e^t$, and hence $\tau(t) = t$, it is easily seen that the functional (20) reduces to (17).

3.3. Connection between the multidimensional and infinite-dimensional cases

When the functions $p(\cdot), q(\cdot)$ in Proposition 6 belong to a parametric family $h(\cdot|\theta)$ with $\theta = [\theta^1, \cdots, \theta^n]$, so that $p(\zeta) = h(\zeta|\theta_p)$, $q(\zeta) = h(\zeta|\theta_q)$, the divergence *functional* taking in functions p, q as its arguments can be viewed as a divergence *function* of their parametric representation θ_p, θ_q. In other words, through parameterizing the functions representing stimuli, we arrive at a divergence function over a multidimensional vector space. We now investigate conditions under which this divergence function have the same form as that stated in Proposition 5.

PROPOSITION 7. *Let $f : \mathbb{R} \to \mathbb{R}$ be strictly convex, and (ρ, τ) be an ordered pair of conjugate scales with respect to f. Suppose the ρ-scaled representation $\rho(h(\zeta)) \equiv \rho_h(\zeta)$ of the stimulus function $h(\zeta)$, $\zeta \in X$, can be represented as*

$$\rho_h = \langle \theta, \lambda(\zeta) \rangle , \tag{21}$$

where $\lambda(\zeta) = [\lambda_1(\zeta), \cdots, \lambda_n(\zeta)]$, with its components representing n linearly independent basis functions, and $\theta = [\theta^1, \cdots, \theta^n]$ is a vector whose components are real numbers. Then

(i) *the function*

$$\Psi(\theta) = \int_X f(\rho_h) \, d\mu$$

is strictly convex;

(ii) *denote* $\eta = [\eta_1, \cdots, \eta_n]$ *as the projection of the τ-scaled representation of $h(\zeta)$, $\tau(h(\zeta)) \equiv \tau_h(\zeta)$, on $\lambda(\zeta)$,*

$$\eta = \int_X \tau_h \, \lambda(\zeta) \, d\mu \, , \tag{22}$$

and denote

$$\tilde{\Psi}(\theta) = \int_X f^*(\tau_h) \, d\mu \, ,$$

then the function $\tilde{\Psi}((\nabla\Psi)^{-1}(\cdot)) \equiv \Psi^*(\cdot)$ is the convex conjugate of $\Psi(\cdot)$;

(iii) *the θ and η parameters are related to each other via*

$$(\nabla\Psi)(\theta) = \eta \, , \quad (\nabla\Psi^*)(\eta) = \theta \, ;$$

(iv) *the divergence functionals $\mathcal{D}_f^{(\lambda)}$ becomes the divergence functions $\mathcal{D}_\Psi^{(\lambda)}$,*

$$\mathcal{D}_f^{(\lambda)}(\rho_p, \rho_q) = \mathcal{D}_\Psi^{(\lambda)}(\theta_p, \theta_q) \, ;$$

(v) *the canonical divergence functional $\mathcal{A}_f$ becomes the canonical divergence function $\mathcal{A}_\Psi$,*

$$\mathcal{A}_f(\rho_p, \tau_q) = \Psi(\theta_p) + \Psi^*(\eta_q) - \langle \theta_p, \eta_q \rangle = \mathcal{A}_\Psi(\theta_p, \eta_q) \, .$$

Proof. Parts (iv) and (v) are natural consequences of part (i), by substituting the expression of $\Phi(\theta)$ for the corresponding term in the definition of $\mathcal{D}$ and $\mathcal{A}$. Parts (i) to (iii) were proved in Proposition 9 of Zhang (2004a).◇

The parameter θ in $h(\cdot|\theta)$ can be viewed as the "natural parameter" (borrowing the terminology from statistics) of parameterized functions representing stimuli. In information geometry, it is well known that an exponential family of density functions can also be parameterized by means of the "expectation parameter," which is dual to the natural parameter; this is our parameter η here. We have thus generalized the duality between the natural parameter and the expectation parameter from the exponential family to stimuli under arbitrary ρ- and τ-embeddings. Proposition 7 specifies the sufficient condition, (21), under which we can use one of the vectors, θ (natural parameter) or η (expectation parameter), to represent an individual stimulus function $h(\zeta)$, and under which the pullback of $\mathcal{D}_f^{(\lambda)}(\rho(\cdot), \rho(\cdot))$ and $\mathcal{D}_{f^*}^{(\lambda)}(\tau(\cdot), \tau(\cdot))$ in the multidimensional parameter space gives rise to the form of divergence functions presented by Proposition 5.

4.   BIDUALISTIC RIEMANNIAN STRUCTURE OF STIMULUS MANIFOLDS

A divergence function, while measuring distance of two points in the large, induces a dually symmetric Riemannian structure in the small with a metric g and a pair of conjugate connections Γ, Γ^*. They are given by what we refer to here as the *Eguchi relations* (Eguchi, 1983, 1992):

$$g_{ij}(x) = -\left.\frac{\partial^2 \mathcal{D}_{\Psi}^{(\lambda)}(x', x'')}{\partial x'^i \partial x''^j}\right|_{x'=x''=x} , \qquad (23)$$

$$\Gamma_{ij,k}^{(\lambda)}(x) = -\left.\frac{\partial^3 \mathcal{D}_{\Psi}^{(\lambda)}(x', x'')}{\partial x'^i \partial x'^j \partial x''^k}\right|_{x'=x''=x} , \qquad (24)$$

$$\Gamma_{ij,k}^{*(\lambda)}(x) = -\left.\frac{\partial^3 \mathcal{D}_{\Psi}^{(\lambda)}(x', x'')}{\partial x''^i \partial x''^j \partial x'^k}\right|_{x'=x''=x} . \qquad (25)$$

Later, we explicitly give the Riemannian metric and the pair of conjugate connections induced by the divergence functions $\mathcal{D}_{\Psi}^{(\lambda)}$ and the divergence functionals $\mathcal{D}_{f}^{(\lambda)}$.

4.1.   Riemannian structure on multidimensional vector space

In the proposition to follow, $\Psi_{ij}(x)$, $\Psi_{ijk}(x)$ denote, respectively, second and third partial derivatives of $\Psi(x)$,

$$\Psi_{ij}(x) = \frac{\partial^2 \Psi(x)}{\partial x^i \partial x^j} , \qquad \Psi_{ijk}(x) = \frac{\partial^3 \Psi(x)}{\partial x^i \partial x^j \partial x^k} ,$$

and $\Psi^{ij}(x)$ is the matrix inverse of $\Psi_{ij}(x)$.

PROPOSITION 8. *The divergence functions* $\mathcal{D}_{\Psi}^{(\lambda)}(x, x')$ *induce on the stimulus manifold a metric* g *and a pair of conjugate connections* $\Gamma^{(\lambda)}, \Gamma^{*(\lambda)}$ *with*

(i) *the metric tensor given by*

$$g_{ij}(x) = \Psi_{ij}(x) ;$$

(ii) *the conjugate connections given by*

$$\Gamma_{ij,k}^{(\lambda)}(x) = (1 - \lambda)\,\Psi_{ijk}(x) , \qquad \Gamma_{ij,k}^{*(\lambda)}(x) = \lambda\,\Psi_{ijk}(x) ;$$

(iii) *the Riemann-Christoffel curvature for the connection* $\Gamma_{ij,k}^{(\lambda)}$ *given by*

$$R_{ij\mu\nu}^{(\lambda)}(x) = \lambda(1-\lambda)\sum_{l,k}(\Psi_{il\nu}(x)\Psi_{jk\mu}(x) - \Psi_{il\mu}(x)\Psi_{jk\nu}(x))\Psi^{lk}(x) \ .$$

Proof. The proof for parts (i) and (ii) and for part (iii) follows, respectively, those in Proposition 2 and in Proposition 3 of Zhang (2004a). ◇

According to Proposition 8, the metric tensor g_{ij}, which is symmetric and positive semidefinite due to the strict convexity of Ψ, is independent of λ, whereas the affine connections are λ-dependent, satisfying the dualistic relation

$$\Gamma_{ij,k}^{*(\lambda)}(x) = \Gamma_{ij,k}^{(1-\lambda)}(x) \ . \tag{26}$$

When $\lambda = 1/2$, the self-conjugate connection $\Gamma^{(1/2)} = \Gamma^{*(1/2)} \equiv \Gamma^{LC}$ is the Levi-Civita connection, related to the metric tensor by

$$\Gamma_{ij,k}^{(1/2)}(x) = \Gamma_{ij,k}^{LC}(x) \equiv \frac{1}{2}\left(\frac{\partial g_{ik}(x)}{\partial x^j} + \frac{\partial g_{kj}(x)}{\partial x^i} - \frac{\partial g_{ij}(x)}{\partial x^k}\right) \ .$$

For any λ, the mutually conjugate connections $\Gamma_{ij,k}^{(\lambda)}$ and $\Gamma_{ij,k}^{(1-\lambda)}$ satisfy the relation

$$\frac{1}{2}\left(\Gamma_{ij,k}^{(\lambda)}(x) + \Gamma_{ij,k}^{(1-\lambda)}(x)\right) = \Gamma_{ij,k}^{LC}(x) \ .$$

When $\lambda \in \{0,1\}$, all components of the Riemann-Christoffel curvature tensor vanish, in which case $\Gamma_{ij,k}^{(0)}(x) = 0 \leftrightarrow \Gamma_{ij,k}^{*(1)}(x) = 0$, or $\Gamma_{ij,k}^{(1)}(x) = 0 \leftrightarrow \Gamma_{ij,k}^{*(0)}(x) = 0$. The manifold in these cases is said to be "dually flat" (Amari, 1985; Amari & Nagaoka, 2000) and the divergence functions defined on it is the unique, canonical divergence studied in Sections 2.2 and 2.3.

Note that the referential duality exhibited by the divergence functions $\mathcal{D}_{\Psi}^{(\lambda)}$, (18), is reflected in the conjugacy of the affine connections $\Gamma \leftrightarrow \Gamma^*$, (26). On the other hand, the one-to-one mapping $y = (\nabla\Psi)(x) \leftrightarrow x = (\nabla\Psi^*)(y)$ between the space $\mathcal{X}$ and its dual $\mathcal{Y}$ indicates that we may view $x \in \mathcal{X}$ and $y \in \mathcal{Y}$ as two coordinate representations for one and the same underlying manifold. Later, we investigate this representational duality. We will relate the Riemannian structures (metric, dual connnections, Riemann-Christoffel curvature) expressed in x and in y.

PROPOSITION 9. *Denote the Riemannian metric, the connection, and the Riemann-Christoffel curvature tensor induced by* $\mathcal{D}_{\Psi^*}^{(\lambda)}(y, y')$ *as, respectively,* $\tilde{g}^{mn}(y)$, $\tilde{\Gamma}^{(\lambda)mn,l}(y)$, *and* $\tilde{R}^{(\lambda)klmn}(y)$, *whereas the analogous quantities without the tilde sign are induced by* $\mathcal{D}_{\Psi}^{(\lambda)}(x, x')$, *as in Proposition 8. Then, as long as*

$$y = (\nabla\Psi)(x) \longleftrightarrow x = (\nabla\Psi^*)(y) \ ,$$

(i) *the metric tensors are related as*

$$\sum_l g_{il}(x)\tilde{g}^{ln}(y) = \delta_i^n \; ;$$

(ii) *the affine connections are related as*

$$\tilde{\Gamma}^{(\lambda)mn,l}(y) = -\sum_{i,j,k} \tilde{g}^{im}(y)\tilde{g}^{jn}(y)\tilde{g}^{kl}(y)\Gamma_{ij,k}^{(\lambda)}(x) \; ;$$

(iii) *the Riemann-Christoffel curvatures are related as*

$$\tilde{R}^{(\lambda)klmn}(y) = \sum_{i,j,\mu,\nu} \tilde{g}^{ik}(y)\tilde{g}^{jl}(y)\tilde{g}^{\mu m}(y)\tilde{g}^{\nu n}(y)R_{ij\mu\nu}^{(\lambda)}(x) \; .$$

Proof. See Proposition 5 of Zhang (2004a). ⋄

4.2. Riemannian structure on infinite-dimensional function space

Similar to the multidimensional case, we can compute the Riemannian geometry of the stimulus manifold for the infinite-dimensional (function space) case. For ease of comparison, we assume here that the stimulus functions $h(\zeta)$ have a parametric representation $h(\zeta|\theta)$, so strictly speaking, "infinite-dimensional space" is a misnomer.

PROPOSITION 10. *The family of divergence functions* $\mathcal{D}_f^{(\lambda)}(\rho(h(\cdot|\theta_p)),$ $\rho(h(\cdot|\theta_q)))$ *induce a Riemannian structure on the stimulus manifold for each* $\lambda \in \mathbb{R}$, *with*

(i) *the metric tensor given as*

$$g_{ij}(\theta) = \int_X \left\{ f''(\rho(h(\zeta|\theta))) \frac{\partial \rho(h(\zeta|\theta))}{\partial \theta^i} \frac{\partial \rho(h(\zeta|\theta))}{\partial \theta^j} \right\} d\mu \; ;$$

(ii) *the conjugate connections given as*

$$\Gamma_{ij,k}^{(\lambda)}(\theta) = \int_X \{(1-\lambda)\, f'''(\rho(h(\zeta|\theta)))\, A_{ijk}(\zeta|\theta)$$
$$+ f''(\rho(h(\zeta|\theta)))\, B_{ijk}(\zeta|\theta)\}\, d\mu \; ,$$
$$\Gamma_{ij,k}^{*(\lambda)}(\theta) = \int_X \{\lambda\, f'''(\rho(h(\zeta|\theta)))\, A_{ijk}(\zeta|\theta)$$
$$+ f''(\rho(h(\zeta|\theta)))\, B_{ijk}(\zeta|\theta)\}\, d\mu \; .$$

Here A_{ijk}, B_{ijk} denote

$$A_{ijk}(\zeta|\theta) = \frac{\partial \rho(h(\zeta|\theta))}{\partial \theta^i} \frac{\partial \rho(h(\zeta|\theta))}{\partial \theta^j} \frac{\partial \rho(h(\zeta|\theta))}{\partial \theta^k},$$

$$B_{ijk}(\zeta|\theta) = \frac{\partial^2 \rho(h(\zeta|\theta))}{\partial \theta^i \partial \theta^j} \frac{\partial \rho(h(\zeta|\theta))}{\partial \theta^k}.$$

Proof. The proof is by straightforward application of (23) to (25). See Proposition 7 of Zhang (2004a) for details. ◇

Note that the strict convexity of f implies $f'' > 0$, and thereby guarantees the positive semidefiniteness of g_{ij}. Clearly, the conjugate connections satisfy $\Gamma_{ijk}^{*(\lambda)}(\theta) = \Gamma_{ijk}^{(1-\lambda)}(\theta)$, and hence reflect referential duality.

As a special case, if we set $f(t) = e^t$ and $\rho(t) = \log t$, then Proposition 10 gives the Fisher information metric

$$\int_X \left\{ h(\zeta|\theta) \frac{\partial \log(h(\zeta|\theta))}{\partial \theta^i} \frac{\partial \log(h(\zeta|\theta))}{\partial \theta^j} \right\} d\mu,$$

and the α-connections associated with the α-divergence mentioned earlier (with $\alpha = 2\lambda - 1$):

$$\int_X \left\{ h(\zeta|\theta) \left((1-\lambda) \frac{\partial \log h(\zeta|\theta)}{\partial \theta^i} \frac{\partial \log h(\zeta|\theta)}{\partial \theta^j} + \frac{\partial^2 \log h(\zeta|\theta)}{\partial \theta^i \partial \theta^j} \right) \right.$$
$$\left. \times \frac{\partial \log h(\zeta|\theta)}{\partial \theta^k} \right\} d\mu.$$

Therefore, the Riemannian structure derived here generalizes the core concepts of classic parametric information geometry as summarized in Amari (1985) and Amari and Nagaoka (2000).

For the next proposition, recall the notion of conjugate scaling of functions we introduced in Section 2.4.

PROPOSITION 11. *Under conjugate ρ- and τ-scaling (with respect to some strictly convex function f),*

(i) *the metric tensor is given by*

$$g_{ij}(\theta) = \int_X \left\{ \frac{\partial \rho(h(\zeta|\theta))}{\partial \theta^i} \frac{\partial \tau(h(\zeta|\theta))}{\partial \theta^j} \right\} d\mu$$
$$= \int_X \left\{ \frac{\partial \tau(h(\zeta|\theta))}{\partial \theta^i} \frac{\partial \rho(h(\zeta|\theta))}{\partial \theta^j} \right\} d\mu;$$

(ii) *the conjugate connections are given by*

$$\Gamma_{ij,k}^{(\lambda)}(\theta) = \int_X \left\{ (1-\lambda) \frac{\partial^2 \tau(h(\zeta|\theta))}{\partial \theta^i \partial \theta^j} \frac{\partial \rho(h(\zeta|\theta))}{\partial \theta^k} \right.$$
$$\left. +\lambda \frac{\partial^2 \rho(h(\zeta|\theta))}{\partial \theta^i \partial \theta^j} \frac{\partial \tau(h(\zeta|\theta))}{\partial \theta^k} \right\} d\mu ,$$

$$\Gamma_{ij,k}^{*(\lambda)}(\theta) = \int_X \left\{ \lambda \frac{\partial^2 \tau(h(\zeta|\theta))}{\partial \theta^i \partial \theta^j} \frac{\partial \rho(h(\zeta|\theta))}{\partial \theta^k} \right.$$
$$\left. +(1-\lambda) \frac{\partial^2 \rho(h(\zeta|\theta))}{\partial \theta^i \partial \theta^j} \frac{\partial \tau(h(\zeta|\theta))}{\partial \theta^k} \right\} d\mu .$$

Proof. See Proposition 8 of Zhang (2004a). ◇

Proposition 11 casts the metric and conjugate connections in dualistic forms with respect to any pair of conjugate scales (ρ, τ). This leads to the following corollary.

COROLLARY 12. *The metric tensor $\tilde{g}_{ij}$ and the dual affine connection $\tilde{\Gamma}_{ij,k}^{(\lambda)}, \tilde{\Gamma}_{ij,k}^{*(\lambda)}$ induced on the stimulus manifold by the divergence functions $\mathcal{D}_{f^*}^{(\lambda)}(\tau(h(\cdot|\theta_p)), \tau(h(\cdot|\theta_q)))$ are related to, respectively, g_{ij}, $\Gamma_{ij,k}^{(\lambda)}$, and $\Gamma_{ij,k}^{*(\lambda)}$ induced by $\mathcal{D}_f^{(\lambda)}(\rho(h(\cdot|\theta_p)), \rho(h(\cdot|\theta_q)))$ as*

$$\tilde{g}_{ij}(\theta) = g_{ij}(\theta) ,$$

with

$$\tilde{\Gamma}_{ij,k}^{(\lambda)}(\theta) = \Gamma_{ij,k}^{*(\lambda)}(\theta) , \qquad \tilde{\Gamma}_{ij,k}^{*(\lambda)}(\theta) = \Gamma_{ij,k}^{(\lambda)}(\theta) .$$

Proof. See Corollary 3 of Zhang (2004a). ◇

Combining Proposition 11 with Corollary 12, we get

$$\Gamma_{ij,k}^{*(\lambda)}(\theta) = \tilde{\Gamma}_{ij,k}^{(\lambda)}(\theta) .$$

This is the *reference-representation biduality* for the Riemannian structure of an infinite-dimensional stimulus space (after parameterization).

4.3. Connection between the multidimensional and infinite-dimensional cases

We have shown in Proposition 7 that when (21) holds, the divergence functionals $\mathcal{D}_f^{(\lambda)}$ become the divergence functions $\mathcal{D}_\psi^{(\lambda)}$ on the finite-dimensional parameter space. This correspondence also holds for the Riemannian geometries they induce.

PROPOSITION 13. *Under representation (21), the metric tensor and the conjugate connections on a stimulus manifold as given by Proposition 10, acquire the form given in Proposition 8:*

$$g_{ij}(\theta) = \frac{\partial^2 \Psi(\theta)}{\partial\theta^i \partial\theta^j} , \qquad \Gamma_{ij,k}^{(\lambda)}(\theta) = (1-\lambda)\frac{\partial^3 \Psi(\theta)}{\partial\theta^i \partial\theta^j \partial\theta^k} , \qquad \Gamma_{ij,k}^{*(\lambda)}(\theta) = \lambda\frac{\partial^3 \Psi(\theta)}{\partial\theta^i \partial\theta^j \partial\theta^k} .$$

Proof. See Proposition 9 of Zhang (2004a). ⋄

According to Proposition 7, θ and η are mutually orthogonal coordinates. They are related to the covariant and contravariant representations of the metric tensor (see Proposition 9):

$$\frac{\partial\eta_i}{\partial\theta^j} = g_{ij}(\theta) , \qquad \frac{\partial\theta^i}{\partial\eta_j} = \tilde{g}^{ij}(\eta) .$$

5. SUMMARY AND DISCUSSION

Understanding the intrinsic asymmetry during referent-probe comparisons was the motivation for this exposition. It was our goal to find a proper mathematical formalism to express the asymmetric difference between a reference stimulus (referent) and a comparison stimulus (probe) in such a way that the assignment of the referent-probe status itself can be "arbitrarily made." This is to say, subject to a change of the representation ("scaling") of the two stimuli, the roles of the reference and the comparison stimuli in expressing the asymmetric difference are "exchangeable" within the formalism. This was the kind of duality we were looking for, namely, to account for the referent-probe asymmetry by scaling the stimulus representations.

To this end, we have made use of some tools in convex analysis and differential geometry. We characterized the asymmetric distance between a reference stimulus and a comparison stimulus by proposing a dually symmetric psychometric differential function measuring the directed difference between them. The principle of regular cross-minimality (Axiom 1) allowed us to establish a one-to-one mapping between the two stimulus spaces. Further requiring the mapping to be symmetric with positive-definite Jacobian (Axiom 2) led to (convex) conjugate scaled representations of these mappings. Making full use of the machineries of convex analysis, we constructed a family of psychometric differentials between any two points (one as referent and one as probe) based on the fundamental inequality of a convex function. The family of psychometric differentials is indexed by the parameter $\lambda \in \mathbb{R}$, with $\lambda \in \{0, 1\}$ cases specializing to the canonical divergence which satisfy the reference-representation biduality (Axiom 3). So what we have accomplished here is to show the convex conjugation (under Legendre transformation) to be the precise mathematical expression of the representational duality and the convex mixture coefficient as expressing the referential duality. We also showed that this kind of biduality — referential duality and representational duality — is fundamentally coupled in defining the Riemannian geometry (metric, connection, curvature, etc.) of the stimulus manifold. The referential duality is revealed as the conjugacy of the connection pair, whereas the representational duality is revealed as the choice of the contravariant and covariant form of a vector to represent the stimulus (for the multidimensional case), or as the choice from a pair of monotone transformations ρ, τ to "scale" the stimulus function (for the infinite-dimensional case).

Throughout our investigation of dual scaling of the stimulus space, in terms of either the psychometric differential (divergence function) in the large or the resultant Riemannian geometry in the small, our treatment has been both in the multidimensional vector space setting and in the infinite-dimensional function space setting. Through an appropriate affine submanifold embedding, namely (21), the infinite-dimensional forms of the divergence measure and of the geometry reduce to the corresponding multidimensional forms. Submanifold embedding not only provides a unified view of duality independent of whether stimuli are defined in the multidimensional space or in the infinite-dimensional space, but also is a window for more intuitive understanding of the kind of dual Riemannian geometry (involving conjugate connections) studied here. It is known in affine differential geometry (Nomizu & Sasaki, 1994; Simon, Schwenk-Schellschmidt, & Viesel, 1991) that conjugate connections arise from characterizing the different ways that hypersurfaces can be embedded into a higher dimensional space. Future research will elaborate how these geometric intuitions may be applied to the bona fide infinite-dimensional function space as well (not merely the parameterized version as done here), and explain how referential duality and representational duality become dualistic themselves.

References

Amari, S. (1982). Differential geometry of curved exponential families — Curvatures and information loss. *Annals of Statistics*, 10, 357-385.

Amari, S. (1985). *Differential geometric methods in statistics* (Lecture Notes in Statistics), 28, New York: Springer-Verlag.

Amari, S., & Nagaoka, H. (2000). *Method of information geometry* (AMS monograph). New York: Oxford University Press.

Bauschke, H. H. (2003). Duality for Bregman projections onto translated cones and affine subspaces. *Journal of Approximation Theory*, 121, 1-12.

Bauschke, H. H., Borwein, J. M., & Combettes, P. L. (2003). Bregman monotone optimization algorithms. *SIAM Journal on Control and Optimization*, 42, 596-636.

Bauschke, H. H. & Combettes, P. L. (2003a). Construction of best Bregman approximations in reflexive Banach spaces. *Proceedings of the American Mathematical Society*, 131, 3757-3766.

Bauschke, H. H. & Combettes, P. L. (2003b). Iterating Bregman retractions. *SIAM Journal on Optimization*, 13, 1159-1173.

Bregman, L. M. (1967). The relaxation method of finding the common point of convex sets and its application to the solution of problems in convex programming. *USSR Computational Mathematics and Physics*, 7, 200-217.

Dzhafarov, E. N. (2002). Multidimensional Fechnerian scaling, pairwise comparisons, regular minimality, and nonconstant self-similarity. *Journal of Mathematical Psychology*, 46, 583-608.

Dzhafarov, E. N., & Colonius, H. (1999). Fechnerian metrics in unidimensional and multidimensional stimulus spaces. *Psychological Bulletin and Review*, 6, 239-268.

Dzhafarov, E. N., & Colonius, H. (2001). Multidimensional Fechnerian scaling: Basics. *Journal of Mathematical Psychology*, 45, 670-719.

Dzhafarov, E. N., & Colonius, H. (2005a). Psychophysics without physics: A purely psychological theory of Fechnerian Scaling in continuous stimulus spaces. *Journal of Mathematical Psychology*, 49, 1-50.

Dzhafarov, E. N., & Colonius, H. (2005b). Psychophysics without physics: Extension of Fechnerian Scaling from continuous to discrete and discrete-continuous stimulus spaces. *Journal of Mathematical Psychology*, 49, 125-141.

Eguchi, S. (1983). Second order efficiency of minimum contrast estimators in a curved exponential family. *Annals of Statistics*, 11, 793-803.

Eguchi, S. (1992). Geometry of minimum contrast. *Hiroshima Mathematical Journal*, 22, 631-647.

Kurose, T. (1994). On the divergences of 1-conformally flat statistical manifolds. *Tōhoko Mathematical Journal*, 46, 427-433.

Murata, N., Takenouchi, T., Kanamori, T., & Eguchi, S. (2004). Information geometry of U-boost and Bregman divergence. *Neural Computation*, 16, 1437-1481.

Nomizu, K., & Sasaki, T. (1994). *Affine differential geometry*. Cambridge, UK: Cambridge University Press.

Roberts, A. W., & Varberg, D. E. (1973). *Convex functions*. New York: Academic.

Rockafellar, R. T. (1970). *Convex analysis*. Princeton, NJ: Princeton University Press.

Shepard, R. N. (1962a). The analysis of proximities, multidimensional scaling with an unknown distance function. I. *Psychometrika*, 27, 125-140.

Shepard, R. N. (1962b). The analysis of proximities, multidimensional scaling with an unknown distance function. II. *Psychometrika*, 27, 219-246.

Simon, U., Schwenk-Schellschmidt, A., & Viesel, H. (1991). *Introduction to the affine differential geometry of hypersurfaces*. Tokyo: Science University of Tokyo.

Townsend, J. T., Solomon, B., & Smith, J. S. (2001). The perfect Gestalt, Infinite dimensional Riemannian face spaces and other aspects of face perception. In M. J. Wenger, & J. T. Townsend (Eds), *Computational, geometric, and process perspectives of facial cognition, contexts and challenges* (pp 39-82). Mahwah, NJ: Lawrence Erlbaum Associates, Inc.

Tversky, A. (1977). Features of similarity. *Psychological Review*, 84, 327-352.

Zhang, J. (2004a). Divergence function, duality, and convex analysis. *Neural Computation*, 16, 159-195.

Zhang, J. (2004b). Dual scaling between comparison and reference stimuli in multidimensional psychological space. *Journal of Mathematical Psychology*, 48, 409-424.

5

Objective Analysis of Classification Behavior: Applications to Scaling

J. D. Balakrishnan

California Center for Perception and Decision Sciences

1. INTRODUCTION

Most psychophysical models are empirically testable only when expressed as a probability space or class of probability spaces, that is, as elementary events and their associated probabilities or probability densities. Within a given experimental milieu, the model attempts to reproduce the probability spaces defined by observable events (or some aspects of the space) by postulating certain unobservable events that "explain" or "give rise to" the behavior. To the extent that the fit between data and model spaces is deemed acceptable, the model is judged to be worthy of further interest and research.

In general, a model is only formulated because the spaces defined by the experiments are relatively "sparse" by themselves, leaving unanswered some important questions about the causes of the behavior. Models make it possible to answer virtually any question about the cognition supporting behavior. The problem, of course, is that there is no guarantee that the answers the models provide are correct in any meaningful sense at all. At least in this respect, their value to the field is subjective.

Recently, we proposed an alternative to the model-building approach that is strictly limited to estimating observable probabilities and considering their implications (Balakrishnan & MacDonald, 2004). We call this an *objective method of analysis*. Instead of estimating model parameters, properties of unobservable probability spaces (cognition) are logically inferred from properties of observable probability spaces, by taking advantage of certain relations that can be shown to hold between the two. Of course, the term *objective* does not mean atheoretical. The notion of a probability space is, after all, a theoretical construct – in this respect, the objective method is theory-based. Moreover, not all (probably not even most) questions can be addressed in an objective manner. However, until the approach is attempted, it is impossible to know whether modeling techniques can be properly justified.

In this chapter, we consider how this objective approach might be applied to the issues of psychophysical scaling. The first section briefly reviews the scaling problem and the motives we ascribe to it. We then introduce the basic concepts of the objective method when applied to a comparative judgment experiment. Three objective analyses are proposed, examining the following:

- the effects of suboptimality and bias of the decision rule (defined as a property of a probability space) on the amount of asymmetry in a comparison matrix.
- decomposition of a subjective confidence report into perceived prior and a posteriori probabilities.
- the information value of one aspect of a stimulus (e.g., the "standard object") under variations of another aspect of the stimulus (e.g., the "comparison object") – in other words, an objective psychophysical scale.

2. SCALING OBJECTIVES

Psychophysical scales can be constructed in different ways and with different purposes. In this chapter, the scales to be defined are observable properties of behavior – that is, probabilities in an observable probability space or probabilities in an unobservable probability space that can be logically inferred from probabilities in an observable space. In this sense, they are non-falsifiable descriptions of behavior. The point of the scaling analysis, therefore, is not to test the hypotheses of a specific behavioral theory or class of theories, but instead to discover interesting relations (e.g., invariances of some kind) between physical dimensions of stimuli and their effects on behavior. If the objective method reveals no interesting relations between stimuli and the properties of a probability space, the results are not invalidated, since they are merely descriptions of the space. However, because it seems unlikely that no interesting relations exist, failure to find them would suggest that the specific objective methods being applied to the data are inadequate, and, if possible, need to be strengthened in some way.

It is also important to recognize that even if this objective method can successfully recover some interesting invariances between stimuli and behavior, it could never replace behavioral theorizing, for at least two reasons.

First, behavioral theories provide a basis for formulating the questions that objective methods may seek to answer – it is difficult if not impossible to think entirely in terms of stimulus conditions and their effects on probability spaces. Second, once an objective result is documented, it is always possible – and usually worthwhile – to ask what implications this result might have for current theories.

3.   The Objective Method: Definitions and Experimental Design

The outcome of a typical behavioral experiment can be expressed as a data table, each row representing the outcome of an individual trial and each column one of the different measures recorded by the experimenter on each trial. Although some of these measures may represent theoretically continuous quantities (e.g., response time), in practice each of them will be discrete (if for no other reason, due to the accuracy limitations of the recording instrument). For the same reasons, the measures will have a lower and upper bound.

We will assume that the experiment is repeatable and that its measures induce a probability space, Γ_1. The elementary events of Γ_1 are the individual lists (the different possible data tables) that could be produced by the experiment. because the measures are discrete and bounded, the sample space has a finite or countably infinite number of elements, depending on how the sample size (the number of trials) of the experiment is determined (i.e., whether the design stipulates it to be a constant or a random variable).

Assuming that a single, random sample is taken from the set of trials observed in a single experiment, another probability space is defined, Γ_2, in which the elementary events are the outcomes of individual trials. This space is more important for us, because the questions we will address will refer to behavior on a single trial rather than a set of trials. The reason for specifically distinguishing the two spaces will become clear later, when we consider what inferences about Γ_1 can be drawn from properties of Γ_2.

3.1.   Classification Tasks

Although the objective method is not logically restricted to any specific class of experimental designs, the results developed in Balakrishnan and MacDonald (2004) and the extensions reported here are mostly limited to classification tasks, defined as follows:

– one of the columns (or some subset of columns) of the data table uniquely identifies the stimulus category, S, where $S = A$ or $S = B$.

- another column (or subset of columns) uniquely identifies the participant's classification (category) response, R, where $R = A$ or $R = B$.
- the classification response is either correct or incorrect on each trial.
Trials in which the response cannot be dubbed correct or incorrect
(e.g., the participant does not respond or the stimulus is not correctly
classified by any of the permissible classification responses) may simply
be ignored. In such cases, however, the interpretation of the results of
the objective tests may need to take this fact into account.

3.2.   The Comparative Judgment Design

We will also assume that there are only two stimulus categories, $S = A$ and
$S = B$, equally likely on each trial, and two classification responses, $R = A$
and $R = B$. Most of the results to be presented generalize easily to unequal
priors and arbitrarily large stimulus and classification response sets. The
only exceptions are the methods specifically tied to scaling of stimuli in a
comparative judgment task, which can be defined as follows:

- the stimulus is identified by the values of two columns, S_1 and S_2.
- S_1 and S_2 are independent random variables uniformly distributed over
the integer values from 1 to n. Thus, in the space Γ_2, $p(S_1 > S_2) =$
$p(S_1 < S_2) = \frac{1}{2}$, that is, the prior probabilities of the two stimulus
categories are equal.
- on a given trial, the response, $R = A$ is correct if and only if $S_1 > S_2$,
and the response $R = B$ is correct if and only if $S_1 < S_2$.
- on the "equal trials," $S_1 S_2$, the classification response is neither correct
nor incorrect – in most of the analyses, these trials are ignored.

When the two aspects of the stimulus that determine which classification
response is correct, S_1 and S_2, represent two physical objects presented in a
temporal sequence, S_1 identifies the first object presented and S_2 identifies
the second object presented.

3.3.   Confidence Ratings

The minimum set of measures needed to define a classification task, the
stimulus, S, and the classification response, R, rarely provide enough information about the participant's behavior to answer interesting questions in
objective terms. The two most common additional measures, response time
and confidence, both greatly increase the possibilities for discovery, and are
generally easy to incorporate into the design. Most of our discussion focuses
on response confidence.

In the ratings paradigm from signal detection theory (Green & Swets,
1974), the participant's integer rating response on a bipolar integer scale

replaces the explicit classification response R. One extreme of the scale represents high confidence that the stimulus was a signal ($S = A$) and the other high confidence that the stimulus was noise ($S = B$). For the data from such a design to be a proper classification task, an explicit cutoff between the two possible classification responses must be stipulated somewhere on the scale. Therefore, in place of, or in addition to, the column identifying the participant's classification response (R), we assume that another column in the data table contains integer values from $-N$ to $+N$, and represents the participant's response on a bipolar scale with $2N$ unique values. We refer to the "directional" or "signed" integer value of the scale as the confidence rating response, C, and the "unsigned" or "non-directional" absolute value of the rating response as the level or degree of confidence, D.

3.4.   Information available at the point of the response

Although the experimenter could stipulate the cutoff on the rating scale without informing the participant, the conclusions that can be drawn from the objective methods are somewhat stronger if the participants know (or at least should know) which classification response they are giving on each trial. A more important issue is the consequence of eliciting both the classification response and the confidence level simultaneously rather than sequentially, as is sometimes done. Whether there are non-trivial differences in the results obtained from the two designs is, of course, an empirical issue. For the purpose of objective analysis, however, the simultaneous method seems preferable because under these conditions the properties of the probability space induced by the two measures provides information about the same deliberate action. Because of this, both of the measures can be said to contain information that is available to the participant at the point of his or her deliberate classification response. This fact has some important consequences with regards to the possible interpretations of the objective results.

3.5.   Properties of a Classification Space: The Decision Rule

Because the experiment we have in mind is a two-choice classification task, each row of the data table (and hence each elementary event in Γ_2) is either an A or a B classification response (and not both). Although the usage may seem odd, we will call this property of Γ_2 the *decision rule* (for a discussion of the use of this term in decision theory and behavioral modeling and its relationship to our definition, see Balakrishnan & MacDonald, 2004).

Let W be any one of the recorded measures in the experiment (i.e., the stimulus category, the classification response, or some other property of the stimulus or the participant's behavior that is recorded on each trial). The first question to be addressed in objective terms is how much of the information (ability to predict the stimulus category) in W is realized by the decision rule. With respect to the measure W, the decision rule is *optimal* if and only if

$$p(S = A | R = A, W = w) \geq \frac{1}{2}, \tag{1}$$

for all values $W = w$ such that $p(R = A, W = w) > 0$, and

$$p(S = B | R = B, W = w) \geq \frac{1}{2}, \tag{2}$$

for all values $W = w$ such that $p(R = B, W = w) > 0$.

If the decision rule is not optimal, then it must be *suboptimal*, that is,

$$p(S = A | R = A, W = w) < \frac{1}{2}, \tag{3}$$

for some values $W = w$, or

$$p(S = B | R = B, W = w) < \frac{1}{2}, \tag{4}$$

for some values $W = w$.

Suboptimality of the decision rule with respect to W implies that the participant's performance (overall probability of a correct response) could be improved by taking proper advantage of the information available in W.

4.   Objective Analysis Step 1: Observation

Because the measures in the data table are discrete and bounded, the probabilities involved in the conditions for optimality and suboptimality with respect to a measure are well-defined and observable. Optimality or suboptimality with respect to one of these measures is therefore an observable property of Γ_2, without qualification. Notice that when $W = S$ (i.e., the column that identifies the stimulus), the decision rule is suboptimal with respect to W unless the probability of an incorrect classification response is exactly zero. This is simply another way of saying that given knowledge of the category of the stimulus on each trial, the optimal decision maker achieves perfect performance. When $W = R$ (i.e., the classification response), suboptimality of the decision rule with respect to W would imply that inverting the participant's decision rule – switching all $R = A$ responses to $R = B$ responses and/or all $R = B$ responses to $R = A$ responses – would improve the participant's observable performance (the overall probability of a correct classification response in Γ_2). In such a case there is information (ability to predict the stimulus category) available in the classification response that is not realized by the actual decision rule that describes Γ_2. Although we will focus on accuracy (probability correct), the optimal-suboptimal dichotomy could easily be defined with respect to other loss functions, including an asymmetric payoff matrix.

It might seem unreasonable to characterize the participant's decision rule as optimal with respect to the classification response, R, merely because inequalities (1) and (2) are satisfied. It is important to recognize, however, that "with respect to R" does not imply "with respect to the decision-making strategy that produces or explains R," however this behavioral construct might be understood. The measure R is in fact a relatively "crude" description of the participant's behavior on a given trial, telling us only which of the two judgments was executed. This "resolution" issue can be reduced to the following statement: optimality of the decision rule with respect to some measure W does not imply optimality with respect to the pair of measures W and V, that is,

$$p(S = A|R = A, W = w) \geq \frac{1}{2},$$

and

$$p(S = B|R = B, W = w) \geq \frac{1}{2},$$

for all values $W = w$ does not imply that

$$p(S = A|R = A, W = w, V = v) \geq \frac{1}{2},$$

and

$$p(S = B|R = B, W = w, V = v) \geq \frac{1}{2},$$

for all w and v.

To give a simple example, in the classical signal detection model (i.e., when two perceptual effects distributions and a decision criterion describe the participant's behavior), setting the decision criterion at a suboptimal location would not usually cause the condition for suboptimality to be satisfied with respect to R. For this to happen, the suboptimality would need to be quite extreme (the reasons for this are discussed later). The condition would be satisfied, however, with respect to the measure defined as the classification response joined with the perceptual effect of the stimulus.

The resolution issue is particularly important when, compared to W, V is a "more precise" measure of the same behavioral quantity or for some other reason is deterministically related to W, that is, $p(W = w|V = v) = 0$ or 1 for all w and v, but $p(V = v|W = w)$ is not 0 or 1 for some values of w and v. We call this a *deterministic* relation between W and V. Note that in such a case, V has higher resolution than W (optimality with respect to V implies optimality with respect to W). Of course, whether two measures are deterministically related because they measure the same behavioral quantity or for some other reason is not always easy to determine. The percept in signal detection theory, for example, might or might not be considered a more precise measure of the same quantity than the classification response R. At least in the standard detection model, however, it does perfectly predict R.

Another pertinent example of perfect prediction is the confidence rating measure C in the ratings paradigm defined earlier. As we defined C, it perfectly predicts R, but R does not perfectly predict C. Moreover, unless accuracy is entirely unrelated to the participant's degree of confidence, that is, neither $p(S = A|R = A, D = d)$ nor $p(S = B|R = B, D = d)$ varies with d, the measure C (which is equivalent to the pair R, D) will have higher resolution than R.

4.1.   Information on which the response is based

From an information processing perspective (at least as we understand this term), for virtually any observed measure of a participant's behavior, there should be other, more detailed (higher resolution) measures that "explain" why the observed measure has a given value on a given trial. Using again signal detection theory as an example, the value of the percept on a given trial combined with the value of the decision criterion and the response assignment rule (i.e., respond A if the percept falls to the left of the criterion and respond B if it falls on the right) explains why the participant chooses a given detection response on that trial. The classification response is strategic and is said to be "based on" the value of the percept.

On any given trial, a myriad of events occurs in the environment, sensory pathways, and central cortex – many of these could be recorded in the data table, and the decision rule will be either optimal or suboptimal with respect to each of them. However, only some of these measures are related to the classification process, that is, only some represent processes that explain why the probabilities $p(S = A|R = A, D = d)$ have their observed set of values (i.e., why the rating responses predict the stimulus to a certain degree). This idea is illustrated graphically in Fig. 1.

Notice that "explanation" of W by V implies perfect prediction of W by V, but perfect prediction does not imply explanation (the rating response, for example, perfectly predicts R, and in fact R itself perfectly predicts R). At least for the types of measures and experimental methods we are considering, it is impossible to define the concept of explanation in an objective fashion, because it would not be a property of a probability space. What is important, however, is that a very large class of theories (i.e., the so-called

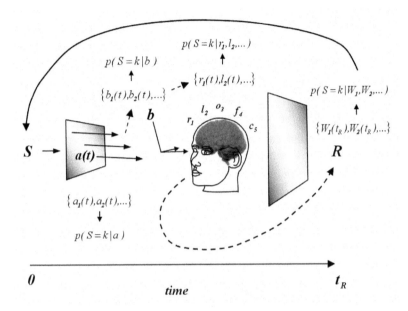

Fig. 1: Illustration of the information processing framework and the behavioral interpretation of observable probabilities. Many aspects of the environment and biological/neurochemical events following on the presentation of a stimulus S could be recorded on each trial of the experiment, including stochastic temporal sequences describing the changing intensities of light sources (pixels) on the display (a), activity at the receptor level of the sensory system (b), the ganglion cells (r_1), the lateral geniculate nucleus (l_2), and other areas of the brain. The decision rule will be either optimal or suboptimal with respect to any recorded measure, irrespective of what physical events it represents. On each trial, the values of some of the measures that could in principle be recorded presumably represent physical events that explain why a given response is executed on a given trial. This idea is represented by the pathway (dashed line) connecting measures at the level of the stimulus to measures at the periphery and the central cortex. Suboptimality of the decision rule with respect to this set of measures would constitute suboptimality of the decision rule with respect to the information on which the classification response is based.

process models) attempt to explain behavior in an important sense, and in such cases, the response is said to be "based on" a measure or set of measures defined in the model. In considering the implications of an objective result for behavior theory, we will frequently refer to this concept of "information on which the response is based."

5.   Objective Analysis Step 2: Inference

The fact that optimality with respect to the response R does not imply optimality with respect to the pair of measures R and V is an example of a property of a larger, perhaps even unobservable probability space (containing both R and V) that cannot be inferred from the smaller, observable one (containing only R). To make a positive inference, properties of the observable space that are logically imposed on the unobservable spaces must be derived. There may be many ways to do this. The method we will employ makes consistent use of a single, in some respects trivial, relation, which we will call the *weighted average principle*. Let W and V be any two measures (recorded or not recorded in the experiment). From the probability rules,

$$p(W = w) = \sum_V p(W = w|V = v)p(V = v). \tag{5}$$

Because the marginal probabilities, $p(V = v)$ add to one across all possible v, $p(W = w)$ is a weighted average of the conditional probabilities $p(W = w|V = v)$, where the $p(V = v)$ values are the weights.

For conditional probabilities,

$$p(W = w|V = v) = \sum_U p(W = w|V = v, U = u)p(U = u|V = v). \tag{6}$$

Again, because

$$\sum_U p(U = u|V = v) = 1,$$

$p(W = w|V = v)$ is a weighted average of the conditional probabilities $p(W = w|V = v, U = u)$, the weights in this case being the values of $p(U = u|V = v)$ for different values of u.

To see how this principle can be profitably applied to draw inferences between two different spaces, suppose that the decision rule is suboptimal with respect to some observed measure V. From expression (6), the decision rule must also be suboptimal with respect to the measure V when it is paired with any other measure U, including measures that in principle could have been but in fact were not recorded in the experiment. Suppose, for example, that V perfectly predicts R. In this case,

$$p(S = A|V = v, R = A) = p(S = A|V = v),$$

and

$$p(S = B|V = v, R = B) = p(S = B|V = v).$$

From expression (6),

$$p(S = A|V = v) < \frac{1}{2}$$

for some v implies that

$$p(S = A|V = v, U = u) < \frac{1}{2}$$

for some pair of values v, u (the result of a weighted average cannot be greater than the largest element in the weighted sum). Thus, when the condition for suboptimality with respect to an observed measure W is satisfied, we can infer a property of some unobserved probability spaces defined by identical experiments containing additional measures. Notice, in particular, that this would include the unrecorded measures that "explain" the observed values of V and hence are deterministically related to it. For example, if the decision rule is suboptimal with respect to R, it must be suboptimal with respect to any measures that purportedly explain R (i.e., the measures in any behavioral model). Thus, optimality with respect to R is relatively uninformative, but suboptimality with respect to R, if it is observed, has important implications for behavioral theories.

5.1. Inferences About Γ_1

Now consider the individual trial numbers in the data table, which are explicitly represented in Γ_1, and could also be a recorded measure in the experiment. Let I denote this measure in Γ_2. The probabilities of the elementary events in Γ_2 are weighted averages over the trial numbers, which are in turn averages over the probabilities of events in Γ_1. For example, the probability $p(S = A|W = w)$ in Γ_2 is

$$p_{\Gamma_2}(S = A|W = w) = \sum_i p_{\Gamma_2}(S = A|W = w, I = i)p_{\Gamma_2}(I = i|W = w)$$

$$= \sum_i p_{\Gamma_1}(S_i = A|W_i = w)p_{\Gamma_2}(I = i|W = w), \tag{7}$$

where $p_{\Gamma_1}(S_i = A|W_i = w)$ is the probability that the stimulus on the ith trial in the data table is $S = A$ given that $W = w$ on this trial (and hence the number of trials is greater than or equal to i).

Thus, the test for suboptimality in Γ_2 does not assume independence, identical distributions, or anything else with respect to the effect of the trial number or the outcomes of other trials on the participant's behavior.

When the suboptimality condition is satisfied with respect to a measure in Γ_2, it implies suboptimality with respect to this measure on at least some trials of the experiment, for whatever reason.[1]

Stated in somewhat more practical terms, unlike optimality, suboptimality with respect to an observed measure W cannot be "excused" or "dismissed" by attributing it to a lack of resolution of the measure W, or to an "artifact" of analyzing data combined across participants or sessions. It unequivocally implies a loss of information in the response R with respect to W.

6.   Objective Analysis Step 3: Interpretation

Apart from estimation error and replicability issues, the results of an objective analysis cannot be wrong. However, they may be uninteresting. Suboptimality with respect to the stimulus S, for example, is easily established (if the participants make errors), but does not provide much information about the cognition supporting the participant's behavior (other than showing that it is not infallible). The final step in the objective analysis is to consider the nature of the measure, and, with this in mind, the implications of the objective results for behavioral theory.

To illustrate, suppose that W_1 is a measure of the pattern of activity of the ganglion cells in a visual discrimination task, whereas W_2 is the participant's deliberate confidence rating response. Suboptimality with respect to W_1 implies suboptimality with respect to the pair W_1 and W_2, but not suboptimality with respect to W_2. In such a case, suboptimality with respect to W_1 could be "excused" – that is, "explained" without being pejorative about the participant's strategic behavior – by supposing that some information at the level of the ganglion cells is lost before it reaches the higher levels of the sensory pathways or the cortex.

Suboptimality with respect to the confidence rating, on the other hand, is a different matter. Because the rating response is deliberate and, in the paradigm we defined, simultaneous with the classification response, it represents information that is available to the participant at the point of the classification response. In this sense, suboptimality with respect to the rating report is not "excusable." In fact, informing the participants of this suboptimality should allow them to correct it, whereas informing them about suboptimality with respect to activity at the receptor level would presumably be useless.

---

[1]The author is grateful to Bill Batchelder for pointing out the need to clarify this issue.

7.   Biased Decision Rules

Because $p(S = B|R = A, W = w) = 1 - p(S = A|R = A, W = w)$, the condition for optimality with respect to W can also be stated as

$$p(S = A|R = A, W = w) \geq p(S = B|R = A, W = w),$$

for all values $W = w$ such that $p(R = A, W = w) > 0$, and

$$p(S = B|R = B, W = w) \geq p(S = A|R = B, W = w),$$

for all values $W = w$ such that $p(R = B, W = w) > 0$.

Reversing the conditional probabilities yields the complementary condition for *bias-unbias* of the decision rule with respect to W. That is, the decision rule is *unbiased* with respect to W if and only if

$$p(R = A, W = w|S = A) \geq p(R = B, W = w|S = A), \qquad (8)$$

and

$$p(R = B, W = w|S = B) \geq p(R = A, W = w|S = B), \qquad (9)$$

for all values $W = w$.

All of the averaging principles and interpretation issues developed earlier apply equally to bias. In general, the decision rule must be biased in order for it to be optimal when the priors are unequal (the priors must be "taken into account" by the decision maker in evaluating the sensory effect of the stimulus). However, because we are assuming equal priors, suboptimality implies and is implied by bias in the decision rule. For example, suboptimality for any subset of $R = A$ responses,

$$p(S = A|R = A, W = w) < p(S = B|R = A, W = w)$$

implies that

$$1 > \frac{p(S = A|R = A, W = w)}{p(S = B|R = A, W = w)} = \frac{p(R = A, W = w|S = A)}{p(R = A, W = w|S = B)},$$

and hence the decision rule is also biased.

We therefore confine our discussion to suboptimality and its implications. It may also be worth mentioning that the sufficient condtions for optimality and bias do not depend on the values of the priors. The value $\frac{1}{2}$ appears in inequalities (1-4) because there are two classification responses in the experiment, not because we are assuming that $p(S = A) = p(S = B) = \frac{1}{2}$ (this assumption is convenient for other reasons).

8.   The Information Value of a Measure

Suboptimality of the decision rule with respect to some measure W implies that the measure contains at least some information about the stimulus category that is not realized by the classification response R (i.e., and hence, by the participant's decision rule). Stated more precisely, if all of the elementary events in Γ_2 that have the two properties, $R = A$ (i.e., the A classification responses in Γ_2), and $p(S = A | R = A, W = w) < \frac{1}{2}$, are converted to $R = B$ responses, the probability of a correct classification judgment in this modified sample space (i.e., with a modified decision rule) will be greater than the probability correct value in the actual probability space Γ_2. "Correcting" any suboptimal values of W for both the $R = A$ and $R = B$ responses would maximize the probability of a correct response with respect to the information available in the pair of measures W and R.

When the value of a measure also determines the classification rating (e.g., the signed confidence rating, C), optimizing with respect to (W, R) is obviously equivalent to optimizing with respect to W. For other measures (e.g., the response time), it is possible to optimize with respect to W alone, that is, to base the correction rule on $p(S = A | W = w)$ rather than $p(S = A | R = A, W = w)$. However, because R is always a measure in Γ_2 and its value defines the participant's decision rule, the resolution of any such "non-directional" measure can always be "doubled" by combining it with R. At least for scaling purposes, there is no reason to consider the information value of a non-directional measure W by itself. With this in mind, we define the information value of the measure W as the probability of a correct classification judgment in the space Γ_2^{opt} created when the decision rule in Γ_2 is optimized with respect to the pair of measures W and R.

In the next section, we consider some of the properties of comparative judgment behavior and the effects of correcting a participant's suboptimal decision rule by optimizing it with respect to the confidence rating.

9.   Objective Analysis of Comparative Judgment Data: Time Errors

In the probability space induced by the comparative judgment experiment (as we defined it), neither of the two allowable classification responses is correct on the "equal trials," that is, when $S_1 = S_2$. These trials must therefore be ignored when applying the test for suboptimality. That is, Γ_2 is defined by assuming that a random sample is drawn from the set of unequal trials $(S_1 \neq S_2)$ in the data table produced by the experiment. We consider the implications of this in the interpretation phase of the objective analysis. In the observation phase, the most obvious question to ask is whether the decision rule in this experiment can be shown (objectively) to be suboptimal with respect to information available at the point of the response.

Apart from general interest in decision-making behavior, the issue is important because of the potential effects that suboptimality could have on an empirically derived psychophysical scale (Hellström, 1979; John, 1975; Masin & Fanton, 1989; McClelland, 1943; Tresselt, 1944; Woodrow, 1935). When the integer values of S_1 and S_2 identify the relative sizes of two "objects" presented in chronological order, the matrix of conditional response probabilities (i.e., the "comparison matrix") is often asymmetric in a manner suggesting that the participants for some reason prefer the $R = B$ response (i.e., the judgment indicating that $S_2 > S_1$),

$$p(R = A|S_1 = i, S_2 = j) < p(R = B|S_1 = j, S_2 = i),$$

when $i \geq j$.

Many interpretations of these time errors, as Fechner called them, have been offered, including intentional or idiosyncratic biases on the part of participants (Erlebacher & Sekuler, 1971; Masin & Agostini, 1990; Masin and Fanton, 1989), effects of presentation sequences on sensation magnitudes (Hellström, 1985; Helson, 1964; Woodworth & Schlosberg, 1954), and accidental biases (John, 1975; Luce & Galanter, 1963; Restle, 1961). Most of these explanations can be reduced to the same "objective" hypothesis, that is, that the time error reflects a suboptimality of the decision rule with respect to the information on which the response is based, and hence would be eliminated if the suboptimality could be corrected.

9.1.   Empirical Results

Results of the objective suboptimality test on data from a comparative judgment experiment reported in Balakrishnan and MacDonald (2000) are shown in Fig. 2. Subjects in this experiment compared the lengths of two horizontal lines, each presented for 1 sec and separated by .5 sec. They gave their comparative judgment and a confidence rating simultaneously on a 14-point bipolar scale. The suboptimality condition – and hence the bias condition as well, because the priors were equal and the $S_1 = S_2$ trials were excluded – was exhibited for only one of the confidence ratings, the lowest confidence $R = B$ response. Although the function is close to $\frac{1}{2}$ at this position, this rating response was selected with relatively high frequency (more than 10% of the trials, see the lower function in the figure), which has two important implications. First, the sample size of the estimated conditional probability is relatively large (1,973 samples), and second, the suboptimality is relatively substantial in the sense that it causes the suboptimality condition to be satisfied for a relatively large "portion" of Γ_2.

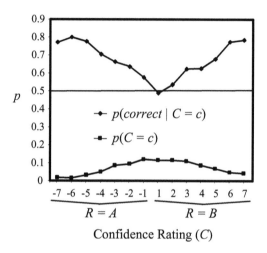

Fig. 2: Results of the test for suboptimality of the decision rule with respect to the confidence rating response. If the conditional probability that the stimulus is $S = A$ given $R = A, D = d$ (i.e., $C = -d$) is less than $\frac{1}{2}$ for any value of d, or if the conditional probability that the stimulus is $S = B$ given $R = B, D = d$ (i.e., $C = +d$) is less than $\frac{1}{2}$ for any value of d, the decision rule is suboptimal with respect to C (and, equivalently, with respect to R, D). The sufficient condition is satisfied in this experiment for one case, $C = 1$ (the lowest confidence $R = B$ response). Since the rating and classification responses were given simultaneously, the decision rule is suboptimal with respect to information available at the point of the response. The lower function in the figure is the marginal probability of the rating response.

In previous applications of this test to discrimination data (Balakrishnan, 1998a, 1998b, 1999; Balakrishnan & MacDonald, 2001), the decision rule was always optimal or virtually optimal when the prior probabilities were equal, and completely or virtually unbiased and hence suboptimal when the priors were unequal. To our knowledge, therefore, the Fig. 2 result is the first empirical observation of a substantively biased decision rule in a perceptual classification task.

9.2.   Inference

In principle, suboptimality of the decision rule and asymmetry of the comparison matrix could be entirely unrelated phenomena, because optimality (suboptimality) of the decision rule neither implies nor is implied by symmetry (asymmetry) of the comparison matrix. In the Balakrishnan and MacDonald (2000) experiment, however, every cell of the comparison matrix was asymmetrical in the direction favoring the $R = B$ response, and only a subset of these responses (i.e., the lowest confidence $R = B$ responses) satisfied the condition for suboptimality. Thus, we can infer that optimizing the decision rule with respect to the confidence rating, because it involves switching only some of the $R = B$ responses to $R = A$ responses, would reduce, eliminate, or change the direction of the asymmetry.

The two comparison matrices – before and after the correction for suboptimality –are shown in Tables 1 and 2. Figure 3 illustrates the effect of the correction as a function of the size of the physical differences between the objects. For reasons to be discussed later, the estimated probabilities in both the table and the figure describe the entire dataset, including the $S_1 = S_2$ trials. With respect to objective inferences about suboptimality, the conclusions are unaffected. In the original matrix, the time error is pronounced in favor of the $R = B$ judgment. It is much weaker and its direction is entirely reversed after the correction.

In order to draw inferences about the unobserved probability spaces induced by the experiment, consider an unrecorded discrete measure, V^*, that is deterministically related to the confidence rating C and higher in resolution (i.e., V^* perfectly predicts C, but C does not perfectly predict V^*). From the observable result (suboptimality with respect to confidence) and the weighted average principle, we may infer that $p(S = B|V^* = v)$ must be less than $\frac{1}{2}$ for at least some values of v. When optimizing with respect to V^*, the total proportion of $R = B$ responses that would need to be switched to $R = A$ responses might be smaller or larger than the proportion switched when optimizing with respect to the confidence rating, but it cannot be zero.

Table 1: Comparison matrix, $p(R = B | S_1 = i, S_2 = j)$, before correction for sub-optimality of the decision rule. Data from the comparative judgment experiment reported in Balakrishnan and MacDonald (2000). (See also Fig. 3).

		Second Line					
		1	2	3	4	5	6
First Line	1	.584	.628	.707	.750	.798	.816
	2	.532	.561	.595	.669	.734	.811
	3	.469	.520	.608	.666	.707	.754
	4	.407	.463	.519	.609	.675	.693
	5	.357	.427	.446	.519	.615	.703
	6	.300	.377	.439	.498	.561	.653

Table 2: Comparison matrix after correction for suboptimality of the decision rule.

		Second Line					
		1	2	3	4	5	6
First Line	1	.461	.462	.576	.652	.697	.723
	2	.377	.434	.490	.559	.638	.712
	3	.330	.407	.481	.531	.594	.655
	4	.293	.332	.379	.471	.552	.558
	5	.256	.316	.319	.390	.497	.575
	6	.230	.272	.339	.408	.435	.516

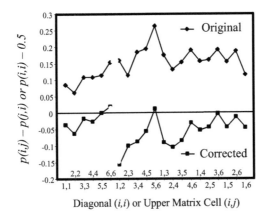

Fig. 3: Effects of the correction for suboptimality of the decision rule on the asymmetric form of the comparison matrix. The first six values of the functions are the comparison probabilities on the diagonal minus $\frac{1}{2}$. The remaining values are differences in the probabilities in the corresponding upper and lower cells of the matrix (row i, column j, versus row j, column i) ordered on the abscissa by the size of the physical difference in the object pair. The asymmetry favors the $R = B$ response in the original matrix (upper function), and reverses with the correction, showing (in the objective sense) that the time error is at least partially due to suboptimality of the decision rule and consistent with the hypothesis that the error would be eliminated if the decision rule were perfectly optimal.

9.3.   Interpretation

From the information processing perspective, suboptimality of the decision rule with respect to the confidence ratings implies, for the reasons given earlier, that the participants fail to take proper advantage of information about the stimulus category that is available to them at the point of the classification response. This is probably the most important implication of the experimental results. To carry the analysis a bit further, however, suppose that V^* is the measure or set of measures in the "true" information processing model, that is, a model that "correctly explains" why the participant makes a given confidence rating and classification response on a given trial of our comparative judgment experiment. The fact that optimizing the decision rule with respect to the confidence ratings reversed the direction of the asymmetry may be taken as evidence to support the hypothesis that the time error is in fact entirely due to suboptimality of the decision rule with respect to V^* (i.e., that the comparison matrix would be perfectly symmetric if the decision rule were optimized with respect to V^*).

The strength of this evidence, however, is a matter of opinion – it depends on the plausibility of an implicit assumption, that is, that the resolution of the observable confidence rating measure is reasonably good with respect to V^*. This issue is illustrated graphically in Fig. 4, using a Thurstonian model of the comparative judgment process to represent the "true" behavioral theory. The example assumes that the effect V^* can be expressed as a pair of sensory values (or sensation magnitudes), one for each object in the pair, and a decision boundary divides these effects into two classification response regions.

Together with two additional boundaries, the decision boundary also divides the sensory effects into four confidence rating categories (i.e., two levels of confidence on a 4-point bipolar scale). The decision boundary is suboptimal (with respect to V^*) in favor of the $R = B$ response (some of the sensory states mapped to the $R = B$ response have higher relative frequency on $S = A$ trials than on $S = B$ trials, and the prior probabilities of the categories are assumed to be equal). The observable conditional probability, $p(S = A|R = B, D = 1)$, will be a weighted average of two values, the probability that $S = A$ given that the sensory state falls in the suboptimally mapped portion of the $R = B, D = 1$ response region and the probability that $S = A$ given that the sensory state falls in the optimally mapped portion of this region.

Now suppose that the suboptimal portion of the $R = B, D = 1$ region is large enough to cause the suboptimality condition to be satisfied for the $R = B, D = 1$ response, that is,

$$p(S = B|R = B, D = 1) < \frac{1}{2}.$$

– – –   Subject's Decision Bound

······   Optimal Decision Bound

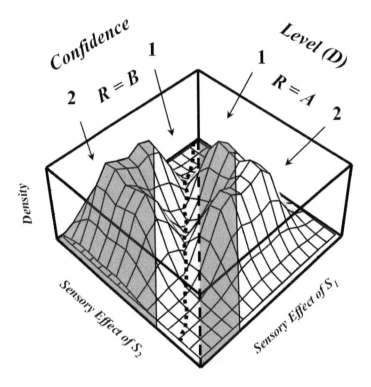

Fig. 4: An illustration of the potential effects of averaging on the objective test for suboptimality. The suboptimal region between the subject's decision boundary and the optimal decision boundary is contained within the region defining the lowest confidence $R = B$ response. If the conditional probability $p(S = B|R = B, D = 1)$ is less than one half, the decision rule is suboptimal with respect to R, D (i.e., with respect to the signed rating response C. Correcting by changing all the $R = B, D1$ responses to $R = A$ responses (at any arbitrary confidence level increases the overall performance (percent correct). However, some of the sensory states that were optimally mapped to the $R = B$ would be, after correction, suboptimality mapped to $R = A$.

Optimizing the decision rule with respect to the confidence rating "correctly" converts all of the suboptimal $R = B$ responses to $R = A$ responses, but also incorrectly converts some of the optimal $R = B$ responses to $R = A$ responses. In other words, it over-corrects the decision rule. In this sense, the observed reversal of the direction of the time error with the correction for suboptimality with respect to confidence can be considered evidence for an overcorrection.

If optimization with respect to an observable measure W reverses the time error because it overcorrects for suboptimality with respect to V^*, increasing the "precision" (number of possible values) of this measure should reduce the size of the overcorrection and hence the size of the time error in the corrected space. Another possibility would be to optimize the decision rule with respect to the measure created by joining the confidence rating response with the response time, if this measure can be recorded. Because response time is also a property of the classification response that is "completed" or "realized" only at the point of the response, it would also represent information available at the point of the response in a behavioral model. Although response time and confidence tend to be correlated (Baranski, & Petrusic, 1998; Emmerich, Gray, Watson, & Tanis, 1972; Katz, 1970; Petrusic & Baranski, 1997; Shaw, McClure, & Wilkens, 2001; Vickers, Smith, Burt, & Brown, 1985; see Link, 1992, for a review of earlier work), the correlation is far from perfect. Response time would almost surely provide information about V^* that is unavailable in the confidence ratings. Combining response time and confidence, therefore, should result in a more powerful empirical test of the hypothesis that asymmetry of the comparison matrix is entirely due to suboptimality of the decision rule with respect to information available at the point of the response.

9.4.   Analysis of the Equal Trials

Objective inferences cannot be drawn between probability spaces induced by two different experiments unless the participant's behavior in the two experiments can be logically inferred to be identical, which means that the only difference between the experiments should be the set of measures recorded in the dataset. It is not possible, therefore, to logically infer how participants would have behaved if the equal trials were removed from the comparative judgment design rather than ignored at the point of the analysis. They may have chosen to adopt a suboptimal decision rule with respect to accuracy on the unequal trials merely because of the presence of the equal trials, for some obscure reason. However, because there is no *rational* reason for adopting a suboptimal decision-making strategy on the unequal trials because some of the other trials will not be scored by the experimenter, the theoretical significance of the suboptimality result is essentially the same;

that is, with respect to the information available to them at the point of their classification responses, the participants did not meet the objective of maximizing the probability of a correct classification response. The question of why the participants did not meet this objective is certainly an interesting one, but such questions are too vaguely formulated to be addressed objectively.

The participants' behavior on the equal trials may also be informative in at least one important respect. Let V^* represent the information on which the classification response is based and assume that the time error is due to suboptimality with respect to V^* (i.e., it would be eliminated if the decision rule were optimized with respect to V^*). Because the participants make errors on the unequal trials, it seems reasonable to suppose that they cannot perfectly distinguish the equal trials from the unequal trials. It seems reasonable to assume, therefore, that the domain of V^* on equal trials is the same as its domain on unequal trials. If so, applying the correction for suboptimality with respect to V^* on the entire data set as opposed to just the unequal trials should "symmetrize" the diagonal of the resulting comparison matrix, causing these values to equal $\frac{1}{2}$ (assuming also that the asymmetry is only due suboptimality of the decision rule). The fact that the asymmetry on the diagonal was smaller and reversed by the correction with respect to the confidence rating is therefore further support for the hypothesis that the asymmetry of the comparison matrix is exclusively due to suboptimality of the decision rule with respect to V^*.

10.   Asymmetry in the Information Available in Subjective Confidence Reports

The fact that the suboptimality condition was only satisfied for an $R = B$ rating response in the comparative judgment experiment implies another kind of asymmetry in the participants' decision-making behavior, which we will call *miscalibration*.[2] For each possible value of any measure W in Γ_2, there is a corresponding pair of conditional stimulus probabilities,

$$p(S = A | R = A, W = w),$$

and

$$p(S = B | R = B, W = w).$$

We will refer to the maximum of these two values as the information value of the event $W = w$.

---

[2] We use this term in a manner similar, but not equivalent, to its use in the subjective probability judgment literature; see, for example, Yates, 1990.

A given measure W is *calibrated* if and only if

$$p(S = A | R = A, W = w) = p(S = B | R = B, W = w), \qquad (10)$$

for all values w such that $p(R = A, W = w)$ and $p(R = B, W = w)$ are both nonzero.

For some (in fact, many) measures, calibration or miscalibration would be uninteresting. When W is the stimulus category S, for example, the two conditional stimulus probabilities will obviously be unequal for each value of W, and when W is the signed confidence rating C, the joint probabilities, $p(R = A, W = w)$ and $p(R = B, W = w)$, will never both be nonzero.

However, when W is a measure whose nominal value should be related to its information value, that is, when $p(S = A | R = A, W = w)$ and $p(S = B | R = B, W = w)$ are expected to be positively correlated with w, the calibration-miscalibration characterization may become an interesting issue.

The most obvious example of such a measure is the participant's reported degree of confidence in the classification judgment (i.e., the "unsigned" value D indicating the degree of confidence but not which response is selected). In crude terms, high (low) subjective confidence should be associated with a high (low) information value. Miscalibration, as we defined it, would imply that the information value associated with a given reported degree of confidence, $D = d$, depends not only on d but also on which classification judgment the value d is assigned to,

$$p(S = A | R = A, D = d) \neq p(S = B | R = B, D = d).$$

Miscalibration suggests that the participants are, at least to some degree, irrational decision makers. To see why, suppose that the participants are able to convert V^* (the information on which their classification response is based) to the maximum conditional stimulus probability,

$$\max \left(p(S = A | V^* = v), p(S = B | V^* = v) \right),$$

where V^* is the information on which they base their classification response.

If they are rational decision makers, they would respond $R = A$ when $S = A$ is more likely and $R = B$ when $S = B$ is more likely. Now suppose that the participants are allowed to report the maximum of the two conditional stimulus probabilities as their degree of confidence, D. In this case,

$$p(S = A | R = A, D = d) = d = p(S = B | R = B, D = d),$$

and hence their confidence reports would be calibrated.

In general, confidence reports are positively correlated with accuracy, but are miscalibrated when the prior probabilities are unequal (see, e.g., Balakrishnan, 1998b; Balakrishnan, 1999). The fact that the confidence reports are miscalibrated only when the priors are unequal suggests that the participants for some reason have trouble taking the priors properly into account, as signal detection theorists and others have sometimes suggested (e.g., Davies & Parasuraman, 1982; Kubovy, 1977; Maloney & Thomas, 1991). In this section, we derive an objective test for the assumption that the miscalibration of a measure W can be attributed exclusively to a misestimation of the prior probabilities of the stimulus categories.

Stated as a modeling issue, the question is whether the confidence rating data can be perfectly fit by assuming that the participants correctly compute the conditional probabilities of the perceptual information, $p(V^* = v|S = A)$ and $p(V^* = v|S = B)$, where V^* is the information on which the rating response, C, is based, but incorrectly assign values for $p(S = A)$ and $p(S = B)$ when estimating $p(S = A|V^* = v)$ and $p(S = B|V^* = v)$ from $p(V^* = v|S = A)$ and $p(V^* = v|S = B)$, that is, when computing their confidence level. Stated in objective terms, the question is whether a pair of prior probability values can be found that transform the observable space Γ_2 into a new space, Γ_2^*, in which the measure D is calibrated. The transformation (changing only the prior probabilities) can be understood as follows.

Each elementary event, $E = e$ in Γ_2, has probability

$$p_{\Gamma_2}(E = e) = p_{\Gamma_2}(E = e|S = A)p_{\Gamma_2}(S = A) + p_{\Gamma_2}(E = e|S = B)p_{\Gamma_2}(S = B).$$

The elementary events in Γ_2^* are the same as in Γ_2, but their probabilities are defined by substituting a different pair of prior probabilities for the "true" values describing Γ_2,

$$p_{\Gamma_2^*}(E = e) = p_{\Gamma_2}(E = e|S = A)p_{\Gamma_2^*}(S = A) + p_{\Gamma_2}(E = e|S = B)p_{\Gamma_2^*}(S = B).$$

The question is whether values of $p_{\Gamma_2^*}(S = A)$ and $p_{\Gamma_2^*}(S = B)$ can be found such that the measure D is calibrated in Γ_2^*. To avoid cumbersome notation, henceforth any conditional probability expression may be assumed to represent a probability in Γ_2 unless otherwise stated. The prior probabilities in Γ_2 will be denoted as p_A and p_B, and in Γ_2^* as p_A^* and p_B^*.

To derive the test, suppose that a measure, D^*, is added to the data table by transforming the degree of confidence, D, using

$$D^*(d) = \frac{p(R = A, D = d|S = A)p_A^*}{p(R = A, D = d|S = A)p_A^* + p(R = A, D = d|S = B)p_B^*}, \quad (11)$$

for some pair of values of p_A^* and p_B^*. Notice that this is simply an application of Bayes's rule with the "wrong" prior probabilities, that is, D^* is

$p(S = A|R = A, D = d)$ computed with p_A^* and p_B^* substituted for p_A and p_B. Under this transformation,

$$1 - D^*(d) = \frac{p(R = A, D = d|S = B)p_B^*}{p(R = A, D = d|S = A)p_A^* + p(R = A, D = d|S = B)p_B^*},$$

for each value d. Again, this is merely Bayes's rule, in this case applied to $p(S = B|R = A, D = d) = 1 - p(S = A|R = A, D = d)$, and following through with the same wrong assumption about the priors.

Finally, suppose that the same transformation to D^* also satisfies

$$D^*(d) = \frac{p(R = B, D = d|S = B)p_B^*}{p(R = B, D = d|S = A)p_A^* + p(R = B, D = d|S = B)p_B^*},$$

and

$$1 - D^*(d) = \frac{p(R = B, D = d|S = A)p_A^*}{p(R = B, D = d|S = A)p_A^* + p(R = B, D = d|S = B)p_B^*},$$

for each value d. Satisfying these conditions ensures that the measure D will be calibrated in Γ_2^*.

If a single transformation from the conditional stimulus probabilities for D to D^* satisfies all of these conditions, then in Γ_2^* (i.e., when the true prior probabilities are in fact p_A^* and p_B^*),

$$D^*(d) = p_{\Gamma_2^*}(S = A|R = A, D = d) = p_{\Gamma_2^*}(S = B|R = B, D = d),$$

and hence D will be calibrated in Γ_2^*.

A testable empirical condition for the existence of such a transformation can be defined by taking the ratios of the different expressions for D^* to cancel out the terms in the denominators,

$$1 = \frac{D^*(1 - D^*)}{(1 - D^*)D^*} = \frac{p(R = A, D = d|S = A)p_A^*}{p(R = A, D = d|S = B)p_B^*} \frac{p(R = B, D = d|S = A)p_A^*}{p(R = B, D = d|S = B)p_B^*}.$$

Therefore, if a suitable transformation from D to D^* exists, then

$$\phi(d) = \sqrt{\frac{p(R = A, D = d|S = A)}{p(R = A, D = d|S = B)} \frac{p(R = B, D = d|S = A)}{p(R = B, D = d|S = B)}} = \frac{p_B^*}{p_A^*}. \quad (12)$$

Constancy of the observable function $\phi(d)$ as a function of d, $\phi(d) = \phi$, implies that the participant's degree of confidence, D, would be calibrated if the prior probabilities were

$$p_B^* = \frac{\phi}{1 + \phi} \quad \text{and} \quad p_A^* = \frac{1}{1 + \phi}.$$

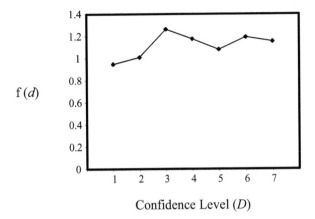

f(d)

Confidence Level (D)

Fig. 5: Results of the test for symmetry in the information value of subjective confidence reports (calibration) under a different pair of prior probabilities of the two stimulus categories. Since the true priors in the experiment were equal, values greater than 1 indicate overestimation of $p(S = B) = p(S_1 < S_2)$. The function should be constant if the observed miscalibration of the confidence level D is entirely due to miscalculation of the prior probabilities.

10.1. Empirical Results

Results of the $\phi(d)$ analysis on the data reported in Balakrishnan and MacDonald (2000) are shown in Fig. 5. Because the bias in this experiment favored the $R = B$ response, the function would be expected to be greater than 1 (participants overestimate the prior probability of $S = B$), which is consistent with the result. The function is also reasonably flat, although it may also be increasing at a small rate. A larger study, ideally one in which the prior probabilities of the categories are varied, would be needed to determine whether misestimation of the priors is truly sufficient to explain the miscalibration of participants' confidence ratings.

10.2. Interpretation

Allowing for estimation error, constancy of $\phi(d)$ as a function of d establishes, in the objective sense, that the miscalibration is due entirely to miscalculation of the prior probabilities. However, when $\phi(d)$ varies with d, the result could be attributed to poor resolution in the confidence rating report with respect to V^*, defined as the information on which the confidence rating response is based. The strength of the evidence afforded by the test would depend, once again, on the resolution of the confidence report with respect to V^*, which presumably means the extent to which $p(S = A|C = c)$ varies as a function of c. If these values are distributed over a reasonably wide range and the constancy condition is clearly violated, the results would strongly suggest that the participant's confidence states are miscalibrated, and further that this miscalibration must be attributed at least in part to miscalculation of the conditional probabilities $p(V^* = v|S = A)$ and $p(V^* = v|S = B)$.

11. Information value and the Odds Distribution

Asymmetry of the comparison matrix and miscalibration of subjective confidence reports are each observable properties of a probability space that would suggest – but not confirm – that the overall probability of a correct classification judgment underestimates the amount of information available to the participant at the point of his or her classification response. Stated another way, such results may be easily accounted for by a relatively pedestrian behavioral model (e.g., signal detection theory) with a suboptimal decision rule, but another model could also be constructed that accounts for these properties of the observable probability space while incorporating an optimal decision rule (cf. Maloney & Thomas, 1991).[3]

Suboptimality of the decision rule with respect to reported confidence, on the other hand, unequivocally establishes a discrepancy between overt performance and the information available at the point of the response (assuming, as we are, that the classification response and the confidence report are simultaneous). Although the suboptimality could be "explained" in a model by mapping one measure to a reported degree of confidence (i.e., to predict the unsigned confidence level) and another measure to the classification response, the decision rule cannot be optimal with respect to each of these measures individually or to their combination. In short, the result establishes that with some nonzero probability, the participant is acquiring perceptual information about the stimulus that is not properly realized in his or her overt classification response.

For any measure, W, that perfectly predicts the participant's classification response, such as the confidence rating C, the maximum potential performance (i.e., the information value of the measure) depends on two factors, the values of $p(S = A|W = w)$ and the relative frequency dis-

---

[3]The term decision rule can be understood here either as a property of a probability space or as a modeling construct, that is, a process that maps perceptual effects to responses – when the position of the criterion is a constant, it does not matter.

tribution of W. Stated crudely, if there is a high probability that when a single random sample of W is taken from Γ_1, the corresponding value of $p(S = A|W = w)$ (i.e., when the expression $p(S = A|W = w)$ is understood as a transformation of the random variable W and hence is itself a random variable) will be close to 1 or 0, then W contains a lot of information about the category to which the stimulus belongs. If the incident value of $p(S = A|W = w)$ is highly likely to be close to $\frac{1}{2}$ on a randomly selected trial, the amount of information afforded by W is relatively small.

Because we are only quantifying the potential or realized accuracy of the participants' classification behavior and not how this accuracy comes about – for example, two different values of W, w_1 and w_2, could have the same information value, $p(S = A|W = w_1) = p(S = A|W = w_2)$ – the information value of W depends only on the possible values of

$$\max(p(S = A|W = w), p(S = B|W = w))$$

and their relative frequencies when W is sampled at random from Γ_2. It is easy to show that the expected value of this "unarticulated odds distribution" (Balakrishnan, MacDonald, & Kohen, 2003) is the information value of W as we defined this term earlier, that is, the probability that the classification response will be correct when an optimal decision rule is applied to a random sample of W from Γ_2. The "articulated odds distribution " is a plot of $p(S = A|W = w)$ (or $p(S = A|W = w)$) against its relative frequency.

Because it is a measure of the difficulty of the actual classification task performed by the participant, which involves a given pair of prior probabilities of the stimuli, the shape of the odds distributions (both articulated and unarticulated), and hence the maximum probability of a correct classification response, will depend on the prior probabilities as well as the probability distribution of W. We are assuming, however, that the priors are equal. Moreover, it is easy to transform the odds distributions to the shapes they would have under equal priors (see Balakrishnan et al., 2003). Henceforth, the information value of a measure is the expected value of the unarticulated odds distribution for W under equal priors.

12. Objective Psychophysical Scales

Having developed a means of converting observable behaviors to an objective measure of information available at the point of the comparative judgment response, we may now consider how such measures could be employed to scale a set of stimuli. To begin, it is helpful to briefly review some of the basic concepts and practices in classical psychophysical scaling, relating them to our analysis in terms of probability spaces and information value.

Scaling stimuli on the basis of comparative judgment behavior presupposes that participants would make errors in assigning a comparative judgment response to at least some stimuli in the set of possible stimuli defined by the physical dimension (or dimensions) of interest. At least in this respect, confusability in a classification task – and hence the information value of a measure – are already well-established concepts in the scaling literature.

The purpose of the comparative judgment task, however, is not to measure the confusability of the two categories, but instead to assign subjective distance values to the individual stimuli within the categories, as well as other stimuli that share the same physical dimensions but were not included in the experiment. Notice that we are defining the stimulus as the physical properties of the participant's environment on a given trial instead of assuming that the trial is composed of a pair of stimuli, or that it induces a pair of perceptual effects. The distance value for a given stimulus is some function of the confusability values of stimuli that represent a path from the physical property represented by S_1 to the property represented by S_2, with respect to a single physical dimension, as in most treatments, or with respect to the full dimensionality of the stimuli, as developed recently by Dzhafarov and Colonius (1999; Dzhafarov & Colonius, 2001, 2005).

Because the distance values often depend on response probabilities assigned to stimuli that were not included in the experiment, this type of analysis cannot be objective – it requires a theory. Thurstonian methods assume that the effect of the stimulus (V^*, the information on which the classification response is based) can be split into two random variables, possibly interdependent but selectively attributed to the two different physical aspects of the stimulus represented by S_1 and S_2 (see Dzhafarov, 2003c). However, Dzhafarov (2003a,b) has recently shown that even in its weakest possible forms, this Thurstonian representation leads to predictions about psychophysical functions that are violated empirically. Although we will make use of the Thurstonian framework, the purpose is to illustrate the logic of the objective scaling method, not to endorse the classical point of view.

Even if the effect of the stimulus on the participant (V^*) cannot be split into two separate effects associated with S_1 and S_2, it must still *depend on* these two physical properties of the stimulus (otherwise, the participant's classification accuracy would be at the chance level). The information value of V^*, as we defined it, is one measure of this dependence, but a crude one, that is, if this value is high, the dependence must be strong in some way. To be more specific about the dependence of V^* (or an observable measure) on the specific values of S_1 and S_2, the information values of the measure must be compared when they are defined by randomly sampling from a subset of the data table containing only two different stimuli.

Let T_1 and T_2 denote two pairs of values of S_1 and S_2, that is, two different stimuli in the comparative judgment task. Suppose that a random sample is drawn only from the set of $S = T_1$ or $S = T_2$ trials of the data table. Let w be the value of W on this randomly sampled trial. With respect to W, the objective measure of the confusability of T_1 and T_2 is the probability that the stimulus, T_1 or T_2, on this randomly sampled trial would be correctly identified when an optimal decision rule is applied to w, that is, when the response is $R = T_1$ if

$$p(S = T_1 | W = w, S = T_1 \text{ or } T_2) \geq \frac{1}{2},$$

and the response is $R = T_2$ if

$$p(S = T_2 | W = w, S = T_1 \text{ or } T_2) > \frac{1}{2}.$$

We will refer to this "inferred" information value of W for a single pair of stimuli as $_{i,j}I_{k,m}$, where i and j identify the values of S_1 and S_2, respectively, for T_1, and k and m identify the values of S_1 and S_2, respectively, for T_2.

If the measure W has good resolution with respect to V^*, $_{i,j}I_{k,m}$ will be a good measure of the information value of V^* when this measure is used to discriminate two specific stimuli from the set in the comparative judgment task. However, because there are as many as four different integer values in the two pairs, (i,j) and (k,m), that identify the two stimuli, the size of the information value $_{i,j}I_{k,m}$ has, in general, many possible interpretations. Now suppose, however, that the two stimuli are chosen so that they share a value on one of the "dimensions," S_1 or S_2, that is, when $i = k$ or $j = m$. Because the stimulus is uniquely identified by the values of S_1 and S_2, the only physical difference between the two stimuli in these cases is the difference implied by the values of S_1 (when S_2 is shared) or of S_2 (when S_1 is shared), that is, on one of the two dimensions. The value of $_{i,j}I_{k,m}$ in these cases can therefore be attributed to the effect of this physical difference on a single physical dimension on the distribution of the measure W. Fixing S_1 in the two pairs, the value $_{i,j}I_{i,m}$ is the confusability of $S_2 = j$ and $S_2 = m$ in the context $S_1 = i$, and fixing S_2, $_{j,i}I_{m,i}$ is the confusability of $S_1 = j$ and $S_1 = m$ in the context $S_2 = i$.

Following a similar logic, it might seem that the value of $_{i,j}I_{k,m}$ when $i = m$ would be an appropriate objective measure of the confusability of the properties $S_1 = j$ and $S_2 = k$, in the context $i = m$. In this set, the information value $_{i,j}I_{k,m}$ is still, of course, an observable property of Γ_2, and the definition is therefore objective. However, the interpretation of these values is considerably more difficult. First, the difference between the two stimuli can no longer be ascribed to a single dimension. The value of $_{i,j}I_{k,m}$ may depend therefore not only on the difference between j and k, but also on the difference in the dimensions these values represent. Second, when the measure W is directional, the information measure $_{i,j}I_{k,i}$ will confound the effects of the differences in the physical aspects represented by j and k with the differences implied by i and j and by i and k. The problem arises because the two stimuli come from different categories. The appropriate interpretation (information value) of a given value of W would therefore be different (and opposite) depending on which stimulus generated it, T_1 or T_2. Because of this, a high (low) value of $_{i,j}I_{k,i}$ would not imply a large (small) difference between $S_1 = k$ and $S_2 = j$. The effects of the confounding are illustrated by example in the Interpretation section that follows. Objective scaling of two physically different aspects of the stimulus would only be appropriate if W is calibrated in the sense defined by (10) or has sufficiently high resolution so that for each value of $p(S = A|W = w)$, there is a value $W = w^*$ for which $p(S = A|W = w^*)$ is equal or very close to $1 - p(S = A|W = w)$. In this case, the values of w on the T_1 (or T_2) trials in the data table can be replaced by their corresponding w^* values, and a high (low) value of $_{i,j}I_{k,i}$ for this modified dataset would then imply a large (small) difference between $S_1 = k$ and $S_2 = j$.

12.1.   Empirical Results

Estimates of $_{i,j}I_{i,m}$ and $_{j,i}I_{m,i}$ are shown in Fig. 6, once again ordering the abscissa by the size of the physical differences between the two lines being compared. Not surprisingly, fixing the size of one of the two lines and increasing the size of the other increases the information value associated with the pair. A more striking result is the apparent invariance of the objective scale with respect to the value of the context. Because there were only seven levels on the confidence rating scale, and presumably therefore a fair amount of averaging in the observed information values, it is somewhat remarkable that the estimated distance between, for example, two of the smallest lines in a given position, is the same when the size of the context line is relatively small or relatively large, dramatically changing the difficulty of the comparative judgment.

To contrast this observed invariance property with the effects of position on the derived distance measures, the upper panel of Fig. 7 shows the average information value for a given pair of sizes when the six contexts were separated into two groups, smaller (1-3) and larger (4-6). In this way the two functions have the same sample sizes as the comparison by position, shown in the lower panel of the figure. The two functions in the comparison of contexts (small versus large) are virtually indistinguishable. Perhaps the

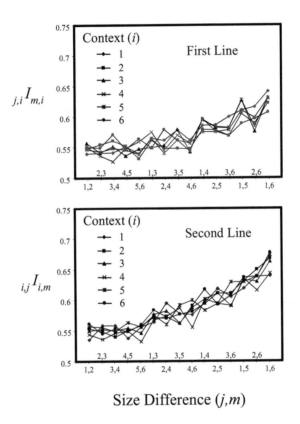

Fig. 6: Estimates of the information value of the confidence rating as a function of the size of the context (denoted by i) when the lines are presented in the first position $(_{j,i}I_{m,i})$ or the second position, $_{i,j}I_{i,m}$. The confusability of two lines of different length presented in the first (second) position of the sequence does not depend on the size of the second (first) line presented.

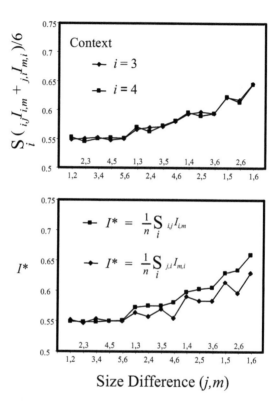

Fig. 7: Upper panel: estimates of the information value of a given size difference between two lines, averaged over their positions and three values of the context, that is, the summation is from $i = 1$ to 3 or from $i = 4$ to 6. The sample sizes of each estimate are comparable to the sizes in the lower panel figure. Lower panel: comparison of the information value for a pair of lines presented in the first versus the second position (averaged over the size of the context line). The values are generally higher, indicating higher discriminability, for the line presented second.

clearest indication of the invariance with respect to context, however, is the results of a two-way analysis of variance comparing position to the size of the context. The main of effect of position was significant, $F(1, 168) = 6.606$, $p < .02$, whereas the main effect of context was quite small, $F(5, 168) = 0.008$, $p > .99$. The interaction was also nonsignificant, $F(5, 168) = 0.266$, $p > .93$. Effect sizes for context and position were .003 and .038, respectively. The direction of the effect of position (lower panel of Fig. 7) is predictable, indicating that objects in the second position (i.e., closer in time to the point of the response) were more discriminable.

12.2.   Interpretation

Invariance of the information values $_{i,j}I_{i,m}$ and $_{j,i}I_{m,i}$ with respect to the context, i, is consistent with the assumption that the effect of the first line presented (S_1) does not depend on the size of the second line, and vice versa. The basic idea is probably clear enough. However, to state it somewhat more precisely, suppose that V^* is the measure on which W is based and further that V^* can be split into two separate measures, ψ_i and ψ_j, the first of which identifies the effect of the first line when $S_1 = i$ and the second the effect of the second line when $S_2 = j$. Invariance with respect to context suggests that the distribution of ψ_i (ψ_j) does not depend on the value of S_2 (S_1). The fact that the information values are smaller for lines presented in the first position of a sequence suggests that the distributions of ψ_i are less discriminable (in the usual Thurstonian sense) than the distributions of ψ_j.

The Thurstonian model also serves to illustrate why $_{i,j}I_{m,i}$ would not be a suitable measure of the confusability between the effects of $S_1 = j$ versus $S_2 = m$. Suppose that W is simply the arithmetic difference between the two (univariate and independent) random variables ψ_i and ψ_j, $W = \psi_i - \psi_j$. Suppose further that the distributions of these subjective effects do not depend on the physical dimension they refer to, that is, the distributions of ψ_i and ψ_j are identical when $i = j$. When stimulus T_1 ($S_1 = i$, $S_2 = j$) is presented,

$$W = \psi_i - \psi_j,$$

whereas when T_2 ($S_1 = m$, $S_2 = i$) is presented,

$$W = \psi_m - \psi_i.$$

Because of the difference in the sign on the variable ψ_i in the two expressions, this "shared" effect does not "cancel out" in the information value $_{i,j}I_{m,i}$. In fact, when $j = m$ (i.e., the two aspects to be compared are presumed to be physically identical), the information value will increase with the difference between i and j. Changing the sign of W for either the T_1 or the T_2 trials would resolve the problem in this particular case. Substituting w^* for w on the T_1 or T_2 trials, as outlined earlier, accomplishes the appropriate change of sign without relying on a specific behavioral model.

13. DISCUSSION

The results of the objective tests and their most important implications can be summarized as follows.

With respect to the information contained in the subjective confidence report, which was a deliberate aspect of the comparative judgment response and therefore represents information available to the participant at the point of the response, the decision rule is suboptimal in the direction of the time error. In the objective sense, therefore, we may conclude that the time error is at least partially due to suboptimality of the decision rule with respect to information available at the point of the response. The fact that the error was reversed once the suboptimality was "corrected" (but possibly overcorrected) is consistent with, but does not objectively confirm, the hypothesis that the time error is in fact entirely due to suboptimality of the decision rule with respect to the information on which the classification response is based. Even assuming that the time error would be eliminated by optimizing the decision rule with respect to this information, the result could still be attributed to either perceptual processes or decision-making strategies. For example, if the perceptual representation of the object in the second of the two sequential positions tends to be greater for some reason but the participant is unaware of this illusory effect, a decision rule that is subjectively optimal would be objectively suboptimal.

The participants' confidence reports are also irrational, in the sense that equal reported degrees of confidence in the A or B classification response do not correspond to equal levels of objective accuracy. The size of the difference is too large to be attributed to the limited resolution of the rating scale, and is in fact simply another manifestation of the time error. Because the test function $\phi(d)$ was roughly independent of the degree of confidence d, it is possible that the time error is entirely due to miscalculation of the prior probabilities of the two categories. However, even if this were true, the error could still be accidental or deliberate.

With respect to the information available at the point of the response (i.e., the information contained in the participant's confidence ratings), the information effect of a horizontal line in the first or second position of a temporal presentation sequence does not depend on the size of the line to which it is compared. This conclusion is objective, in the sense that the information measure $_{i,j}I_{k,m}$ is an observable property (a derived probability) of the probability space induced by the experiment. Obviously, it is impossible to objectively show that there is zero effect of context. However, if there is an effect, it must be quite small or for some reason averaged out in the translation from effects of the stimuli to integer confidence ratings. Because accuracy and confidence were strongly correlated, and the effect of position on the scale was easily detectable from the same dataset, it would probably be difficult to sustain the argument that the invariance merely reflects a lack of power in the analysis.

13.1.   Extensions of the method: Stochastic decision rules and other decision processes

Suboptimality with respect to a measure W in Γ_2 implies suboptimality on at least some trials, that is, with respect to W in Γ_1. However, suboptimality of the decision rule in Γ_2 is only identifiable when it is systematic or consistent in some way. To illustrate, suppose that the decision criterion, X_c, in a standard signal detection model (i.e., with equal variance Gaussian distributions of the perceptual effect, X), is itself Gaussian with its mean at the midpoint between the means of the two perceptual effects distributions. If the confidence rating, C, is defined, say, as the absolute value of the distance between the percept X and the criterion X_c on a given trial, the decision rule (as we defined this term) would be suboptimal with respect to X but optimal with respect to C. The suboptimality of the decision rule with respect to X is "balanced out" in C.

To detect a suboptimality of this kind, X_c need not be observable: it would suffice to find an observable measure, U, that is correlated to some degree with X_c. In the space that includes this measure, the decision rule would be suboptimal with respect to the pair C and U, and the information value of C would be independent of U. In other words, the stochasticity of the decision rule (defined in the signal detection theory sense) would be objectively established.

Judging from previous theoretical work, sequential effects ought to provide a means of establishing stochasticity of the decision rule in objective terms (e.g., Lockhead & King, 1983; Luce, Nosofsky, Green, & Smith, 1982; Mori, 1998; Treisman & Williams, 1984). In general, classification judgments are positively correlated with the participant's recent response history, suggesting (in signal detection theory terms) that the criterion for choosing a given response becomes more lenient when this response was recently selected. Figure 8 compares the asymmetry of the comparison matrix when conditioning on the response of the immediately previous trial, $R_{i-1} = A$ versus $R_{i-1} = B$. The time error is considerably more pronounced on the trials that follow an $R = B$ response, accounting in fact for almost the entire effect. Figure 9 shows the rating receiver operating characteristic

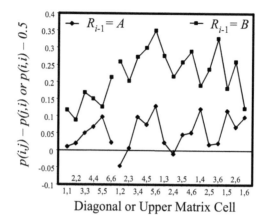

Fig. 8: Asymmetry of the comparison matrix when selecting trials following an $R = A$ versus an $R = B$ response. The time error is substantially greater following a response in the direction of the bias $(R_{i-1} = B)$.

(ROC) curves for the two conditions and compares this traditional signal detection analysis to a plot of the articulated odds distribution.

Although the ROC functions appear to be quite similar, and are virtually indistinguishable with respect to the area beneath them, this traditional graphic device, like the z-ROC curve, appears to have relatively little power to distinguish different pairs of distributions when they are estimated at different quantiles (cf. Balakrishnan et al., 2003). The articulated odds distribution is similar to a plot of the slopes of the ROC curve – that is, the likelihood ratios associated with each rating response – against the relative frequency of the ratio. In this respect, it provides more visual information. The task is difficult if the participant often has relatively high uncertainty (objectively), that is, when the density or mass of the distribution is concentrated near the middle of the scale (maximum uncertainty). Differences between these two distributions are more discernable, indicating a shift in the balance of information toward the $S = A$ category when $R_{i-1} = B$. The effect of R_{i-1} on the information distribution is even more evident in the derived distance measures, which are shown in Fig. 10. For each stimulus pair, the distance value averaged across position and context is greater when $R_{i-1} = A$. Whatever their proper interpretation might be, sequential effects of this kind cannot be attributed merely to variation of the decision rule with respect to C.

Because the two prime candidates for experimentally manipulating only the decision rule – prior probabilities and payoff matrices – appear instead

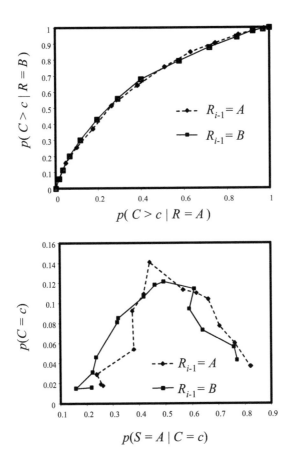

Fig. 9: Comparison of the rating ROC and odds distributions for responses on trials following an $R = A$ versus an $R = B$ response. The rating ROC curves (upper panel) are quite similar, suggesting that the outcomes of a previous trial only affect the decision rule, as is often proposed. However, the ROC representation is a relatively weak visual test of this hypothesis. Plots of the odds distributions under the two different conditions (lower panel) reveal a shift in the balance of information from right (indicating higher ability to identify the $S = B$ event than the $S = A$ event) to left (higher ability to identify the $S = A$ event than the $S = B$ event) when the response on trial $i - 1$ was in the direction of the time error ($R_{i-1} = B$).

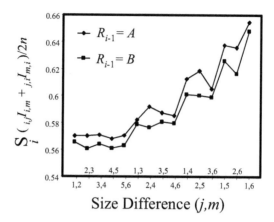

Fig. 10: Effects of the response on a previous trial on the information value of a given pair of lines, averaged over their (two) positions and (six) contexts. The lines are more discriminable on trials following a response in the opposite direction of the time error ($R_{i-1} = A$).

to affect primarily or exclusively the shape of the information effects distributions (Balakrishnan, 1998a, 1998b; Balakrishnan, 1999; Van Zandt, 2000), it appears to be difficult to find any measure that has the properties that are taken for granted in classical perception theories. Presumably, other aspects of the decision process, such as the factors that determine when the participant terminates the deliberation process and executes a response (i.e., the "stopping rule") are also involved in determining the probabilities in Γ_2. At least in this respect, response time models (e.g., Diederich, 1997; Link & Heath, 1975; Luce, 1986; Ratcliff & Rouder, 2000; Ratcliff, Van Zandt, & McCoon, 1999; Smith, 2000; Townsend & Ashby, 1983; Van Zandt, 2000; Vickers, et al., 1985), because they allow for the possibility that biases in the decision-making attitudes of the participants may influence the amount of information available at the point of the response – and hence the distribution of the information effect – may be a more fruitful basis for formulating objective questions about classification structure.

Acknowledgment: This work was supported by NASA grant NRA2-37143 (Intelligent Systems). Address correspondence to J. D. Balakrishnan, California Center for Perception and Decision Sciences, 2251 Shell Beach Road, Pismo Beach, CA 93449.

References

Balakrishnan, J. D. (1998a). Some more sensitive measures of sensitivity and response bias. *Psychological Methods, 3*, 68-90.

Balakrishnan, J. D. (1998b). Measures and interpretations of vigilance performance: Evidence against the detection criterion. *Human Factors, 40*, 601-623.

Balakrishnan, J. D. (1999). Decision processes in discrimination: Fundamental misrepresentations of signal detection theory. *Journal of Experimental Psychology: Human Perception and Performance, 25*, 1-18.

Balakrishnan, J. D., & MacDonald, J. A. (2000). Effects of bias on the psychometric function: A model-free perspective. *Purdue Quantitative Division Technical Report* No. 31, Purdue University, West Lafayette, IN.

Balakrishnan, J. D., & MacDonald, J. A. (2001). Misrepresentations of signal detection theory and an alternative approach to human image classification. *Journal of Electronic Imaging, 10*, 376-384.

Balakrishnan, J. D., & MacDonald, J. A. (2004). Objective analysis of classification behavior. Manuscript submitted for publication.

Balakrishnan, J. D., MacDonald, J. A., & Kohen, H. S. (2003). Is the area measure a historical anomaly? *Canadian Journal of Experimental Psychology, 57*, 238-256.

Baranski, J. V., & Petrusic, W. M. (1998). Probing the locus of confidence judgments: Experiments on the time to determine confidence. *Journal of Experimental Psychology: Human Perception & Performance, 24*, 929-945.

Davies, D. R., & Parasuraman, R. (1982). *The psychology of vigilance*. London: Academic.

Diederich, A. (1997). Dynamic stochastic models for decision making under time constraints. *Journal of Mathematical Psychology, 41*, 260-274.

Dzhafarov, E. N. (2003a). Thurstonian-type representations for "same-different" discriminations: Deterministic decisions and independent images. *Journal of Mathematical Psychology, 47*, 208-228.

Dzhafarov, E. N. (2003b). Thurstonian-type representations for "same-different" discriminations: Probabilistic decisions and interdependent images. *Journal of Mathematical Psychology, 47*, 229-243.

Dzhafarov, E. N. (2003c). Selective influence through conditional independence. *Psychometrika, 68*, 7-26.

Dzhafarov, E. N., & Colonius, H. (1999). Fechnerian metrics in unidimensional and multidimensional stimulus spaces. *Psychonomic Bulletin and Review, 6*, 239-268.

Dzhafarov, E. N., & Colonius, H. (2001). Multidimensional Fechnerian scaling: Basics. *Journal of Mathematical Psychology, 45*, 670-719.

Dzhafarov, E. N., & Colonius, H. (2005). Psychophysics without physics: A purely psychological theory of Fechnerian Scaling in continuous stimulus spaces. *Journal of Mathematical Psychology, 49*, 1-50.

Emmerich, D. S., Gray, J. L., Watson, C. S., & Tanis, D. C. (1972). Response latency, confidence, and rocs in auditory signal detection. *Perception & Psychophysics, 11*, 65-72.

Erlebacher, A., & Sekuler, R. (1971). Response frequency equalization: A bias model for psychophysics. *Perception & Psychophysics, 9*, 315-320.

Green, D. M., & Swets, J. A. (1974). *Signal detection theory and psychophysics.* Huntington, NY: Krieger.

Hellström, Å. (1979). Time errors and differential sensation weighting. *Journal of Experimental Psychology: Human Perception and Performance, 5*, 460-477.

Hellström, Å. (1985). The Time-order error and its relatives: Mirrors of cognitive processes in comparing. *Psychological Bulletin, 97*, 35-61.

Helson, H. (1964). *Adaptation-level theory.* New York: Harper & Row.

John, I. D. (1975). A common mechanism mediating the time-order error and the cross-over effect in comparative judgments of loudness. *Australian Journal of Psychology, 6*, 51-60.

Katz, L. (1970). A comparison of Type II operating characteristics derived from confidence ratings and from latencies. *Perception & Psychophysics, 8*, 65-68.

Kubovy, M. (1977). A possible basis for conservatism in signal detection and probabilistic categorization tasks. *Perception & Psychophysics, 22*, 277-281.

Link, S. W. (1992). *The wave theory of difference and similarity.* Hillsdale, NJ: Lawrence Erlbaum Associates, Inc.

Link, S. W., & Heath, R. A. (1975). A sequential theory of psychological discrimination. *Psychometrika, 40*, 77-105.

Lockhead, G. R., & King, M. C. (1983). A memory model of sequential effects in scaling tasks. *Journal of Experimental Psychology: Human Perception and Performance, 9*, 461-473.

Luce, R. D. (1986). *Response times: Their role in inferring elementary mental organization.* New York: Oxford University Press.

Luce, R. D., & Galanter, E. (1963). Discrimination. In R. D. Luce, R. Bush, & E. Galanter (Eds.), *Handbook of mathematical psychology* (*vol. 1*, pp. 191-243). New York: Wiley.

Luce, R. D., Nosofsky, R. M., Green, D. M., & Smith, A. F. (1982). The bow and sequential effects in absolute identification. *Perception & Psychophysics, 32*, 397-408.

Maloney, L. T., & Thomas, E. A. C. (1991). Distributional assumptions and observed conservatism in the theory of signal detectability. *Journal of Mathematical Psychology, 35*, 443–470.

Masin, S. C., & Agostini, A. (1990). Time errors in the method of pair comparisons. *American Journal of Psychology, 103*, 487-494.

Masin, S. C., & Fanton, V. (1989). An explanation for the presentation-order effect in the method of constant stimuli. *Perception & Psychophysics, 46*, 483-486.

McClelland, D. C. (1943). Factors influencing the time error in judgments of visual extents. *Journal of Experimental Psychology, 33*, 81-95.

Mori, S. (1998). Effects of stimulus information and number of stimuli on sequential dependencies in absolute identification. *Canadian Journal of Experimental Psychology, 52*, 72-83.

Petrusic, W. M., & Baranski, J. V. (1997). Context, feedback, and the calibration and resolution of confidence in perceptual judgments. *American Journal of Psychology, 110*, 543-572.

Ratcliff, R., & Rouder, J. N. (2000). A diffusion model account of masking in two-choice letter identification. *Journal of Experimental Psychology: Human Perception and Performance, 26*, 127-140.

Ratcliff, R., Van Zandt, T., & McCoon, G. (1999). Connectionist and diffusion models of reaction time. *Psychological Review, 106*, 261-300.

Restle, F. (1961). *Psychology of judgment and choice.* New York: Wiley.

Shaw, J. S., McClure, K. A., & Wilkens, C. E. (2001). Recognition instructions and recognition practice can alter the confidence- response time relationship. *Journal of Applied Psychology, 86*, 93-103.

Smith, P. L. (2000). Stochastic dynamic models of response time and accuracy: A foundational primer. *Journal of Mathematical Psychology, 44*, 408-463.

Townsend, J. T., & Ashby, F. G. (1983). *Stochastic modeling of elementary psychological processes.* Cambridge, England: Cambridge University Press.

Treisman, M., & Williams, T. C. (1984). A theory of criterion setting with an application to sequential dependencies. *Psychological Review, 91*, 68-111.

Tresselt, M. E. (1944). Time errors in successive comparison of simple visual objects. *American Journal of Psychology, 57*, 555-558.

Van Zandt, T. (2000). ROC curves and confidence judgments in recognition memory. *Journal of Experimental Psychology: Learning, Memory & Cognition, 26*, 582-600.

Vickers, D., Smith, P., Burt, J., & Brown, M. (1985). Experimental paradigms emphasizing state or process limitations: II. Effects on confidence. *Acta Psychologica, 59*, 163-193.

Woodrow, H. (1935). The effect of practice upon time- order errors in the comparison of temporal intervals. *Psychological Review, 42*, 127-152.

Woodworth, R. S., & Schlosberg, H. (1954). *Experimental psychology.* New York: Holt.

Yates, J. F. (1990). *Judgment and decision making.* Englewood Cliffs, NJ: Prentice Hall.

6

General Recognition Theory and Methodology for Dimensional Independence on Simple Cognitive Manifolds

James T. Townsend[1], Janet Aisbett[2], Jerome Busemeyer[1], and Amir Assadi[3]

[1] Indiana University
[2] The University of Newcastle
[3] University of Wisconsin

1. INTRODUCTION

This chapter concerns the issue of whether and how perceptual dimensions interact from a differential geometric standpoint. Earlier efforts in this direction initiated depiction of percepts, viewed "in the large," that is, where the percepts are sufficiently separated that discrimination is virtually perfect (Townsend & Spencer-Smith, 2004). Hence, the percepts can be treated in that framework as deterministic. In this investigation, we take up the same type of question when discrimination is imperfect due to noise or closeness of the stimuli. This is accomplished as a generalization of General Recognition Theory (GRT) (Ashby & Townsend, 1986; see also, Ashby, 1992; Maddox, 1992; Thomas, 1999, 2003). The original GRT dealt with percepts as points lying in an orthogonally coordinated space associated with distinct densities associated with the stimulus set.

We have found that the present explorations in non-Euclidean spaces tend to bring up novel aspects of relationships between stimulus dimensions and perceptual dimensions that were not immediately evident in the usual Euclidean milieu. Thus, in addition to providing some "first-order" extensions of GRT to elementary manifolds, we view this chapter as propaedeutic to several potential new lines of inquiry.

Until we are deeper within the chapter, it may seem that we are studying systems devoid of response properties. However, within the early deterministic framework, it is assumed, as in Townsend and Thomas (1993) or Townsend, Solomon, and Spencer-Smith (2001), that standard psychophysical responses are acquired. Later, as we enter the hard-to-discriminate, and therefore probabilistic milieu, we will discuss an identification paradigm (readily generalizable to categorization) where an observation point in a manifold leads inexorably to a response. A word about our conception of perceptual entities seems in order. We believe that, in fact, most objects in physical stimulus space are things like shapes, sounds, and so forth, that lie in infinite dimensional spaces. We also think that people can process these as complex percepts sometimes homeomorphic or even diffeomorphic to the physical stimulus. For instance, think of perceiving or internally imaging a friend's face. Some of our previous articles have begun to deal with this aspect of perception (see, e.g., Townsend et al., 2001; Townsend & Thomas, 1993).

However, it is also evident that somehow perceiving organisms are able to filter out dimensions (e.g., brightness or color) and categorical entities (e.g., stripes on a tiger, or the orthographic RED, independent, say, of print color) from the original object. Further, most of psychology in general and psychophysics in particular treats perceptual stimuli as points in a relatively simple space, usually a space with orthogonal coordinates and often with a Euclidean or sometimes a Minkowski power metric. Other possibilities, such as tree metrics (e.g., Tversky, 1977), are occasionally considered, too; Dzhafarov and Colonius (1999) built a theory based on Finsler and more general metrics that derive from discriminability functions.

We focus on points from two continua, assuming either elementary stimulus presentation (e.g., sound intensity and sound frequency), or that dimensional reduction through filtering (e.g., attentional) has already taken place (e.g., as in abstracting the color from an object). Thus, we treat the problem of stimulus continua with a finite number of response assignments (i.e., a type of category). However, many of the later statements concerning common experimental paradigms are true for stimuli as discrete categories (e.g., letters of the alphabet, words, and so forth).

The format of our study is somewhat tutorial in form with occasional references to instructive volumes, because many readers may not be conversant with differential geometry.[4] Although there are many terms which involve several modifiers, we give acronyms for very few of them to lessen

---

[4]Probability theory and stochastic processes, and, especially for psychometricians, linear algebra, remain the modal mathematical education for social scien-

opportunities for confusion. Also, we drop some of the modifiers when it is transparent to which theoretical object we are referring.

Following Townsend and Spencer-Smith (2004), we take the concept of a coordinate patch or simply "patch" in differential geometry as forming an appropriate level of description for a beginning treatment of dimensional independence on manifolds. First, we require a definition of a stimulus domain, which, for simplicity, we restrict to two dimensions. It is explicit that all possible pairs of stimulus dimension values be potentially available for perception.

Definition 1. *A two-dimensional stimulus domain is an open set in the plane: $D = U \times V \subseteq \Re^2$, where U and V may be finite or infinite open intervals, $\Re$ is the real line, and $\Re^2$ is the plane with the Euclidean metric.*

We should note that $\Re^n$, $n = 1, 2$ and so forth, will not be armed with the Euclidean metric unless so stated, as in Definition 1. $\Re^n$ unadorned with a metric denotes the usual set of orthogonal coordinates. Note that the presence or absence of physical units is left open. The next definition adapts the notion of a proper coordinate patch that is also a diffeomorphism (that is, a map between manifolds that has an inverse such that both the map and the inverse are smooth – see the following, for example, more or less in order of increasing sophistication: O'Neill, 1966; Boothby, 2003; Kobayashi & Nomizu, 1991, 1969; Lang, 1985). Our assumptions in this treatise will be rather tight and may in some instances be considerably loosened. For instance, the diffeomorphic assumption in Definition 2, shown later, is fairly demanding. This constraint helps keep matters relatively straightforward, but these aspects should be generalizable in the future (e.g., as the case demands, to immersions, submersions, or nonsmooth mappings – see Summary and Discussion).

Here, we investigate cognitive modeling using the simplest type of differential manifold, namely spaces that can be represented as orientable surfaces. One way that such spaces might be produced in the brain is by mapping, say, a physical object of n dimensions into a space of $n + k$ dimensions. For instance, a pair of fundamental frequencies w_1, w_2, as a stimulus may produce sounds involving the overtones of w_1 and w_2 through nonlinearities. There may be other psychological dimensions produced by the same two stimulus dimensions. Thus, even a finite distribution of colors on a piece of art or in a room can stimulate distinct values in aesthetics scales simply by apparently minor rearrangement of the color placements.

Alternatively, it could be that any such psychological manifold is more chimerical. For example, if the psychological metric is non-Euclidean, say

---

tists. However, this state of affairs is changing with increasing influences of many areas of applied and pure mathematics into social and especially cognitive science.

Riemannian, then it could be associated with a certain kind of manifold, although the manifold as a surface might be rather a "second-thought" construction. In any event, we keep the material simple by invoking only one extra dimension, assuming that the manifold is two-dimensional and lies in three-dimensional space. Generalization to higher dimensional embeddings (e.g., a two-dimensional surface in a k-dimensional Euclidean space) is easy, if more tedious.

Definition 2. *A proper perceptual patch* $X : D \to M \subset \Re^3$ *is a one-to-one, diffeomorphic map of an open set D of $\Re^2$ into $\Re^3$, and onto M. Thus we specify X by a coordinate function*

$$X(u, v) = (x(u, v), y(u, v), z(u, v))$$

in $\Re^3$. *Let us call the psychological coordinates $\phi \in \Phi$ and $\psi \in \Psi$, respectively, where $\Phi \times \Psi$ is a subset of $\Re^2$. In general, ϕ and ψ are functions of (u, v), but neither is necessarily identical to any of x, y, or z. If we focus on the coordinates produced by holding v or u constant, respectively, and vary the other, the proper perceptual patch X is interpreted as a parameterization of D.*

There is an induced diffeomorphism $Y : \Pi \to M$ for

$$\Pi = \{\phi(u, v) : (u, v) \in D\} \times \{\psi(u, v) : (u, v) \in D\} \subset \Re^2,$$

which provides the coordinate chart for the manifold M. Through this map and its inverse, the psychological experiences being studied can be considered as either points in M or as points in the set Π. Moreover, we occasionally require the map $Z : D \to \Pi$ defined by $Z = Y^{-1}(X)$. In cases where a psychological coordinate is identical to a coordinate in the embedding space or a monotonic function of it (e.g., as in the patch $x = \phi(u, v), y = \psi(u, v), z = \gamma(u, v)$), the coordinate is directly readable from M itself.

Fig.1 illustrates the general relationship between the stimulus domain D, the psychological space M, and the psychological coordinates. In this example, the manifold M is the modified geographical upper half-sphere of radius 1. A perceptual patch might be defined as the map

$$X(u, v) = (cos(u)cos(v), sin(u)cos(v), sin(v)),$$

with $U = (-\pi/2, \pi/2)$ and $V = (-\pi/2, \pi/2)$.

As mentioned earlier, deterministic separability has been introduced by Townsend and Spencer-Smith (2004). We present a slightly modified form here. There are two fundamental classes of deterministic separability in their

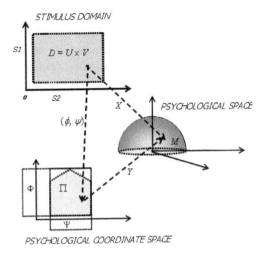

STIMULUS DOMAIN

$S1$

$D = U \times V$

0

$S2$

X

(ϕ, ψ)

PSYCHOLOGICAL SPACE

M

Y

Φ

Π

Ψ

PSYCHOLOGICAL COORDINATE SPACE

Fig. 1: Example of proper perceptual patch X from two-dimensional physical stimulus space to a hemisperical manifold in psychological space, with coordinate map Y from psychological coordinate space to the same manifold. The induced mapping (ϕ, ψ) to the coordinate space $\Phi \times \Psi$ is not neccesarily Cartesian, and is not necessarily onto $\Phi \times \Psi$.

scheme, one called domain-range separability. This notion captures the traditional emphasis on whether perceptual dimensions interact as functions of specified physical dimensions. For instance, suppose $M = \Re^2$, and let $X(u,v) = (\phi(u), \psi(v))$; this is a trivial example of domain range separability. In contrast, the fact that equiloudness contours in sound perception are functions of both intensity and frequency implies that loudness is not deterministically a separable function of intensity.

The second class of separability is called range-alone separability and this concept pertains to properties that adhere to M itself, without reference to the map X. An example of a property associated primarily with M itself is local orthogonality; that is, the tangent vectors to the coordinates ϕ, ψ are always orthogonal at every point of M (see Townsend & Spencer-Smith, 2004). We are mainly concerned with domain-range separabilty in this study, but range-alone separability is expanded on later.

It is worth remarking that some of our developments require a metric and some do not, rendering them more general objects. For instance, local orthogonality requires an inner product in the tangent space, which then readily produces a metric. However, the following definition, as well as Definitions 1 and 2, do not necessitate a metric.

Definition 3. *Deterministic domain-range, parameterization, perceptual separability (DDR-PPS) of two stimulus dimensions is defined by the condition that the proper perceptual patch X be a parameterization of $D = U \times V$, with the perceptual coordinates ϕ, ψ corresponding respectively to functions of u, v.*

Thus, irrespective of how the nervous system does it, we can think of the map X as a composition of maps from U, V to Φ, Ψ, and then from there onto M via Y. That is,

$$X(u, v) = Y(\phi(u), \psi(v)) = m \in M.$$

See Fig.2.

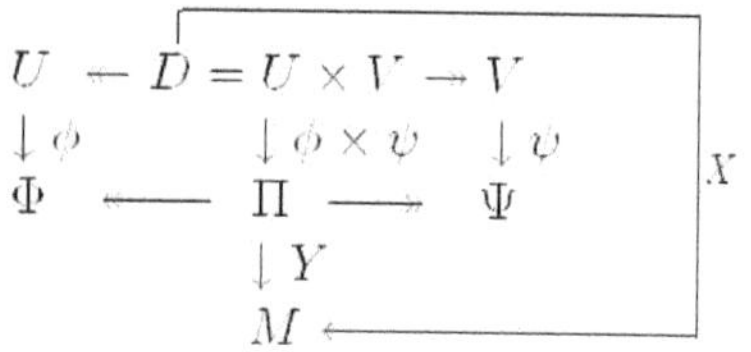

Fig. 2: X has deterministic domain-range parametrized perceptual separability (DDR-PPS) when the diagram exists and commutes. Here, all maps are onto, the horizontal maps are the projections onto the Cartesian components, and $Y : \Phi \times \Psi \to M$ exists such that $X = Y \circ (\phi \times \psi)$.

In Townsend and Spencer-Smith (2004), the designation of domain-range separability was given to the case where $M \subset \Re^3$ and $x = x(u) = \phi(u)$ and $y = y(v) = \psi(v)$, with z being an arbitrary function of u, v. We now think parameterization separability should, in contrast to the earlier treatment, be featured, because this earlier situation, now called "embedding coordinate perceptual separability," is obviously a special instance of parameterization separability (Definition 3). Proposition 1, whose proof is obvious, keeps this new characterization in order. Fig.3 illustrates this concept.

Proposition 1. *Deterministic domain-range embedding coordinate perceptual separability is a special case DDR-PPS of Definition 3.*

Is there any sense to thinking of any kind of separability notion when we focus entirely on the image space and the psychological coordinates

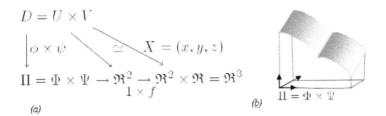

$D = U \times V$

$\phi \times \psi$

$\simeq \quad X = (x, y, z)$

$\mathrm{II} = \Phi \times \Psi \rightarrow \mathfrak{R}^2 \rightarrow \mathfrak{R}^2 \times \mathfrak{R} = \mathfrak{R}^3$

$1 \times f$

(a)

$\mathrm{II} = \Phi \times \Psi$

(b)

Fig. 3: (a) X is a deterministic domain-range embedding if for some $f : \mathfrak{R}^2 \rightarrow \mathfrak{R}$ the diagram exists and commutes, where ϕ is defined on U and ψ is defined on V. (b) Example of an embedding in which the two-dimensional coordinate space is mapped to a surface in three-dimensional space.

therein, ignoring the $D \rightarrow M$ map? It has been suggested that the answer to this query is "yes" (Townsend & Spencer-Smith, 2004). The idea is that although the psychological dimensions may be intricate functions of the manipulated physical variables, there are some properties that are suggestive of separability. Local orthogonality, mentioned earlier, is one such option because whether the tangents to the psychological coordinates are at right angles does not depend on whether they are parameterizations of the physical coordinates, u, v. In another elemental kind of separability that depends only on the properties of the range space, Townsend and Thomas (1993) suggested that one simple type of deterministic perceptual separability might demand that the perceptual space can be expressed as

$$\{\phi(u, v) : u \in U\} \times \{\psi(u, v) : v \in V\} = \Phi \times \Psi,$$

that is, as the Cartesian product of the possible values of the psychological coordinates regardless of whether ϕ, ψ are each functions only of u, v respectively. This observation leads to the following definition.

Definition 4. *Cartesian range separability is defined by the condition that the perceptual coordinates consist of the Cartesian product $\Phi \times \Psi$.*

The upshot here is that there is a kind of deterministic nonseparability when certain combinations of the psychological variables cannot occur. To see how Cartesian range separability can fail to hold even when the stimulus space is $D = U \times V$ and the specified coordinates are functions on D, consider the map

$$(\phi(u, v), \psi(u, v)) = (u \ln(v), v e^u), \, u > 0, v > 1.$$

A level surface is created by solving for $v = e^{\phi_o/u}$ and then finding that $\psi = e^{\phi_o/u + u}$. We see that ψ is bounded below by $e^{2\sqrt{\phi_o}}$, and hence the range is not equivalent to

$$\Phi \times \Psi \equiv \{\phi(u,v) : (u,v) \in D\} \times \{\psi(u,v) : (u,v) \in D\} = (0,\infty) \times (1,\infty).$$

The next proposition establishes the relationship between Cartesian range separability and DDR-PPS.

Proposition 2. *DDR-PPS implies that $\Pi = \Phi \times \Psi$ and therefore that Cartesian range separability is in force; and Cartesian range separabilty does not imply DDR-PPS.*

Proof. Given DDR-PPS, each value of ϕ corresponds to a specific v-trajectory in M, say $\phi(u) = X(u_\phi, V)$ and similarly each $\psi(v) = X(U, v_\psi)$. Then clearly,

$$\Pi = \cup_\phi X(u_\phi, V) \times \cup_\psi X(U, v_\psi) = \Phi \times \Psi.$$

To show that Cartesian range separabilty does not imply DDR-PPS, consider the maps $\phi(u,v) = vu^a$ and $\psi(u,v) = uv^b$ where u, v, a, b are positive on the real line, a, b fixed parameters, say, $a, b > 1$. In this case, ϕ is primarily a function of u, for instance, loudness as a function primarily of intensity, secondarily of $v =$ frequency; and vice versa for $\psi =$ pitch. One can then solve for a given level surface, $\phi = \phi_o$, $v = u^{-a}\phi_o$ and find that $\psi = u$ $(u^{-a}\phi_o)^b$, so that for every $\phi_o \in \Re^+$, all legitimate values of ψ are produced. Similar results obviously occur in the reverse function, and Cartesian range separability occurs, because $\{(\phi(u,v),\psi(u,v))\} = \Phi \times \Psi$. But, observe that coordinate domain-range perceptual separability does not hold.

In principle, an investigator can empirically determine whether DDR-PPS holds through various psychophysical methods, such as variations on Stevens's direct scaling methods. Equiloudness contours are an example. However, even if DDR-PPS is valid, it could be that probabilistic mechanisms, including correlation of noise in the two-dimensional channels, could invalidate separability at the local, tough-to-discriminate stochastic level. We turn to this question next.

2. PROBABILISTIC DOMAIN-RANGE PERCEPTUAL SEPARABILITY AND PERCEPTUAL INDEPENDENCE

In general, we refrain from specifying the source of probabilism - it may be from the outer environment, internal noise, and so forth. Any such specification will depend on more microlevel or process-oriented interpretations.

As far as our present technical considerations are concerned, it matters little, although the technical difficulty can vary. Next, we have a couple of evident propositions.

The earlier Ashby and Townsend (1986) work, as in the present, is descriptive to a point, in the sense that we are deliberating at a geometric level, without direct reference to underlying time-oriented dynamics. The reader is referred to MacMillan and Creelman (2005) for a survey of the current state of multivariate detection theory and methods in Cartesian coordinates. We assume that the perceptual activity and decisions in, say, a 2 x 2 factorial design take place in a way equivalent to some type of decision rule on M itself. For instance, if, as we shall postulate, M is partitioned into a set of four mutually exclusive regions, then the probability measures over those regions determine the stochastic structures of interest in our endeavor. On the other hand, if the decision occurs after filtering operations are performed that map the psychological point to a different space, such as the plane, then it could be that the topological or geometric aspects of M are inherited by this tertiary space, or not.

Next, we require the probabilistic structure obtained by placing probability densities on M. This approach stipulates that associated with each stimulus $(u, v) \in D$ is a probability density function on M given point-wise by $p(x, y, z | u, v)$, with the understanding that any such point (x, y, z) resides on M via the map X. Also, there is a function $p(\phi, \psi | u, v)$ that depends conjointly on (u, v). We abuse the notation in using the same symbol "p" for both functions, allowing that there is a 1-1 relation between $(x, y, z) \in M$ and $(\phi, \psi) \in \Pi$. Indeed, the distribution on M can also be pulled back to D. In any event, we can think of p as being a member of a family depending on u, v, each pair (u, v) of which determines a unique probability density function. As discussed more later and as suggested by Fig. 1, we can discuss the psychological coordinates as they exist in planar Π, or as they exist through a mapping Y from Π onto M. This facilitates the following definition.

Definition 5. *Every setting of u, v engenders a joint probability distribution on ϕ, ψ in Π, that is $p(\phi, \psi | u, v)$. Because a setting of u, v (say $u = u_o$, $v = v_o$) leads, in the deterministic sense, to values ϕ_o, ψ_o of ϕ, ψ, we can also express*

$$p(\phi, \psi | u_o, v_o) = p(\phi, \psi | \phi_o, \psi_o).$$

It is an interesting sidelight of this picture that although a number of parameters dependent on u could be defined on Π, the parameter space will still be one-dimensional. For instance, suppose the probability density on Π is normal with the mean and variance being functions of u. Then the mean and variance are clearly functionally dependent due to their dependence on u. Perhaps the relationships of stochastic model parameters and their dependence may be of aid in the geometrical side of matters (but see, e.g., Levine, 2003, for a discussion of the complexity of relations between quantity of latent variables and dimensionality). The succeeding definition establishes a potential linkage between the stochastic and deterministic milieus but it is not seen much in the following material.

Definition 6. *The distribution on M is said to satisfy convergent determinism if there exists a converging sequence of p as a function of a magnitude parameter I such that*

$$p(\phi, \psi | u_o, v_o; I) \rightarrow p(\phi_o, \psi_o | u_o, v_o; I)$$

as I grows large, where (ϕ_o, ψ_o) is the image of (u_o, v_o).

Convergent determinism then ensures a connection between the stochastic situation and the high signal-to-noise ratio situation when perception becomes deterministic. The parameter I can refer to any physical dimension(s) that increase discriminabiliity such as contrast, salience, and so forth Yet, Definition 6 does not imply that reports, say, in magnitude estimation will be deterministic although discrimination among the presented stimuli is high.

Next, we require an apparatus for integration in the manifold M. We have interest in the geometric aspects of spaces and hence an approach based on the exterior calculus of Grassman and Cartan (e.g., Kobayashi & Nomizu, 1969, 1991; see also, Lang, 1993, for a discussion of the relationship of measures to exterior forms on manifolds) seems called for. The latter immediately and elegantly provides for the institution of the metric into the integral.

Thus, we define a volume form (which is always possible if M is orientable, which we take as a postulate), or in our elementary case, an area form, which we denote by $\mathrm{d}M$.[5] The idea is that $\mathrm{d}M$ is an operator (technically, a covariant tensor of order 2) which operates on a pair of vectors (contravariant tensors) to measure an infinitesimal area. In a Riemannian manifold, this operator will be closely linked to the metric function $g_{ij}(m)$ defined at a point m of M, which determines scale.

---

[5]Using forms for integration necessitates keeping track of the orientation of M, so that the oriented volume, $\mathrm{Vol}^o(\mathrm{v}_1, \mathrm{v}_2, ..., \mathrm{v}_n)$ where the v_i span the parallelepiped, is $+ \mathrm{Vol}(\mathrm{v}_1, \mathrm{v}_2, ..., \mathrm{v}_n)$ if $\mathrm{DET}(\mathrm{v}_1, \mathrm{v}_2, ..., \mathrm{v}_n) > 0$ and $- \mathrm{Vol}(\mathrm{v}_1, \mathrm{v}_2, ..., \mathrm{v}_n)$ if $\mathrm{DET}(\mathrm{v}_1, \mathrm{v}_2, ..., \mathrm{v}_n) < 0$. Because of this facet, some writers call such forms, "pseudoforms". It is assumed in our text that the orientation has been accounted for and the form properly "signed".

Because $m = X(u, v)$ for some (u, v) in D, we can also write $g_{ij}(u, v)$. In addition, the prime vectors to employ in the computation are, in fact, the basis vectors of a tangent space fixed at point m. These basis vectors yield a parallelogram whose area is the local infinitesimal measure for which we are looking.

In the event that the metric is inherited from the map X, which would naturally be of interest to us, it is known as a Riemannian metric or first fundamental form. It turns out that we can then express

$$\mathrm{d}M(X_u, X_v) = \sqrt{g_{11}g_{22} - g_{12}^2}\,\mathrm{d}u\,\mathrm{d}v,$$

where X_u and X_v are the partial derivatives of X and $g_{ij} = \langle X_i, X_j \rangle$, the inner product of the partial derivatives with regard to i or j where either is equal to u or v. Note that we have successfully "pulled back" the computation from M to $D = U \times V$. The role of the factor

$$\sqrt{g_{11}g_{22} - g_{12}^2}$$

is to expand or shrink various parts of M relative to D.

In our case, however, we are more interested in ϕ, ψ as the psychological coordinates rather than the stimulus values u, v. We don't know, of course, if something like a direct map from stimulus space D to psychological coordinate space Π, for instance via Z, occurs, or if, more likely, the latter are "picked off" or interpreted from M, as in

$$(\phi, \psi) = Y^{-1}X(u, v) = Z^{-1}.$$

In any event, we can express the partial derivatives of Y as

$$Y_\phi = X_u \frac{\partial u}{\partial \phi} + X_v \frac{\partial v}{\partial \phi}$$

and

$$Y_\psi = X_u \frac{\partial u}{\partial \psi} + X_v \frac{\partial v}{\partial \psi}.$$

Having restructured the coordinates in terms of ϕ, ψ, we now refer the developments in the previous paragraph to the psychological coordinates. Thus, the stimulus set D, for example, is replaced by Π in the ϕ, ψ plane.

Regardless of the specific metric, the area of the region B on M can then be found from computing

$$\int_{B'} \mathrm{d}M = \int_{B'} \mathrm{d}M(Y_\phi, Y_\psi),$$

where B' is the area corresponding to B in the planar set $\Phi \times \Psi$. The terms Y_ϕ and Y_ψ refer to the standard coordinate basis vectors in the tangent space of M, $TM_{(m)}$ at an arbitrary point $m = Y(\phi, \psi)$ of M. They correspond to (1,0) and (0,1) in $\Re^2$ in the plane and in fact are the push forward of these basis vectors to M. Finally, the density function, p, on M can simply be instated in the integrals above analogously to the situation in $\Re^n$.

The earlier Ashby and Townsend (1986) concept of "perceptual separability" can be viewed as a probabilistic realization of a two-dimensional domain-range coordinate separability (see also Townsend, Hu, & Ashby, 1981; Townsend, Hu, & Evans, 1984; Townsend, Hu, & Kadlec, 1988). Observe again that the fact that the results or models can be plotted in the plane does not imply flatness unless a flat metric is imposed.

How should we formulate the probabilistic version of domain-range separability on M? We can take a hint from the earlier construction in ordinary rectangular coordinated space by Ashby and Townsend (1986). They considered the 2 x 2 table of settings of the two stimulus dimensions; these, in effect, form (i.e., map to) a parameter space. It was assumed that the stimulus dimensions were associated with psychological variables, although allowing that each of the latter variables might, in effect, be functions of both stimulus variables. The psychological space was assumed to be two-dimensional. Because typically, only a 2 x 2 performance matrix containing the relative frequencies of responses to the four stimuli are gathered from an experiment, the location of the probability distributions in this space have to be estimated in a sense from the data. This procedure is analogous to how one carries out Thurstone scaling, or signal detection or discrimination in one-dimensional settings.

In any event, each cell in the stimulus table then was associated with a hypothetical joint probability distribution in $\Re^2$. Ashby and Townsend (1986) next defined probabilistic perceptual separabilty of the psychological dimension (e.g., ϕ) paired with stimulus dimension u, as the requirement that the marginal distribution on that dimension (ϕ), after integrating out the psychological dimension associated with stimulus variable v (e.g., ψ), would be constant over the other stimulus settings of variable v. Notice that this definition does not imply stochastic independence, or vice versa.

To initiate the proceedings, we may simply reiterate the Ashby and Townsend (1986) definition with the present notation.

Definition 7. *Probabilistic domain-range parameterization perceptual separability (PDR-PPS) of ϕ against ψ holds if and only if, for each physical stimulus value u, the marginal distribution for ϕ, namely $p(\phi|u, v)$, is invariant across settings of v. If this is the case, we can write $p(\phi|u, v) =$*

$p(\phi|u)$. *Separability of ψ against ϕ likewise holds when $p(\psi|u, v)$ is independent of u for each v and ψ.*

Identifying coordinate space with psychological space M, PDR-PPS of ϕ from ψ is seen to be equivalent to the condition that

$$\int_V p(x, y, z|u, v)\mathrm{d}M = \int_\Psi p(\phi, \psi|u, v)\mathrm{d}\psi = p(\phi|u, v) = p(\phi|u),$$

where the first term may be interpreted as the integral over

$$\{X^{-1}Y(\phi, \psi) : \psi \in \Psi and(\phi, \psi) \in \Pi\}$$

in the pull back to $U \times V$. Separability of ψ from ϕ on M is defined in the same manner.

As an example in this context, Definition 7 suggests that a parameter set associated with one psychological dimension, say ϕ, is a function of only one physical dimension u and not the other, v. Hence, for instance, if the mean and variance were established to be the defining parameters for ϕ, then they would be functions only of u and not v. Integrating over ψ would then erase the mean and variance associated with v and leave a distribution on ϕ depending only on Φ (and implicitly on u and not v).

One way to think of what is happening in separability is that in perceiving the "coordinates" in M in a separable fashion, the observer is performing in a way that is equivalent to mapping M into the $\Phi \times \Psi$ plane.

Proposition 3. *PDR-PPS holds if DDR-PPS holds and, for any stimulus value (u_s, v_s) and any fixed $u \in U$, the "marginal" distribution obtained by integrating $p(x, y, z|u_s, v_s)$ over*

$$\{(x, y, z)|X^{-1}(x, y, z) \in (u, V)\}$$

is independent of v_s.

Proof. Simply reform $Z^{-1}: \Phi \times \Psi \to D$ as before, $Z^{-1}(\phi, \psi) = X^{-1}Y(\phi, \psi)$. Then

$$Z^{-1}(\phi(u), \psi(v)) = (u, v)$$

and so

$$Z^{-1}(\phi, \psi) = X^{-1}(x, y, z).$$

Note that if the marginal condition in M stipulated in Proposition 3 is abrogated, then even if DDR-PPS is in force, PDR-PPS can fail to hold.

To this point, we have the following setup: We can investigate the properties of the stochastics on M via the plane $\Phi \times \Psi$. The geometric properties of M as expressed in the metric g_{ij} are transferred there. Separability is defined as the invariance of a marginal distribution on either of the psychological dimensions when integrating out the other. These concepts are illustrated in the example in the penultimate section.

3. EVIDENCE ASSESSMENT

Somehow a decision must be made. Of course, the decision must be a function of the observations. As we learned from univariate signal detection theory, the decision plays an important role in performance. Within the literature on multivariate psychophysics and perception, there was scant consideration of this aspect of behavior. Ashby and Townsend (1986) showed that, in some ways, decisional structure played an even more critical role than stimulus structure in studying various types of perceptual independence. Thus, decisional structure could obscure perceptual independencies, reveal them authentically, or in rare cases, render an appearance of perceptual independence where there was none.

The observations in Π have to be mapped into the appropriate set of decisions. A natural intermediary is the "evidence space," which may include a bias that is response oriented (e.g., Luce, 1963; Townsend, 1971a) or stimulus oriented (Lappin, 1978; Nosofsky, 1992). Then a subsequent function on the biased evidence maps the latter into one of the finite set of decisions. We see more on evidence space later.

Ashby and Townsend (1986) found that an assumption of "decisional separability" is crucial in readily exposing the underlying perceptual interactions among dimensions. Decisional separability requires that an implicit or explicit decision based on a dimension be independent of the decision about the other dimension. In a space with orthogonal coordinates, this requirement implies that the decision boundaries are straight lines that are parallel to one axis and orthogonal to the other. However, orthogonality is not a necessary prerequisite, as our new definition indicates.

Definition 8. *Decisional separability of ϕ from ψ is the condition that the criterion that ϕ exceed (or fail to exceed) a certain value ϕ_0, is defined by a boundary in M identified with the constant ϕ_0 trajectory (i.e., varying ψ while holding ϕ constant). So, the response variable on ϕ is a_1 if the observed ϕ is to the "left" of ϕ_0 and a_2 if it is to the "right" of ϕ_0. Decisional separability of ψ from ϕ is defined analogously. (See Fig.4.)*

Thus, each decision bound is itself a value of the psychological variable and simultaneously a trajectory of the other variable holding the first constant. Patently, just as with perceptual separability, the notion is not

$$\Psi \xrightarrow{\quad Y(\phi_0,\psi) \quad} B$$

$$\Big\downarrow \phi_0 \times 1 \qquad\qquad \Big\downarrow identity$$

$$\Pi_i = \Phi_i \times \Psi \xrightarrow[Y|_{\Pi_i}]{} B \cup M_i \subseteq M$$

Fig. 4: Decisional separability of ϕ from ψ exists if the commutative diagram exists for $i = 1$ and 2 and $\Phi_1 = \{\phi : \phi \leq \phi_0\}$ and $\Phi_2 = \{\phi: \phi \geq \phi_0\}$ and where $M_1 \cup M_2 \cup B = M$ and $M_1 \cap M_2 = \varnothing$. B is the decision boundary and response a_i is observed for stimulus (u,v) whenever $X(u,v) \in M_i$.

a symmetric relation. Of course, in Π we immediately find that decisional separability is true if and only if the decision boundaries are appropriately parallel to the ϕ, ψ axes. Next, we see some relations of decisional separability to certain other important notions.

Proposition 4. *Decisional separability does not require Cartesian range separability, or any type of domain-range separability.*

Proof. Merely observe that selecting an arbitrary criterion on either Φ, Ψ does not depend on what values exist on the other dimension; and clearly, the notion of decisional separability is independent of what transpires with respect to the map from D to Π. That is, decisional separability is a range type of property.

How might such a property be generated? We must now consider how the percepts (ϕ, ψ) relate to evidence regarding the response alternative. The evidence space records the evidence in favor of each alternative and permits a decision to be made on some comparison based on this evidence. The mapping of the psychological space into the evidence space assumes the role of the so-called discriminant function in pattern recognition theory (e.g., Nilsson, 1965; Townsend & Landon, 1982). Set the evidence map $e : M \rightarrow E_p$ where the range space is a subset of $\Re^4$ so that

$$e(m) = (e_{11}(m), e_{12}(m), e_{21}(m), e_{22}(m))$$

and e_{ij} maps an observation into $\Re$ as the strength of perceptual indication for response $a_i b_j$. Assume that the evidence map and its inverse are continuous.

In general, the evidence function can include learning and motivational biases; and in fact, biases based on either the responses (most common, e.g., as in Luce's recognition choice theory, 1963) or as noted earlier, on stimulus bias (e.g., Lappin, 1978; Nosofsky, 1992). To constrain the theoretical development, we adopt the MAX rule of decision, that is, response $= a_i b_j$ if and only if $e_{ij} = \max_{kl}(e_{kl})$. This decision rule covers an enormous number of decision possibilities including both optimal and nonoptimal strategies (for some of these, see Townsend & Landon, 1982). It does not include certain probabilistic decision strategies such as probability matching.

Consider the pairs of functions

$$e_{22} - e_{12} = e_1, e_{22} - e_{21} = e_2, e_{22} - e_{11}$$
$$= e_3, e_{12} - e_{21} = e_4, e_{12} - e_{11}$$
$$= e_5, e_{21} - e_{11} = e_6.$$

Let

$$E_{22} = \{m \in M : e_1(m) > 0, e_2(m) > 0, e_3(m) > 0\}$$
$$= \cap_{i=1,2,3}\{m \in M : e_i(m) > 0\},$$

that is, E_{22} is where e_{22} dominates the other functions so that response $a_2 b_2$ will be made in this region. And so on, for the other response alternatives.

Proposition 5. *If*

$$S = \{m \in M : e_1(m) = 0, e_j(m) \neq 0 \, for \, j \neq 1\}$$

and $de_i/dm \neq 0$, *then S is a one-dimensional closed submanifold between a region E_{22} and E_{12}, and similarly for other regions E_{ij}; and each region E_{ij} is connected.*

Proof. The first claim is a generalization into differential manifolds of the inverse function theorem (see, e.g., Hirsch, 1976); and the second claim follows from the topological fact that a continuous image of a connected manifold is connected (e.g., Munkres, 1975).

As yet, we have no means of enforcing decisional separability. The next definition opens a path to this end.

Definition 9. *Discriminant decomposability on both dimensions obtains if there exist two independent, one-dimensional discriminant functions α_i, β_j, $i, j = 1, 2$, where α_i is a function only of ϕ and β_j is a function only of ψ, such that $e_{ij} = \max_{kl}[e_{kl}]$ holds if and only if $\alpha_i = \max_k[\alpha_k]$ and $\beta_j = \max_k[\beta_k]$.*

Proposition 6. *If discriminant decomposability holds on both dimensions and the differences $\alpha = \alpha_2 - \alpha_1$ and $\beta = \beta_2 - \beta_1$ are monotonic functions of their respective arguments ϕ, ψ, then decisional separability holds.*

Proof. We can simply compute $\alpha_2 - \alpha_1$ and $\beta_2 - \beta_1$ and partition M into regions where these differences are negative or positive. Further, under the stipulations, either difference will be 0 on a tie between the α or β values, and the ties partition $\Phi \times \Psi$ space into two disjoint sections apiece. They can both be 0 only once where the two straight and orthogonal lines cross. The lines of separation and the intersection point, being of dimension 1 or 0, must be of measure 0 relative to the underlying densities.

A natural example forms when α_i is the likelihood of alternative u_i and β_j is the likelihood of v_j and α_1/α_2 is monotonic decreasing and similarly for the β ratio. These likelihoods can be taken from the marginal densities, whether or not independence of ϕ, ψ holds.

The next assignment is to formulate analogues to the Ashby and Townsend (1986) observable implications of separability. In that article, it was shown that under decisional separability, an earlier statistic, marginal response invariance (earlier employed in testing for feature independence in a test then called "across-stimulus invariance"; Townsend, Hu, & Ashby, 1981; Townsend & Ashby, 1982; Townsend, Hu, & Evans, 1984; Townsend, Hu, & Kadlec, 1988), was equivalent to perceptual separability.

Let the probability of giving a response identified with level "i" of physical dimension U and level "j" of dimension V be $P(a_i, b_j | u_i, v_j)$. The usual complete factorial identification paradigm has two levels on each dimension and four responses overall corresponding to the four stimulus combinations of the 2 x 2 values. For generality, let k' be the complement to k, that is, if there are two levels and $k = 1$ then $k' = 2$ and vice versa. Then, following Ashby and Townsend (1986), we can state the definition of marginal response invariance as follows.

Definition 10. *Marginal response invariance is defined as the satisfaction of the condition*

$$P(a_i | u_k, v) = P(a_i, b_j | u_k, v) + P(a_i, b_{j'} | u_k, v)$$
$$= P(a_i, b_j | u_k, v') + P(a_i, b_{j'} | u_k, v')$$
$$= P(a_i | u_k, v')$$

for any v, $v' \in V$, and likewise for pairs u, $u' \in U$.

Note that indeed, the marginal probability of responding that u is at level "i" depends on u, but not on the level of v. Next comes a proposition that indicates the conditions under which PDR-PPS is revealed by marginal response invariance. Naturally, the stipulation concerns decisional variables, because marginal response invariance involves response frequencies whereas PDR-PPS only involves the perceptual distributions themselves.

Proposition 7. *If decisional separability holds, then PDR-PPS implies marginal response invariance; and if marginal response invariance holds everywhere in the presence of decisional separability, then PDR-PPS is implied. Thus, under decisional separability, perceptual separability and marginal response invariance are basically equivalent.*

Proof. Assume that decisional separability holds for ϕ over ψ, and that two stimulus values of v have been specified. Decisional separability entails that the decision pertaining to an observed value ϕ depends only on which side of a criterion ϕ_0 it falls. Then, one integrates over the proper range of ψ (i.e., summing over the response probability for reporting either b_j or its alternative) and the "i" side of the division of the space by ϕ_0 to calculate the marginal probability of a_i (i.e., level "i" for dimension ϕ) under the two stimulus settings. Marginal response invariance states that for two distinct settings of v, the marginal probability of reporting a_i will be the same. But, it must be that the integrals formed under the two settings of v are indeed the same because the probability measure is identical as

$$P(a_2, b_1|u_i, v_j) + P(a_2, b_2|u_i, v_j) = \int_\Psi \int_{\phi_0}^\infty p(\phi, \psi|u_i, v_j) \mathrm{d}\phi \mathrm{d}\psi$$

$$= \int_{\phi_0}^\infty p(\phi|u_i) \mathrm{d}\phi = \int_\Psi \int_{\phi_0}^\infty p(\phi, \psi|u_i, v_{j'}) \mathrm{d}\phi \mathrm{d}\psi$$

$$= P(a_2, b_1|u_i, v_j') + P(a_2, b_2|u_i, v_j').$$

If marginal response invariance is in force for all settings of v and for any decisional boundary for u (and therefore ϕ), then because of decisional separability,

$$\int_V \int_{u_o}^\infty p(x, y, z|u_i, v_j) \mathrm{d}M = \int_\Psi \int_{\phi_0}^\infty p(\phi, \psi|u_i, v_j) \mathrm{d}\phi \mathrm{d}\psi$$

$$= \int_V \int_{u_o}^\infty p(x, y, z|u_i, v_j') \mathrm{d}M = \int_\Psi \int_{\phi_0}^\infty p(\phi, \psi|u_i, v_j') \mathrm{d}\phi \mathrm{d}\psi$$

so that

$$\int_{\phi_0}^\infty p(\phi|u_i, v_j) \mathrm{d}\phi = \int_{\phi_0}^\infty p(\phi|u_i, v_j') \mathrm{d}\phi$$

for all v_j and v_j' and ϕ_0. Because of the uniqueness of the relation of the distribution with the parameter sets, it follows that both sides are invariant across v, for all ϕ_0, which implies PDR-PPS.

Strictly speaking, without decisional separability, marginal response invariance and PDR-PPS are logically unrelated. There is an asymmetry in what one might conclude from data. If separability is not experimentally supported, that is, marginal response invariance fails, then one cannot know from this analysis alone if perhaps the absence of decisional separability might not have ruined the chances for true underlying separabilty to manifest itself in the data. But, if perceptual separability is supported by the success of marginal response invariance, then there are fewer cases where a combination of a certain kind of decisional bound and failure of perceptual separability might nevertheless lead to a misleading appearance of separability. An example of such an anomaly is mean shift integrality (e.g., Kadlec & Townsend, 1992; Maddox, 1992).

4.   PERCEPTUAL INDEPENDENCE

Along with the perceptual and decisional separabilities, the other founding concept of general recognition theory is "perceptual independence." Independence is a notion that is so ubiquitous that it is probably impossible to confine it to one concept even in highly related areas of discourse. Ashby and Townsend (1986) chose to assign the term, with a modifier "perceptual," to represent the finest grain level with which we were dealing, that of probabilistic independence of perceptual dimensions, within a single stimulus. That is, perceptual independence is a within-stimulus condition and as is perhaps befitting, this usage coincides with that in probability and stochastic processes theory. Observe again, that in contrast, perceptual separabilty refers to across-stimulus invariances (see, e.g., Townsend & Ashby, 1982). Hence, logically, perceptual independence has nothing to do with domain-range considerations. Nevertheless, later discussion indicates how the domain-range map could indeed play a strategic role, despite the logical distinction.

It is straightforward to define perceptual independence for manifolds more general than the Euclidean. But on region Π, we can express matters analogously to Ashby and Townsend (1986).

Definition 11. *Perceptual independence will be said to hold for a given experimental condition* (u, v) *if* $p(\phi, \psi | u, v) = p(\phi | u, v) p(\psi | u, v)$.

Again, notice that it is not automatically assumed that the marginal probability density on ϕ is a function only of u, for that would be tantamount to forcing perceptual separability as well, which is a logically distinct concept. Unfortunately, psychologists have frequently conflated separability and independence.

What is the commonly observable relation from experiments pertaining to the theoretical notion of perceptual independence? It is a statistic called sampling independence deriving from earlier usage in probing independence of feature processing (e.g., Ashby & Townsend, 1986; Townsend et al., 1981). At the risk of confusing previous readers of GRT, we would like to alter the name of "sampling independence" to "report independence" to emphasize that this statistical property is an observable. We again use the aforementioned definitions relating to experimentally observable response probabilities.

Definition 12. *Consider an experimental setting of the stimulus dimensions u, v. Then, report independence is defined by the property that*

$$P(a_i, b_j | u, v) = [P(a_i, b_j | u, v) + P(a_i, b'_j | u, v)][P(a_i, b_j | u, v) + P(a'_i, b_j | u, v)].$$

Hence, report independence requires that the joint likelihood of reporting a_i and b_j equals the product of the marginal probabilities of reporting them. This definition is in line with the notion of probabilistic independence, but of course, the report probabilities, both joint and marginal, are integrals over the underlying probability densities. Note that it is not necessary to require that the observer explicitly report each value of the two dimensions. As long as there is a 1-1 assignment of stimulus pairs to responses, report independence can be checked. Thus, in the first instance, the experimenter could require that the observer respond as follows: "This trial I saw dimension A at level 1 but dimension B at level 2." Alternatively, he or she could require that the observer respond R_i, $i = 1,2,3,4$, with R_1 corresponding to level 1 on both dimensions, R_2 to level 1 on dimension A but level 2 on dimension B, and so on. In either case, it is straightforward to assess report independence.

Next, we require a proposition to link up perceptual independence and report independence. The natural proposition depends strongly on decisional separability, as it did earlier. Obviously, just as in the case of separability, in M the densities are "perturbed" by the stretching factor. However, given a stimulus (u_0, v_0), on integration the independence of, say, the ψ trajectory representing the psychological value say, ϕ' and the ϕ trajectory representing psychological value ψ', will be established, even if we were directly integrating in x, y, z on M.

Proposition 8. *If decisional separability holds for a given experimental setting, then perceptual independence and report independence are equivalent.*

Proof. Assume decisional separabilty. Perceptual independence implies report independence. With decisional separability,

$$P(a_2, b_2|u, v) = \int_{\psi_0}^{\infty} \int_{\phi_0}^{\infty} p(\phi, \psi|u, v) d\phi d\psi$$

$$= \int_{\phi_0}^{\infty} p(\phi|u, v) d\phi \int_{\psi_0}^{\infty} p(\psi|u, v) d\psi$$

$$= [\int_{-\infty}^{\psi_0} \int_{\phi_0}^{\infty} p(\phi, \psi|u, v) d\phi d\psi + \int_{\psi_0}^{\infty} \int_{\phi_0}^{\infty} p(\phi, \psi|u, v) d\phi d\psi]$$

$$[\int_{\psi_0}^{\infty} \int_{-\infty}^{\phi_0} p(\phi, \psi|u, v) d\phi d\psi + \int_{\psi_0}^{\infty} \int_{\phi_0}^{\infty} p(\phi, \psi|u, v)) d\phi d\psi]$$

$$= [P(a_2, b_2|u, v) + P(a_2, b_1|u, v)][P(a_1, b_2|u, v) + P(a_2, b_2|u, v)].$$

Report independence for all u, v implies perceptual independence. Because of decisional separability, just noting

$$P(a_2, b_2|u, v)$$
$$= [P(a_2, b_2|u, v) + P(a_2, b_1|u, v)][P(a_1, b_2|u, v) + P(a_2, b_2|u, v)]$$

and reversing the argument used in the first part of the proof establishes the result.

We have concentrated on how things look in Π space, which is virtually identical to the Cartesian circumstances in Ashby and Townsend (1986). Moreover, unless PDR-PPS is true, the map Y carrying $\Phi \times \Psi$ into M will not coincide with the X map. Some further remarks concerning the relation between separability and independence are made in the next section.

5. PROBABILISTIC RANGE-ALONE SEPARABILITY AND PERCEPTUAL INDEPENDENCE

What happens when we move from a tight linkage of each physical dimension to their respective perceptual images? Can, for instance, such notions as separability and independence still have any empirical referent? These issues are explored in this section.

We begin with the fairly minimalist assumption that there exist two psychological dimensions everywhere which possess tangents that are linearly independent. Further, we continue to assume that there exists a mapping that carries the equimagnitude trajectories of each dimension into a psychological plane $\Phi \times \Psi$. Obviously, however, these no longer need be co-incident with the original physical dimensions, u and v. That is, no longer will $X(u, V) = Y(\phi, \Psi)$, where ϕ is the image of u.

First, because DDR-PPS obviously does not hold, could there exist probability distributions such that PDR-PPS still is true? This appears to be an open problem. Basically, a functional equation that captures this general issue is, for separability of ψ over ϕ, and when ψ depends on both u, v but ϕ only depends on u,

$$\frac{\partial}{\partial u} \int p(\phi, \psi | u, v) d\phi = \int \frac{\partial p(\phi, \psi | u, v)}{\partial u} d\phi$$

$$= \int \frac{\partial p(\phi, \psi | \phi(u), \psi(u, v))}{\partial \phi(u)} \frac{\partial \phi(u)}{\partial u} d\phi +$$

$$\int \frac{\partial p(\phi, \psi | \phi(u), \psi(u, v))}{\partial \psi(u)} \frac{\partial \psi(u)}{\partial u} d\phi.$$

The first term is always zero but the second being zero establishes the condition for PDR-PPS. If perceptual independence holds, then the critical equation is

$$\int \frac{\partial p(\psi | \psi(u, v))}{\partial \psi(u, v)} \frac{\partial \psi(u, v)}{\partial u} d\phi = 0.$$

Because we assumed that p is a function of the parameter $\psi(u, v)$ and ψ is a function of v, both nontrivial, then it's clear that these two functions must tradeoff in such a way over $\Phi \times \Psi$ that the integral is nil.

As noted earlier, if ϕ, ψ are dependent under p, even if the parameters are separate functions only of u, v, $\phi(u)$ and $\psi(v)$, then this dependence may ruin PDR-PPS. Yet, it is also possible that PDR-PPS is true although perhaps unlikely. This situation is akin to what has been defined as "marginal selective influence" (Townsend & Schweickert, 1989; see also, Townsend, 1984; Townsend & Thomas, 1993) in response time theory.

Next, we turn to the issue of redefining the stimulus dimensions in order to enforce DDR-PPS. If we had access to the internal sites of $\Phi \times \Psi$, in principle we might be able to ascertain if the marginal distributions of ϕ and ψ were invariant over the parameter settings, say ϕ', ψ' respectively. However, behaviorally, there is no way to make this stipulation empirical without creating a new stimulus domain (or doing something logically equivalent). Thus, we can now establish a new physical domain D^*, actually a diffeomorphism of the old one, D, such that the new physical coordinates u^*, v^* in D^* now correspond respectively to functions of ϕ, ψ, and hence are PDR-PPS with regard to ϕ, ψ. Consider two settings (u, v) and (u', v') of D that result in the respective joint densities $p(\phi, \psi | u, v)$ and $p(\phi, \psi | u', v')$. Suppose further that these settings are such that, according to the scales,

ϕ remains the same whereas ψ is changed. This situation corresponds to that in the domain-range situation where u is held constant.

Definition 13. *Consider that two different settings of the stimulus are presented such that the ϕ sensations would be the same if no noise were present - the stimulus has been altered so that only the ψ dimension changes. Then range-alone probabilistic perceptual separability of ϕ from ψ is defined as the requirement that the marginal distribution on ϕ, after integrating over the ψ variable, will be the same for both settings.*

Because we have stipulated that ϕ is unchanged by integrating over the other variable, we can simply write this requirement in terms of the respective densities under the two settings:

$$p(\phi, \psi | u, v) = p(\phi, \psi | u_1^*, v_1^*)$$

for the first and

$$p(\phi, \psi | u', v') = p(\phi, \psi | u_1^*, v_2^*)$$

for the second. Note that ϕ, as one of the two sensory parameters of the density, is unchanged as is u^*. Similarly, in general, an absence of **PDR-PPS** finds that

$$\int_\Psi p(\phi, \psi | u, v) \mathrm{d}\psi = p(\phi | u, v) \neq p(\phi | u', v')$$

$$= \int_\Psi p(\phi, \psi | u', v') \mathrm{d}\psi.$$

Is there any empirical content left in this situation? The answer is clearly "yes" as long as the scientist has some guide as to the possible underlying dimensions as functions of u, v. The idea would be to use macroscopic methods (e.g., magnitude estimation, cross-modality matching, and so forth) first to map out the way in which two physical dimensions interact (e.g., as in equiloudness contours) to produce the psychological dimensions (e.g., Baird, 1977; see also, Townsend & Spencer-Smith, 2004). Then, in principle, one can carry out tests such as those for marginal response invariance. Naturally, some aspects of marginal response invariance will have to change to reflect the fact that u does not accurately represent ϕ any longer and similarly for v and ψ.

Nevertheless, for each distinct combination of values of ϕ and ψ, there will still be a unique u, v that produce exactly that psychological pairing. Now that D^* is defined, such notions as marginal response invariance and decisional separability follow immediately, and at least in principle and perhaps in practice with effort, range along probabilistic perceptual separability can still be tested.

The situation for perceptual independence is a bit different, in that because we are working with a single stimulus setting, the report independence test can be carried out immediately, without fretting about a remap of $D \rightarrow D^*$ first. Everything is as before in the domain-range milieu.

6. A PSYCHOLOGICAL SPACE AND TWO DISTRIBUTIONS

A strong contender for the most studied pair of dimensions, with regard to issues of independence, are the orientation and size of a line-at-an-angle, often in the context of a definite 0-angle line and an arc, producing pie-slice like figures (Shepard, 1964). Most published studies have assessed the orientation and size dimensions to be separable. Thus, Shepard (1964) and Nosofsky (1985) found multidimensional scaling (MDS) plots to be reasonably rectangular, which, within the deterministic milieu, suggests separability. MDS fits using a city block metric, again in highly discriminable stimuli, have generally been more successful than a Euclidean metric (e.g., Dunn, 1983; Hyman & Well, 1967, 1968; Shepard, 1964). More recently, using GRT methodology, Kadlec and Hicks (1998) substantiated both perceptual independence and perceptual separability as well as decisional separability. Potts, Melara and Marks (1998) provided a thorough parametric investigation of experimental conditions that do or do not lead to separability with the Shepard (1964) stimuli.

We present a simple space M that can capture the topological and probabilistic aspects of the data and serve as a guide to potential assay of the metric, as well as of so far unexplored issues such as curvature and existence - or not - of paths and geodesics in the perceptual space for orientation and size. Then we impose two distinct probability densities on M.

Let ϕ correspond to psychological size, presumably mainly a function of physical radius u, and ψ correspond to psychological orientation, presumably mainly a function of physical orientation v. We think of u as standing for size and contained in the interval (a, b), a > 0, not necessarily bounded on the right in general, and v as angles in $(0, 2\pi)$, say. Psychological space M in $\Re^3$ is then assumed to be the surface of revolution produced by the formula

$$X(u, v) = (s(u, v), \phi(u, v) \cos \psi(u, v), \phi(u, v) \sin \psi(u, v)).$$

Here, the $s(u, v)$ term deforms the psychological parameters so as to describe distortion orthogonal to the cross section of the surface, along the x

axis, say. We assume s is psychological size ϕ, so that

$$X(u,v) = (\phi(u,v), \phi(u,v)\cos\psi(u,v), \phi(u,v)\sin\psi(u,v)).$$

For well-behaved functions ϕ and ψ, X is 1-1 and onto and is further a diffeomorphism. The various mappings are illustrated in Fig.5.

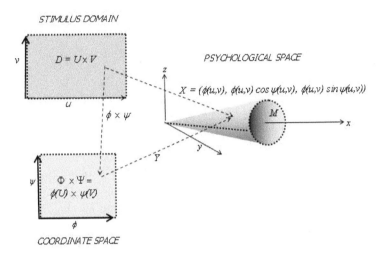

Fig. 5: Example of patch mapping to a conic surface of revolution. Equisized squares in coordinate space map to different sized areas (two-dimensional volumes) in psychological space M, due to the distortion factor of $\sqrt{2}\phi$.

Assuming ϕ, ψ are perceptually separable, as suggested by Kadlec and Hicks (1998; and under certain circumstances, Potts et al., 1998), then we have at the deterministic level,

$$X(u,v) = (\phi(u), \phi(u)\cos(\psi(v)), \phi(u)\sin(\psi(v)))$$

and coordinate space $\Pi = \Phi \times \Psi$. By Definition 3, ϕ and φ are then DDR-PPS (deterministically domain-range separable), and by Definition 8 they are decisionally separable from each other with the boundaries effectively slicing the cone through the y-z plane, or forming a sector along the x-axis. To go further, we need to retrieve some more differential geometry.

Ultimately, we need the metric. Obviously, we don't know that to begin with. We do know that the set of points in a space and the metric are independent. For illustration sake, we employ the metric inherited from the mapping Y, as Riemannian metric. In our example,

$$Y_\phi = (1, \cos\psi, \sin\psi) \text{ and } Y_\psi = (0, -\phi\sin\psi, \phi\cos\psi).$$

Hence

$$g_{11} = \langle(1, \cos\psi, \sin\psi), (1, \cos\psi, \sin\psi)\rangle = 1 + (\cos\psi)^2 + (\sin\psi)^2 = 2.$$

Similarly, $g_{12} = g_{21} = 0$, and $g_{22} = \phi^2$. Then, as observed earlier, the map Y distorts the ϕ, ψ plane in a way captured by

$$\sqrt{g_{11}g_{22} - g_{12}^2} = \sqrt{2}\phi.$$

We can further conclude two immediate points from the fact that $\langle Y_\phi, Y_\psi\rangle = 0$. First, Y_ϕ and Y_ψ are the basis vectors for a coordinate system in T_pM, and their inner product being 0 implies that they are orthogonal at every point m. Hence, this system also obeys the tenet of local orthogonal separability (Townsend & Spencer-Smith, 2004).

Furthermore, there is no interaction in the sense that, although the speed depends on ϕ, ψ (degenerately in ψ, to be sure), the off-diagonal is 0. This statement can be appreciated in the expression for the infinitesimal increment

$$ds = \sqrt{g_{11}(\phi, \psi)(d\phi)^2 + 2g_{12}(\phi, \psi)(d\phi)(d\psi) + g_{22}(\phi, \psi)(d\psi)^2}$$
$$= \sqrt{2(d\phi)^2 + \phi^2(d\psi)^2}.$$

Thus, observe that even if one is, for instance, traveling on the diagonal in the plane, only the weighted Euclidean values determine magnitude - there is no interaction of the product of $d\phi \times d\psi$. The rate of progression along the ϕ or x axis is uniform at rate 2 whereas if we move around a circle, the rate of change is a function of how far out we are along the x-axis (i.e., how big the size is). This makes sense because the circumference is larger the farther out we are. Note that even if DDR-PPS holds as functions of the physical stimuli values, the apparent rate of change along the x-axis may not be uniform as it is moderated by the term $(\partial\phi/\partial u)^2$.

A deficiency of the inherited metric of our map from some points of view may be that it is not the city block metric. Many studies, although far from all, have found that the city block fits in MDS scaling of perception of Shepard stimuli are superior to fits by the Euclidean metric. However, the studies only test members of the power metric class and sometimes only city block versus Euclidean. As far as we know, no general Riemannian metrics have been attempted with these stimulus patterns. The Euclidean metric is the only power metric that is also a Riemannian metric. One property that all the power metrics share is the noninteraction across dimensions (see Beals, Krantz, & Tversky, 1968; Townsend & Thomas, 1993; and Summary and Discussion later).

Distribution A

Suppose initially that probability density p on the manifold M depicted in Fig.5 is Gaussian about the determinate mapping of stimulus (u, v). That is, we suppose that for points (x, y, z) in M,

$$p(x, y, z|u, v) = N exp(-\alpha((x - x(u, v))^2 + (y - y(u, v))^2 + (z - z(u, v))^2))$$

with normalizing function $N = N(u, v)$. In deriving the associated probability distribution p in coordinate space Π, it is necessary to account for the distortion in M. Setting $(\phi_0, \psi_0) = Y^{-1}X(u, v)$, we have

$$p(\phi, \psi|u, v) = \sqrt{2}\phi N(\phi_0, \psi_0)exp(-\alpha((\phi - \phi_0)^2 +$$
$$(\phi \cos(\psi) - \phi_0 \cos(\psi_0))^2 + (\phi \sin(\psi) - \phi_0 \sin(\psi_0))^2)),$$

which by standard trigonometric relations reduces to the following:

$$p(\phi, \psi|u, v) = \sqrt{2}\phi N(\phi_0, \psi_0)exp(-2\alpha(\phi^2 + \phi_0^2 - \phi\phi_0 - \phi\phi_0 \cos(\psi - \psi_0))).$$

Figures 6a and 6b illustrate this probability density on coordinate space $\Phi \times \Psi$ for two physical stimulus values (u, v).

This is an example when perceptual independence (Definition 11) fails to hold. If ϕ is a function only of u, however, the example demonstrates probabilistic separability (PDR-PPS) of ϕ from ψ. To see this, observe first that the normalizing function $N(\phi_0, \psi_0)$ must be independent of ψ_0 because

$$N(\phi_0, \psi_0)^{-1} \equiv \int_\Phi \int_\Psi N(\phi_0, \psi_0)^{-1} p(\phi, \psi|u, v)$$

$$d\psi d\phi = \sqrt{2} \int_\Phi \phi exp(-2\alpha(\phi^2 + \phi_0^2 - \phi\phi_0)) \int_\Psi exp(-2\alpha(\phi\phi_0 cos(\psi - \psi_0)))d\psi d\phi,$$

which is independent of ψ_0. Then

$$\int_\Psi p(\phi, \psi|u, v)d\psi$$

$$= \sqrt{2}N(\phi)\phi exp(-2\alpha(\phi^2 + \phi_0^2 - \phi\phi_0)) \int_\Psi exp(-2\alpha(\phi\phi_0 cos(\psi - \psi_0)))d\psi$$

is independent of ψ_0 and hence of v.

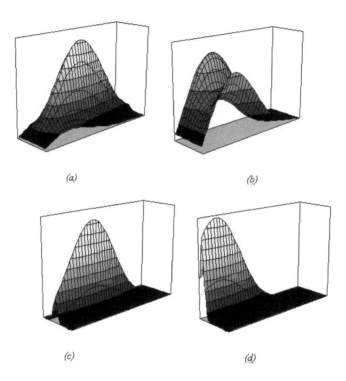

(a)   *(b)*

(c)   *(d)*

Fig. 6: Unnormalized densities on $\Phi \times \Psi$ plane given stimulus (ϕ_0, ψ_0). For (a) and (b): $p(\phi, \psi | u, v) = \phi \exp(-\alpha((\phi - \phi_0)^2 + (\phi \cos(\psi) - \phi_0 \cos(\psi_0))^2 + (\phi \sin(\psi) - \phi_0 \sin(\psi_0))^2))$. (c) and (d): $p(\phi, \psi | u, v) = \exp(-3\alpha((\phi - \phi_0)^2 + (\psi - \psi_0)^2))$.For (a) and (c): $(\phi_0, \psi_0) = (0.7, 3)$; for (b) and (d): $(\phi_0, \psi_0) = (0.3, 1)$.

Even if DDR-PPS holds and ϕ is basically linear in u with slope 1, as the data suggest (e.g., Baird, 1997, p.34), and we assume also that $\psi(v) = v$, then probabilistic separability of ψ from ϕ still will not hold. If psychological size varies from 0 to infinity, and ψ is separated from ψ_0 by π radians so that $\cos(\psi - \psi_0) = $ -1, then

$$\int_\Phi p(\phi, \psi | u, v) d\phi = \sqrt{2} N(\phi_0) exp(-2\alpha\phi_0^2) \int_\Phi \phi exp(-2\alpha\phi^2) d\phi$$

$$= \sqrt{2} N(\phi_0) exp(-2\alpha\phi_0^2)(4\alpha)^{-1}.$$

For this term to be independent of ϕ and hence of u, necessarily $N(\phi_0)$ is proportional to $exp(-2\alpha\phi_0^2)$, say $N(\phi_0) = c \exp(2\alpha\phi_0^2)$. However, if $\psi = \psi_0$ so that $\cos(\psi - \psi_0) = 1$, then substituting for $N(\phi_0)$ gives

$$\int_\Phi p(\phi, \psi | u, v) d\phi = \sqrt{2}c \int_\Phi \phi \exp(-2\alpha\phi(\phi - 2\phi_0))) d\phi,$$

which is not independent of ϕ_0. So for any ψ, we have demonstrated that the marginal distribution $\int_\Phi p(\phi, \psi | u, v) d\phi$ cannot be independent of u for all physical stimulus values $v = \psi_0$.

Distribution B

In contrast, consider the case when the probability density p is Gaussian on Π about the determinate mapping of stimulus (u, v). That is, we suppose that $p(\phi, \psi | u, v)$ is proportional to $exp(-\alpha(\phi - \phi)^2 + (\psi - \psi_0)^2))$, where again we suppose that $\phi(u, v) = \phi_0$ and $\psi(u, v) = \psi_0$. (This density function is illustrated in Figs. 6c and 6d; note that scaling on the ϕ or size axis has visually distorted the circularly symmetric functions.) With this assumed probabilistic structure, perceptual independence obviously holds. With DDR-PPS, probabilistic separability also holds in both directions, because, for example,

$$\int_\Psi p(\phi, \psi | u, v) d\psi$$

$$= exp(-\alpha(\phi - \phi_0)^2) \int_\Psi exp(-\alpha(\psi - \psi_0)^2) d\psi / \int_\Phi \int_\Psi p(\phi, \psi | u, v) d\psi d\phi$$

$$= exp(-\alpha(\phi - \phi_0)^2) \int_\Phi exp(-\alpha(\phi - \phi_0)^2) d\phi$$

is independent of $v = \psi_0$.

These two distributions, A, B, along with the definitions and propositions, illustrate several aspects of the theory. Note that Example A has the joint density as independent in x, y, z, as might happen if independent noise sources are intimately tied to the separate x, y, z dimensions. When interpreted in terms of Π, independence is severed between ϕ and ψ. Example A also points up potential relationships between independence and separability, even though the concepts are logically distinct: With non-independence, it takes a kind of balancing act to rid, say, the marginal distribution on ϕ, from contamination via the "wrong" stimulus dimension, in this case v. This balancing act does not occur in this example.

Example B sees independence between ϕ and ψ, for instance, as we might expect if independent noise sources are connected with the perceptual coordinates ϕ, ψ. Of course, independence in ϕ, ψ will not transfer to independence among x, y, z. Furthermore, if DDR-PPS holds, then Distribution B leads directly to PDR-PPS.

Decisional separability, then, in the case of Distribution B, will eventuate in marginal response invariance and report independence. However, decisional separability will expose the lack of PDR-PPS in the case of Distribution A through a failure of marginal response invariance. And, it will also expose an absence of perceptual independence via failure of report independence.

7. SUMMARY AND DISCUSSION

7.1. Roles of the Map X

We have developed the structures for GRT that are suitable for its use on simple two-dimensional manifolds. We used coordinates but did not resort to extrinsic concepts (e.g., a normal to a surface). Thus, although we have emphasized surfaces, the developments immediately generalize to two-dimensional Riemannian manifolds with diffeomorphic physical-sensory maps; and, with obvious complexification of the notation, from two-dimensional physical Euclidean space to n-dimensional manifolds.

We have found it useful in this enterprise to accentuate the macroscopic picture of the physical-to-sensory map X which would be deterministically visible when discrimination is high (e.g., the psychophysical loudness as a function of sound intensity, as opposed to the discrimination of two neighboring tones). This perspective was not so obviously central in Ashby and Townsend (1986), although it lay in the background of the separability concepts. But here, it makes clear the distinction between the map X and the stochastic structure (e.g., see Definition 6). Thus, we demonstrated in the last section on range-alone separability, that even if the physical space were recoordinatized from D to D^* so that a new X^* is deterministically separable (DDR-PPS), it may not be probabilistically separable (PDR-PPS).

The underlying map X plays other strategic roles as well. Consider the question of decisional separability. It is certainly a highly critical aspect of performance and is exceedingly important in observing the internal structure. On the encouraging side is the likelihood that the decision bounds might be easier for an observer to align with the perceptual axes when the coordinates are perceptually separable. In fact, in categorization research, it is has been found that observers first try to establish decision bounds that are aligned with the simple and evident psychological dimensions and only if that strategy is ineffectual or highly nonoptimal to attempt other strategies (Ashby & Maddox, 1990, 1992). To be sure, it has been found in categorization experiments that observers can establish separable decision bounds with stimuli thought to be integral (Ashby & Gott, 1988) and nonseparable decision bounds with perceptually separable stimuli, if in each case the bounds are optimal within the experimental setting (Ashby & Maddox, 1990, 1992). Yet, it does appear that it is easier for people to set up decisionally separable bounds if the experimental dimensions are indeed perceptually separable (e.g., Ashby, 1992, pp.459ff.). Hence, it seems not unlikely that the assumption of decisional separability might be reasonable in a number of circumstances.

In another role for X, although perceptual independence is formally untied to separability X, in actuality they may be intertwined. As a simple example, suppose $M = \Pi = \Re^2$ and X is a linear orthogonal map of $D = \Re^2$ to Π but with a rotation so that ϕ, ψ are orthogonal. On the one hand, if the noise source is independent in u and v, then it will be correlated in ϕ and ψ. If decisional separabilty holds, then both the failure of perceptual separability as well as the failure of perceptual independence can be discovered.

If X is deterministically perceptual separable as in DDR-PPS, but the noise is correlated then again, with the presence of decisional separability, the satisfaction of probabilistic perceptual separability will be experimentally detectable as will the failure of independence.

7.2. Roles of Metrics

A few remarks are worth making concerning the role of metrics in our proceedings. We employed the inherited metric as a natural approach. First, the actual mappings from sensory organs to brain with the various distortions could be directly related to the way in which the Euclidean metric, typically employed in the physical sciences, is distorted on the way to the psychological representation. However, it could also be that a particular manifold M is simply one of an equivalence class of isometric spaces that capture the psychological metric. Of course, it also could be that the actual metric (assuming one exists) bears little or no relation to the "form" of the psychological manifold.

In another interesting aspect, despite the presence of a metric, the main properties of the aforementioned theory are (differentially) topological in nature. This feature is associated with the usual change-of-variables invariance of Lesbegue or Riemannian integration. Hence, diffeomorphic alterations of either the psychological or the physical coordinates that do not mix coordinates will not disturb the main results concerning separability. That is, if $\phi = f(\alpha)$ and $\psi = g(\beta)$, where α and β are independent parameters and f, g are 1-1, differentiably invertible, then the conclusions regarding perceptual and decisional separability will be unharmed. Independence will not be distorted to dependence. In contrast, coordinate transformations that mix the coordinates, for instance, $\phi = f(\alpha, \beta)$, will ordinarily affect both separability and independence.

Metric issues can also intrude when various questions arise in, for instance, combating mimicking. A case in point regards the attempt by Kadlec and Townsend (1992) to rule out a perceptually nonseparable configuration by applying an empirical test based on measurement of a line in the perceptual space. However, this was shown to be inappropriate except when perceptual independence was in force by Thomas (1999, 2003). In oversimplified form, the metric needs to take the variance of the attendant distributions into account in making such measurements. The potential relations of such questions to the "true" underlying psychological metric appear intriguing but lie beyond the present scope.

With regard to the metric that was emitted from the map in our application to the Shepard (1964) stimuli in the previous section, some particular and general observations can be made. First, the usually preferred city block metric being a member of the class of power metrics as noted, it is only one member of a set of general structures that are in a sense, independent functions of the distinct dimensions. Following Beals et al. (1968; see also Suppes, Krantz, Luce, & Tversky, 1989), we can write a dissimilarity (not necessarily a metric) function $D(x, y) = F(f_1(x_1, y_1), f_2(x_2, y_2))$ where F is strictly monotonic in the two arguments from the two dimensions, a property they called "decomposability." Note that F does not mix the coordinate contributions as it would say if

$$D(x, y) = F(f_1(x_1, y_1), f_2(x_2, y_2), f_1(x_1, y_1).f_2(x_2, y_2)).$$

Our metric follows this precept by virtue of $g_{12} = 0$. However, it can also be observed that F is invariant across the points in the space, except as the coordinates appear under the f_i. Our metric does not obey this stricture because $g_{22} = \phi^2$.

Townsend and Thomas (1993) made the point that qualitative properties put forth by Beals et al. (1968), such as decomposability (above), which is shared by all the power metrics, may be a more appropriate criterion for separability than the very strict city block metric per se. However, we believe that the relations among the various notions of independence and separability, including what we might call "metric separability" (which would presumably invoke properties such as forms of decomposability) and DDR-PPS or PDR-PPS, deserve more thought and study. Both their interrelations and their direct relations to task and response structure may be important considerations.

7.3.   Other Approaches to Separability

Clearly this is not the place for a global review of this important but already vast topic. Ashby and Townsend (1986) provided a few linkages with earlier (and continuing) approaches such as Garner and colleagues' and Shepard and his group, and Townsend and Thomas (1993) provided a more extensive, if not so current, survey. And, we have to neglect the massive psychometric literature that has stemmed from the innovations of Shepard (1964), Kruskal and Wish (1979), and Carroll and Arabie (1980). However, much more could be done even excluding the latter realms. For instance, in one sector, we are collaborating with the laboratory of D. Algom in Israel to integrate GRT, Garner's approach, and our response time technology (e.g., Algom, Eidels, Kadlec, & Townsend, 2005; Melara & Algom, 2003; Townsend & Nozawa, 1995; Townsend & Wenger, 2004), in investigation of the famous Stroop effect. Whenever there is indication of significant inhibition (as in the Stroop effect) or facilitation (as in, say, redundant signal experiments) (Colonius & Townsend, 1997; Miller, 1982; Mordkoff & Egeth, 1993; Mordkoff & Yantis, 1991) across dimensions, there is prima facie evidence for non-separability.

In fact, we envision a taxonomic "space" where various types of independence and separability hold sway in part of the space. Contextual influences in general will be viewed as disabling certain of the independence conditions. "Pure" nonindependence systems of interest include configurality where we conceive that positive dependences may dominate (e.g., Townsend & Wenger, 2004; Wenger & Townsend, 2001) and highly inhibitory interactions such as is posited for the Stroop effect.

Multidimensional Fechnerian Scaling

Dzhafarov (2002) applied his and Colonius's Multidimensional Fechnerian Scaling (MDFS) to perceptual separability, within the same-different matching setting, rather than identification experiments as is the present work. His approach is also distinctive in several other more substantive respects. Notwithstanding, it does appear possible to make a few informal comparative observations in the spirit of scientific communication.

Dzhafarov's modus operandi is to place conditions on functions of probabilities associated with coordinates. And, the coordinates are stimulus coordinates alone - no perceptual coordinates. Both these aspects differ from the GRT approach which is to deal with psychological factors like dissimilarity or distance and bias within a multidimensional signal detection (identification) environment. In GRT, perceptual coordinates are present, and the probabilities are placed on these. These diversities are not necessarily at odds by any means but they do indicate quite distinct strategies. Perhaps an apt analogy is the relationship of functional equations on choice probabilities versus random utility theory (whose scales represent a state space). For instance, Luce's choice axiom is an example of the former in its purest form. Later, investigators sought conditions in random utility theory that satisfied the choice strictures (e.g., Holman & Marley, cited in Yellott's 1977 article). Obviously, GRT is more akin to the random utility approach but could be associated with functional equations expressing certain regularities.

The first condition of Dzhafarov's theory, called "weak perceptual separability," assumes that increments of probability of detection of a stimulus difference is a function of each of the dimensional differences, for instance, on u, v in our terms. So it could be written something like the following:

Pr[increase in detecting a difference in going from (u, v) to $(u + su, v + sv)$; s positive real and small | stimulus (u, v)] $= F$(increase in detecting a difference in going from u to $u + su$, increase in detecting a difference in going from v to $v + sv$ | stimulus (u,v)).

Note that even though F separates out the stimulus dimensions, the probabilities for both dimensions can still depend on the entire stimulus point (u, v). In most interpretations in terms of GRT, it appears that this would engender a failure of PDR-PPS in our machinery, except perhaps for special cases where v becomes "ineffective" relative to the u probabilities and vice-versa.

The second condition, called "detachability," is that when all the dimensions but one are held fixed and the one varied, then the probability of increase in detecting a difference does not depend on the values of the fixed dimensions. Again, informally

Pr[increase in detecting a difference in going from (u, v) to $(u + su, v)$; s positive real and small | stimulus (u, v)] is the same for all values of v.

In this condition, contrary to the first, natural transitions to GRT would seem to imply PDR-PPS. For instance, if the individual dimensional probabilities are interpreted as marginals as is natural, then the transference from MDFS to GRT seems reasonable.

It appears of interest to investigate these relationships more deeply, but these comments appear to intimate some intriguing hints.[6] Because MDFS is presently occupied mostly with same-different designs as opposed to identification, study of the relations may require additional definitions or assumptions (and Robin Thomas's work on interpretations of GRT in same-different designs may be of assistance).

Potential Extensions of theTheory

Generalization to many-one maps X is a clear direction to take in the future, given the phenomena of perception. For instance, when sensory dimensions map into preference scales, it is typically expected that these functions are nonmonotonic (e.g., Coombs, 1964).

However, in some cases, the need is merely apparent, not real. One instance is the constancy of many percepts, typically best handled within invariance of say, perceptual operators. In other cases, it is fair to first negotiate the early downsizing map, and then to figure in the nature of the early sensory→perceptual map. This does not shortchange the early physical→sensory function, but provides a division of labor. For instance, the laws of establishment of hues as functions of the infinite dimensional light spectrum, might act somewhat independently of the geometry of the hue-brightness-saturation manifold.

When actually requisite, the theory of immersions is likely a first consideration. Thus, these may be appropriate for nonmonotonic perceptual to preference maps. They permit many-one and nonhomeomorphic (even if the map is one-one) maps but assume local one-one structure, that is, that the differential $(dX : T_{(u,v)}D \to T_m M)$ to the range space (i.e., the coordinate Jacobian) is of the same rank as the domain. Because Rank(dX) $\leq$ min(Rank D, Rank M), in our present milieu, an immersion suggests that certain aspects of the physical world, in particular the point-to-point correspondence, is maintained at least locally. The natural alternative to immersions would be to assume a submersion where dX is of the same rank as M. It follows that locally the full scope of the perceptual space is being utilized. Immersions are typically more useful than submersions. For instance, if X is a one-one homeomorphic immersion, then locally it is an

---

[6]Dzhafarov (2003a, 2003b) has shown that certain conditions on discrimination probabilities rule out natural Thurstonian (and therefore perhaps GRT) models of same-different discrimination. Discussion of this result exceeds the present scope.

embedding and therefore locally shares the resident topology of M (e.g., Boothby, 2003). Further, if the points of D that map to the same points of M are not too close, the probability densities map enjoys the sufficient properties that allow, say, separability to be present and measurable.

It seems inevitable that more sophisticated spaces will ultimately be required in the cognitive, social, and even biological sciences than have hitherto been the mainstays. There have been scattered examples of efforts to expand psychology's spatial purview over the past 50 years but we suspect that the well has hardly been tapped in this regard. Fifty years from now could see spatial models very different from even the most exotic offerings from today's cafeteria, including the present approach. One exceedingly critical feature that has been scarce in cognitive science has been the invention of direct experimental tools that permit, encourage, and interact with evolving theories of psychological spaces. At present, short of specific geometric model fitting, there is little to aid us in direct implementation of the notions proffered here. We do, however, hope that the kinds of issues that arise in this development will help to move us forward toward pursuit of an expanded set of perspectives and tools.

References

Algom, D., Eidels, A., Kadlec, H., & Townsend, J. T. (2005). *Dull news travels fast: A separate channel theory of the Stroop effect.* Manuscript submitted for publication.

Ashby, F. G. (1992). Multidimensional models of categorization. In F. G. Ashby (Ed.), *Multidimensional models of perception and cognition* (pp. 449-484, Scientific Psychology Series). Hillsdale, NJ: Lawrence Erlbaum Associates, Inc.

Ashby, F. G., & Gott, R.E. (1988). Decision rules in the perception and categorization of multidimensional stimuli. *Journal of Experimental Psychology: Learning, Memory, and Cognitin, 14,* 33-53.

Ashby, F. G., & Maddox, W. T. (1990). Integrating information from separable psychological dimensions. *Journal of Experimental Psychology: Human Perception and Performance, 16,* 598-612.

Ashby, F. G., & Maddox, W. T. (1992). Complex decision rules in categorization: Contrasting novice and experienced performance. *Journal of Experimental Psychology: Human Perception and Performance, 18,* 50-71.

Ashby, F. G., & Townsend, J. T. (1986). Varieties of perceptual independence. *Psychological Review, 93,* 154-179.

Baird, J. C. (1977). *Sensation and judgment.* Mahwah, NJ: Lawrence Erlbaum Associates Inc..

Beals, R., Krantz, D. H., & Tversky, A. (1968). Foundations of multidimensional scaling. *Psychological Review, 75,* 127-142.

Boothby, W. M. (2003). *An introduction to differentiable manifolds and Riemannian geometry.* San Diego, CA: Academic.

Carroll, J. D., & Arabie, P. (1980). Multidimensional scaling. *Annual Review of Psychology, 31,* 607-649.

Colonius, H., & Townsend, J. T. (1997). Activation-state representation of models for the redundant-signals-effect. In A. A. J. Marley (Ed.), *Choice, decision and measurement,* (pp. 245-254) Mahwah, NJ: Lawrence Erlbaum Associates, Inc.

Coombs, C. H. (1964). *A theory of data.* New York:Wiley.

Dunn, J. C. (1983). Spatial metrics of integral and separable dimensions. *Journal of Experimental Psychology: Human Perception & Performance, 9,* 242-257.

Dzhafarov, E. N. (2002). Multidimensional Fechnerian scaling: Perceptual separability. *Journal of Mathematical Psychology, 46,* 564-582.

Dzhafarov, E. N. (2003a). Thurstonian-type representations for "same-different" discriminations: Deterministic decisions and independent images. *Journal of Mathematical Psychology, 47,* 208-228.

Dzhafarov, E. N. (2003b). Thurstonian-type representations for "same-different" discriminations: Probabilistic decisions and interdependent images. *Journal of Mathematical Psychology, 47,* 229-243.

Dzhafarov, E. N., & Colonius, H. (1999). Fechnerian metrics in unidimensional and multidimensional stimulus spaces. *Psychonomic Bulletin & Review, 6,* 239-268.

Hirsch, M. W. (1976). *Differential topology.* New York: Springer-Verlag.

Hyman, R., & Well, A. (1967). Judgments of similarity and spatial models. *Perception & Psychophysics, 2,* 233-248.

Hyman, R., & Well, A. (1968). Perceptual separability and spatial models. *Perception & Psychophysics, 3,* 161-165.

Kadlec, H., & Hicks, C. L. (1998). Invariance of perceptual spaces and perceptual separability of stimulus dimensions. *Journal of Experimental Psychology: Human Perception and Performance, 24,* 80-104.

Kadlec, H., & Townsend, J. T. (1992). Signal detection analysis of multidimensional interactions. In F. G. Ashby (Ed.), *Probabilistic multidimensional models of perception and cognition (pp. 181-227).* Scientific Psychology Series, Hillsdale, NJ: Lawrence Erlbaum Associates, Inc.

Kobayashi, S., & Nomizu, K. (1969). *Foundations of differential geometry* (Vol. 2). New York: Wiley.

Kobayashi, S., & Nomizu, K. (1991). *Foundations of differential geometry* (Vol. 1). New York: Wiley.

Kruskal, J. B., & Wish, M. (1979). *Multidimensional scaling.* Beverly Hills, CA: Sage.

Lang, S. (1993). *Real and functional analysis* (3rd ed.). New York: Springer-Verlag.

Lappin (1978). The relative of choice behavior and the effect of prior knowledge on the speed and accuracy of response time like experiments. In N. J. Castellan, Jr., & F. Restle (Eds.), *Cognitive theory* (Vol. 3, pp. 139-168) Hillsdale, NJ: Lawrence Erlbaum Associates, Inc.

Levine, M. V. (2003). Dimension in latent variable models. *Journal of Mathematical Psychology, 47,* 450-466.

Luce, R. D. (1963). Detection and recognition. In R. D. Luce, R. R. Bush, & E. Galanter (Eds.), *Handbook of mathematical psychology* (Vol. 1, pp. 103-189). New York: Wiley.

MacMillan, N. A., & Creelman, C. D. (2005). Detection theory: A user's guide. Mahwah, NJ: Lawrence Erlbaum Associates, Inc.

Maddox, W. T. (1992). Perceptual and decision separability. In F. G. Ashby (Ed.), *Multidimensional models of perception and cognition* (pp. 147-180, Scientific Psychology Series). Hillsdale, NJ: Lawrence Erlbaum Associates, Inc.

Melara, R.D., & Algom, D. (2003). Driven by information: A tectonic theory of Stroop effects. *Psychological Review, 110*, 422-471.

Miller, J. (1982). Divided attention: Evidence for coactivation with redundant signals. *Cognitive Psychology, 14*, 247-279.

Mordkoff, J. T., & Egeth, H. E. (1993). Response time and accuracy revisited: Converging support for the interactive race model. *Journal of Experimental Psychology: Human Perception & Performance, 19*, 981-991.

Mordkoff, J. T., & Yantis, S. (1991). An interactive race model of divided attention. *Journal of Experimental Psychology: Human Perception and Performance, 17*, 520-538.

Munkres, J. R. (1975). *Topology: a first course.* Englewood Cliffs, N.J., Prentice-Hall.

Nilsson, N. J. (1965). *Learning machines: Foundations of trainable pattern classifying systems.* New York, NY: McGraw-Hill.

Nosofsky, R. M. (1985). Overall similarity and the identification of separable-dimension stimuli: A choice model analysis. *Perception & Psychophysics, 38*, 415-432.

Nosofsky, R. N. (1992). Similarity, scaling and cognitive process models. *Annual Review of Psychology, 43*, 25-53.

O'Neill, B. (1966). *Elementary differential geometry.* New York: Academic.

Potts, B. C., Melara, R. D., & Marks, L. G. (1998). Circle size and diameter tilt: A new look at integrality and separability. *Perception & Psychophysics, 60*, 101-112.

Shepard, R. N. (1964) Attention and the metric structure of the stimulus space. *Journal of Mathematical Psychology, 1*, 54-87.

Suppes, P., Krantz, D. M., Luce, R. D., & Tversky, A. (1989). *Foundations of measurement Vol. 2: Geometrical, threshold, and probabilistic representations* San Diego, CA: Academic.

Thomas, R. D. (1999). Assessing sensitivity in a multidimensional space: Some problems and a definition of a general d'. *Psychonomic Bulletin & Review, 6*, 224-238.

Thomas, R.D. (2003). Further considerations of a general d' in multidimensional space. *Journal of Mathematical Psychology, 47*, 220-224.

Townsend, J. T. (1971a). Theoretical analysis of an alphabetic confusion matrix. *Perception & Psychophysics, 9*, 40-50.

Townsend, J. T. (1971b). A note on the identifiability of parallel and serial processes. *Perception & Psychophysics, 10*, 161-163.

Townsend, J. T. (1984). Uncovering mental processes with factorial experiments. *Journal of Mathematical Psychology, 28*, 363-400.

Townsend, J. T., & Ashby, F. G. (1982). An experimental test of contemporary mathematical models of visual letter recognition. *Journal of Experimental Psychology: Human Perception and Performance, 8*, 834-864.

Townsend, J. T., Hu, G. G., & Ashby, F. G. (1981). Perceptual sampling of orthogonal straight line features. *Psychological Research,43*, 259-275.

Townsend, J. T., Hu, G. G., & Evans, R. (1984). Modeling feature perception in brief displays with evidence for positive interdependencies. *Perception & Psychophysics, 36*, 35-49.

Townsend, J. T., Hu, G. G., & Kadlec, H. (1988). Feature sensitivity, bias, and interdependencies as a function of energy and payoffs. *Perception & Psychophysics, 43*, 575-591.

Townsend, J. T., & Landon, D.E. (1982). An experimental and theoretical investigation of the constant ratio rule and other models of visual letter recognition. *Journal of Mathematical Psychology, 25*, 119-163.

Townsend, J. T., & Nozawa, G. (1995). On the spatio-temporal properties of elementary perception: An investigation of parallel, serial and coactive theories. *Journal of Mathematical Psychology, 39*, 321-360.

Townsend, J. T., & Schweickert, R. (1989). Toward the trichotomy method: Laying the foundation of stochastic mental networks. *Journal of Mathematical Psychology, 33*, 309-327.

Townsend, J. T., Solomon, B., & Spencer-Smith, J. B. (2001). The perfect Gestalt: Infinite dimensional Riemannian face spaces and other aspects of face cognition. In M. J. Wenger & J. T. Townsend (Eds.), *Computational, geometric and process issues in facial cognition: Progress and challenges.* (pp. 39-82, Scientific Psychology Series). Mahwah, NJ:Lawrence Erlbaum Associates, Inc.

Townsend, J. T., & Spencer-Smith, J. B. (2004). Two kinds of global perceptual separability and curvature. In C. Kaernbach, E. Schröger, and H. Müller (Eds.), *Psychophysics beyond sensation: Laws and invariants of human cognition.* (pp. 89-109, Scientific Psychology Series). Mahwah, NJ: Lawrence Erlbaum Associates, Inc.

Townsend, J. T., & Thomas, R. (1993). On the need for a general quantitative theory of pattern similarity. In S. C. Masin (Ed.), *Foundations of perceptual theory* (pp. 297-368). Amsterdam: Elsevier Publishers.

Townsend, J. T., & Wenger, M. J. (2004). A theory of interactive parallel processing: New capacity measures and predictions for a response time inequality series. *Psychological Review, 111*, 1003-1035.

Tversky, A. (1977). Features of similarity. *Psychological Review*, 84, 327-352.

Wenger, M. J., & Townsend, J. T. (2001). *Computational, geometric, and process issues in facial cognition: Progress and challenges.* (pp. 67-99, Scientific Psychology Series). Mahwah, NJ: Lawrence Erlbaum Associates, Inc.

Yellott, J. (1977). The relationship between Luce's choice axiom, Thurstone's theory of comparative judgment, and the double exponential distribution. *Journal of Mathematical Psychology, 15*, 109-144.

Author Index

Subject Index

www.ingramcontent.com/pod-product-compliance
Ingram Content Group UK Ltd.
Pitfield, Milton Keynes, MK11 3LW, UK
UKHW020432010325
455677UK00029B/1122